INTERNATIONAL SHORT-TERM CAPITAL MOVEMENTS

INTERNATIONAL SHORT-TERM CAPITAL MOVEMENTS

BY

CHARLES POOR KINDLEBERGER

NEW YORK : MORNINGSIDE HEIGHTS
COLUMBIA UNIVERSITY PRESS
1937

Published 1937

Foreign Agents
OXFORD UNIVERSITY PRESS
Humphrey Milford, Amen House
London, E.C.4, England

KWANG HSUEH PUBLISHING HOUSE
140 Peking Road
Shanghai, China

MARUZEN COMPANY, LTD.
6 Nihonbashi, Tori-Nichome
Tokyo, Japan

OXFORD UNIVERSITY PRESS
B. I. Building, Nichol Road
Bombay, India

Printed in the United States of America

To S. M. K.

PREFACE

During the last few years a change has taken place in the character of the problems involved in international short-term capital movements. This change, which has only recently been generally recognized, is not in the "heat" of "hot money," now and prior to 1933, but in the amounts of liquid funds available and ready to move between countries. Banking systems the world over have been reflated with government paper; and gold has been transformed into money by sales to monetary authorities from Indian and continental hoards, and from the increased production of the Witwatersrand and the alluvial deposits of the U. S. S. R.

The actual and potential increase in the volume of funds thus made available for use or for the gratification of their wanderlust is now the most pressing issue facing resolution at the hands of monetary authorities throughout the world. It does not, however, receive particular attention in this book. While some attention is devoted in Chapter XIII to the question of sterilization, the analysis there is set forth in terms of an economy in which there are not redundant supplies of money operating at low velocities.

It is to be hoped, however, that this volume will be none the less useful owing to its failure to be up to the minute. The basic principles, the exposition of which form the central theme of the discussion, are: (1) that short-term capital in the balance of payments and in a national banking system should be regarded as equivalent to gold (from which the corollary follows that when gold flows are due solely to movements of short-term funds their effects on the banking system should be offset), and (2) that equilibrium in the foreign-exchange market and in the balance of payments can be said to obtain when at a given rate of exchange the balance of payments exerts neither an inflationary nor a deflationary force on the national money income—

and these principles are believed to have a wide validity and to be of use in the present gold dilemma. Especially will this be the case if the redundancy of gold in present-day banking systems leads it to follow silver into demonitization, with the consequent necessity of evolving a new international monetary system probably based on foreign exchange reserves.

Another apology is due the reader because of the time that must elapse between the writing of a book and its appearance. Had I attempted to halt the completion of the manuscript to study each addition to the literature, this volume would never have been completed. As it is, a vast amount of excellent material has not been sifted because of lack of opportunity.[1]

I am indebted particularly to Professor James W. Angell, of Columbia University, and to Emile Despres, of the Federal Reserve Bank of New York, for the light they have given me on the problems covered below and for their patience in reading and suggesting improvements in the manuscript. In addition, thanks are due to Professor John M. Chapman and Professor B. Haggott Beckhart, both of Columbia University, who have read the manuscript with friendly, critical eyes. I wish to make special acknowledgment of the inspiration I received as a student from the late Professor H. Parker Willis, who encouraged my initial interest in the subject. Finally, a full measure of my gratitude is due to my wife, who has taken an important share in the final preparation of the manuscript for publication and who has compiled the index.

CHARLES P. KINDLEBERGER

New York, N. Y.
October 4, 1937

[1] See especially *Explorations in Economics—Notes and Essays Contributed in Honor of F. W. Taussig*, 1936, of which I have had an opportunity to refer only to the essays of Angell and Currie; "Banking Policy and the Balance of International Payments," by F. W. Paish (*Economica*, III, 404-22), which expresses aptly and concisely a good deal of what I have tried to say below under the transfer problem; *Studies in the Theory of International Trade*, 1936, by Jacob Viner; *International Aspects of the Business Cycle*, 1936, by Hans Neisser; *International Economic Reconstruction*, 1936, two reports of a group of experts to the Joint Committee of the Carnegie Endowment for International Peace and of the International Chamber of Commerce; *Prosperity and Depressions*, 1937, by Gottfried Haberler, especially chap. xi; and *The Theory of the Forward Exchanges*, 1937, by Paul Einzig.

CONTENTS

Part I

THE FOREIGN EXCHANGES AND THE NATIONAL MONEY INCOME

I

TYPES OF INTERNATIONAL SHORT-TERM CAPITAL MOVEMENT

The problem of isolating short-term capital movements from the rest of the balance of international payments and then breaking them down into various types is difficult, both in theory and in practice. A number of methods of classification have been and may be used, dependent upon the type of credit instrument employed, the intention of the investor, the motivation of the investor or the effect of the movement on other items in the balance of payments.

Previous Attempts at Classification. The usual distinction between long- and short-term capital movements turns on the form in which the financial operation takes place. Movements of long-term credit instruments such as bonds, mortgages, titles to property, and so forth, are considered as entailing movements of long-term capital. Changes in open-book credits, foreign deposits, bills of exchange, or other investments payable in foreign short-term money markets represent shifts in short-term capital. A further customary distinction is that obligations with maturities of more than a year constitute long-term credit instruments, and those payable within a year's time are short-term.

This classification is, however, unsuitable from the theoretical point of view. That which should determine the category into which a particular capital movement falls is the intention of the investor.[1] On this basis, a dealer engaged in international security speculation is moving international short-term capital. On the other hand, if the foreign exchange reserves of a central bank are shifted from New York to London for

[1] See Carl Iversen, *Aspects of the Theory of International Capital Movements*, 1935, p. 29 n.; H. D. White, *The French International Accounts, 1880-1913*, 1933, p. 6 n. Ragnar Nurkse (*Internationale Kapitalbewegungen*, 1935, pp. 219-20) distinguishes between short-term capital from the point of view of the

a period of time stretching indefinitely into the future, a long-term capital movement has been effected. This basis of distinction is troublesome, since many instances can be thought of, particularly in connection with international movements of funds between stock markets, in which the investor himself is not sure how long he will hold a particular foreign investment. The practical problems involved in this issue will be reserved for future discussion. For the present, it will necessarily be sufficient to say that where funds are moved internationally with the intention of changing or reversing the direction of the movement within a short period of time, or even at an indeterminate but opportune future date, the capital movement falls under the head of "short-term."

Within the category of short-term loans, however, further subdivisions must be made. Certain economists have attempted this, using various bases for classification.

Iversen makes a distinction between "real" capital movements which represent instances "in which capital moves from countries where it is abundant to countries where it is scarce in order to take lasting advantage of the higher rates of interest prevailing in those countries," and "equalizing" movements, where "a disturbance in the balance of payments through its influence on the foreign exchanges or on short-term interest rates call [sic] forth temporary flows of capital between countries."[2] He specifically denies Machlup's contention that the theory of capital flight provides another type of movement, "the motive of which is to avoid risk rather than to obtain a higher rate of return." Such a movement, he holds, is "real," since "the wish to avoid risk of taxation, currency depreciation, political upheavals and what not, and the desire to get the highest possible return are not two different or even two conflicting motives but merely two aspects of the same calculation."[3]

Nurkse makes a somewhat similar differentiation between

individual and from that of the economy (working capital). We are here dealing only with the former.

[2] *Op. cit.*, p. 30.

[3] *Ibid.*, p. 107.

"induced" and "autonomous" short-term capital movements. The former are results of changes in other items in the balance of payments, while the latter are themselves independent variables.[4] The line between the two is not clear,[5] but Nurkse suggests that "induced" movements can be graded with reference to the degree to which they are passive adjustments to other items. He distinguishes, first of all, trade credits. These vary with changes in the trade balance, if it can be assumed that a fairly stable proportion of all international merchandise transactions is financed through open-book credit facilities granted by exporter to importer.[6] Secondly, he lists the deposit of the proceeds of long-term loans which are held in the creditor country for the account of the debtor preparatory to being transferred into the currency of the latter. These deposits constitute a short-term loan by the long-term debtor to the long-term creditor, in the amount of the average deposit for the period.[7] On the border of the induced group come those short-term capital shifts which can be attached to no particular variation in an item in the balance, but which are the result of a concurrence of changes. Such are the speculative capital movements which appear in response to changes in the rate of exchange within the limits imposed by gold points (on the gold standard).[8] Even less "induced" are capital movements resulting from alterations in central bank discount rates.[9] These, together with short-term capital movements of the exchange speculation variety, offset possible gold flows and for this reason fall into the class of induced, rather than that of autonomous, capital movements.[10]

In the category of autonomous short-term capital movements Nurkse groups all those that spring from extra-economic motives and that are not concerned with the desire to maximize the return on capital. He admits the difficulty of distinguishing between his two principal types of capital movements, but suggests that some sort of differentiation can be made between

[4] *Op. cit.*, p. 225.
[5] *Ibid.*, p. 225 n.
[6] *Ibid.*, p. 226.
[7] *Loc. cit.*
[8] *Ibid.*, p. 227.
[9] *Loc. cit.*
[10] *Ibid.*, p. 228.

those capital movements resulting from interest-rate differences and those due to discrepancies in risk. Where the risk is a measurable one, as in the case of a risk on which an insurance company would quote a rate, the payment for risk bearing must be included as a part of the gross return to the creditor. But where the risk is unmeasurable, and even not clearly distinguishable, an adjustment for risk bearing is not possible. Such risks cut off capital from capital-importing countries and stimulate capital outflows from capital-exporting nations.[11]

The lines drawn between short-term capital movements of the types designated by Nurkse may become shadowy in theory when pursued to their ultimate justification. Moreover, it may be admitted that seeking the greatest rate of interest on capital and avoiding possible losses are both parts of the process of maximizing returns, minimizing losses being only the reverse of the same shield. Nevertheless, the distinctions Nurkse sets up are useful as a first approximation in the vast majority of cases where a proximate cause or an immediate motivation is sought.

Iversen does not attempt to pursue his distinction between equalizing and real capital movements. From one viewpoint it may be suggested that equalizing movements are those which obviate the necessity for gold movements in the opposite direction, while real movements are those that call forth gold flows or further equalizing movements. Yet this distinction, pursued to its logical end, breaks down. In pre-war England, for example, short-term rates of interest were varied upon occasion to check a threatened movement of gold. At times these movements in interest rates induced gold flows in the direction opposite to that of the potential gold movements

[11] Nurkse, following F. H. Knight's analysis (*Risk, Uncertainty and Profit*, 1921), distinguishes among three classes of risk on the basis of their effects on capital movements: (1) diversification (Raumlichen Risikoverteilung), which increases capital movements as investors seek to spread their risks geographically; (2) measurable risk (schätzbaren Risiko harmlosen Ursprung), which is neutral in its effects on capital movements, since a price is paid for bearing it; and (3) the unmeasurable risk of uncertainty (messbare Risiko destruktiver Herkunft), which cuts off capital from importing nations and drives it out of capital-exporting countries. See *ibid.*, p. 30.

they were designed to forestall. An outflow of short-term funds in response to a lowering of the rate of interest is just as much a real movement, or just as much an equalizing movement, as an inward movement occasioned by a rise in short-term interest rates. Iversen's distinction between real and equalizing short-term capital movements is perhaps not without meaning when a broad point of view is taken. If it be examined in the light of the technique of the foreign-exchange markets, however, it appears to be of little use for closely reasoned analytical purposes.

Nurkse's division of short-term capital movements into induced and autonomous varieties produces difficulties of which he is aware, but with which he does not attempt to cope. Distinctions between various types of movements of capital induced for various reasons must be made before the term "induced" is to have any content. We may agree with Nurkse that the most useful basis for classification is that of proximate motivation and at the same time hold that a more elaborate system of definition, integrated with foreign-exchange market practice, will produce more satisfactory results.

Classification by Motivation. For the purposes of the present analysis international short-term capital movements may be divided into four general categories: equilibrating, speculative, income, and autonomous. The basis for distinction is entirely that of convenience in terminology and rests upon the theoretically unsatisfactory ground of proximate motivation. From a number of points of view the lines of differentiation cross and merge into one another. Yet some general system of classification, loosely set up, will prove helpful.

Equilibrating capital movements are those resulting directly from changes in other items in the balance of payments. The amount of trade credits extended and received, on balance, is thus seen to involve a movement of short-term capital. Even if such trade credits be covered so far as the exchange risk is concerned by the purchase or sale of foreign currencies in the forward exchange market, a movement of short-term capital results from the change in the net balance of such credits, since short-term capital movements refer to the market for spot exchange. The extension of credit, by postponing the necessity for a purchase of exchange, therefore constitutes a short-term capital movement.

Another type of equilibrating capital movement is that involved in the deposit of funds received by a borrower on long-term account to his own credit in the lending country. So far as the balance of payments is concerned, this action offsets the long-term capital movement with an opposite short-term shift of funds. Later, when the borrower draws down these deposits, an additional movement of short-term capital takes place, but in the opposite direction to the equilibrating one.

Finally, we may include in the same category the movement of funds at the conscious direction of stabilization account managers.[12] These are not, it is true, the passive result of a change in one item in the balance of payments, but nevertheless are used directly to offset movements in one or more items. Perhaps the greatest use for this type of short-term capital movement—and the purchase of foreign currencies by this means only remains a short-term capital movement so long as foreign balances (not gold) are held—is to offset other movements of short-term funds.

Speculative movements of capital are those inspired by changes or prospective changes in the price of foreign exchange. They merge on the gold standard, into income movements, since the rate of interest is figured in. They differ, however, from income movements in that the exchange risk is not covered. On an inconvertible paper basis they resemble autonomous capital movements, since they may be cumulative without having a limit such as the gold points imposed upon them. They differ, however, from autonomous movements in that they are conducted by professional speculators who plan to reconvert their foreign holdings to their domestic currency

[12] Changes in the foreign-exchange reserve account of the central bank or government operating wholly or partly on a foreign-exchange standard should likewise be placed in this category. These equilibrating movements differ from those of present-day stabilization funds in that they are not immediately converted into gold, but act, instead, as a substitute for it.

after the elapse of a period of time which may be estimated. In no case is the speculative movement of short-term capital covered by an opposite transaction in forward exchange, since the primary purpose of the transaction is to run an exchange risk, not to avoid one.

Income short-term capital movements may be defined as those which have as their immediate motivation the pursuit of a higher rate of income than can be earned in the domestic money market. Two main types may be broadly recognized. In the first place, funds may be moved from one center to another for investment in short-term evidences of debt, such as deposits, bills of exchange, acceptances, call loans, and so forth, with the operation covered by a forward sale of the currency bought. In the absence of speculation in the forward exchange market these movements will generally take place from money markets with low rates of interest to those with higher rates. If, however, a currency is at a wide discount in the forward exchange market, capital may move from the country concerned even though its short-term rate of interest is higher than that abroad. The gain in income will then be made by the forward purchase of the currency at a discount, rather than from the higher rate of interest earned abroad.[13] In the second place, movements of funds between security markets of various countries come under the category of income transactions. The exchange risk involved is seldom covered, and the direction of the capital flow is not necessarily from the money market with the low rate of interest to that with a higher rate. The motivating force is the prospect of capital appreciation. The fact that an exchange position is generally taken makes the movement somewhat akin to speculative capital flows. As an example, British investors may purchase American securities in New York, partly because they entertain more optimistic notions concerning the value of those securities than do Americans and partly as a short sale of sterling. At a given time one or another motive may predominate. Under the gold standard, however, the primary fac-

[13] The theory of forward exchanges will be discussed below, in chap. xii.

tor inducing movements of funds between national stock markets is a difference of opinion between countries as to the value of the securities in a given nation.

The two types of income movement are evidently related at times. When foreign short-term capital is invested in the New York Stock Exchange in equity securities, other foreign funds may be pouring into New York to be placed in the call-loan market. In the former case it is the prospective rate of profit[14] which acts as the magnet or repellent of funds. In the latter, it is the actual income to be received from the loan operation, at a rate known in advance.

Autonomous movements of international short-term capital are those which arise in response to fears for the safety of principal. Capital flight or movements of "bad money" are the terms usually applied to them. These hurried departures of capital from one country or another are generally uncovered, involve assuming an exchange position, and are usually undertaken by private owners of capital rather than by banks and dealers. The latter are more likely to operate through the forward exchange market, earning high rates of return on their funds, but avoiding an exchange position. Autonomous capital movements are essentially speculative movements in that a profit or, more usually, the minimization of a loss is sought in taking advantage of prospective changes in exchange rates. But the operations are usually conducted with the capital of the principal, not with borrowed funds. The motivation, if not the actual results, differs from that of highly professional exchange speculation.

Functional Application of Classes. These four general cat-

[14] The rate of profit on securities is not to be confused with the price-earnings ratio, to which, in the short run, it bears no necessary connection. The price-earnings ratio generally has some relation to the rates of interest current in the money market, but a varying one at best. The rate of profit is probably a misnomer, since speculators are apt to think of opportunities for capital appreciation in absolute terms. It is, of course, possible to reduce these prospective, absolute increases in capital value to a rate, by consideration of the prospective amount of time which the capital appreciation will take. So considered, the "rate of profit" may be compared with a rate of interest. See Bertil Ohlin, *Interregional and International Trade,* 1933, pp. 334-35.

egories, set up in terms of their proximate motivation, may also be examined from the point of view of the functional role they fill in the balance of payments. This question is of primary interest in the present study and will receive extended treatment below. At the present juncture a few broad generalizations may help serve to clarify the distinctions already made. The functional relationships of short-term capital movement types may perhaps best be demonstrated in connection with the complex interaction of gold and short-term capital movements as means of international payment.

Equilibrating movements postpone the necessity for gold movements on the gold standard and for exchange-rate fluctuations on the paper standard. In the case of stabilization fund operations this need not be demonstrated; the equilibrating capital movement has changed its form if gold is demanded for otherwise uncovered purchases of foreign exchange. In the case of the two other main types of equilibrating movements, however, it is evident that the short-term credit transaction takes the place of other means of payment, whether it be a trade credit extended to finance a merchandise transaction or a deposit created in the lending country by the borrower with the proceeds of an international long-term loan. When the trade credit becomes due or the deposit is drawn down, other means of payment are necessary. But for the period during which the equilibrating movement exists, it obviates the necessity for gold movements or of other means of international payment.

Speculative movements of short-term capital, when they are related to changes in the rate of foreign exchange between the gold points on the gold standard, likewise reduce gold flows. By buying sterling at the lower gold point for future sale when it has risen in price New York banks and dealers prevent the flow of gold to London. In the transfer process, which will be explored in some detail in Part II, below, "secondary" movements of capital from the debtor country or a third country to the creditor country, as the latter's currency depreciates to the gold export point, may take place, with the effect of reducing the gold flow necessary to accomplish the transfer of buying power.[15] On the paper standard, however, speculative movements may operate either to increase or to reduce the range of the exchange-rate fluctuations themselves. This point is one requiring complex and extended analysis, given below.[16] For the present it may be said that if the exchange rates are fluctuating within narrow range, whether because of exchange control or because of the absence of long-term capital movements and other short-term movements, speculative movements will reduce the range of fluctuations. If, however, the exchange rates are fluctuating wildly, because of large swings of autonomous short-term capital, the speculative movements may operate in such a fashion as to increase the width of the exchange-rate gyrations.

Income short-term capital movements may serve to restore the demand for foreign exchange and the balance of payments and hence may eliminate the necessity for gold shipments on the gold standard if the rate of discount is operated to this end and if no disturbing factors are present. A rise in the discount rate when gold exports are threatened may bring a flow of income short-term capital, and may thus stop the fall of the foreign-exchange rate short of the gold export point. Conversely, a reduction in bank rate may stimulate an exodus of short-term capital in time to prevent an inflow of gold.[17] There are, however, important limitations to this relationship. The rate of discount may be moved to an extent serving not only to prevent gold movements in one direction but also to stimulate them in the other. Again, the rate of discount may be altered for reasons other than to care for changes in the banking system's gold reserves.[18] Finally, the rate of profit may move independently and with no close relation to the

[15] See Ohlin, *op. cit.*, p. 391; Nurkse, *op. cit.*, p. 227; Iversen, *op. cit.*, p. 521.

[16] See below, pp. 91-96; and chap. x.

[17] See Gottfried Haberler, *Der internationale Handel*, 1933, p. 45; also Ohlin, *op. cit.*, pp. 384-90.

[18] See Iversen, *op. cit.*, p. 514: ". . . it is realized by modern economists . . . that the gold standard under modern conditions is a 'managed' currency just as well as the paper standard."

rate of discount. In the latter two cases the income short-term capital movements may obviate gold movements or may stimulate them. In the case of pre-war England the second of these alternatives seems to have been in operation. Gold flowed cyclically into England during prosperity and out during crisis and depression.[19] The prospective rate of profit appears to have been the important factor in bringing this about, although possibly, on occasions, the manipulation of the discount rate may have been too extensive when regarded from the standpoint of eliminating gold flows.

Autonomous movements of short-term capital have a clearer relationship to gold flows and to exchange-rate fluctuations. On the gold standard a serious outward or inward movement of capital as the result of fear will produce a flow of gold unless offset by other capital movements in the opposite direction. Inasmuch as during a currency depreciation or a war scare, say, private short-term capital is hesitant to take advantage of speculative or income opportunities, the principal type of offsetting flow is that of official equilibrating funds. In the absence of official support of sufficient extent, on the gold standard, autonomous capital movements lead to gold flows. Similarly, on the paper standard they lead to exchange-rate fluctuations. In the case of capital flight the movement of short-term capital is apt to be cumulative, since an outflow of gold, when the gold standard is endangered, renders the maintenance of the standard more doubtful. In the same fashion a movement of the rate of exchange, under the impetus of a movement of "bad money," induces other holders of capital in the country with the depreciating currency to believe that the currency may sink lower and therefore induces them to hasten its fall by exporting capital.[20]

Credit Instruments. It is less interesting theoretically, perhaps, to classify short-term capital transactions from the view-

[19] See W. Edwards Beach, *British International Gold Movements and Banking Policy, 1881-1913*, 1935, *passim*, especially chap. ix. This study will receive our further attention below, in chap. ix.

[20] See R. G. Hawtrey, *Currency and Credit*, 3d ed., 1927, pp. 254-55.

point of the different types of credit instrument in which they may be embodied. Yet for some purposes these distinctions are important. Professor Angell's analysis of the effects of variations in short-term lending on the money supply runs in terms of the bill discount market.[21] Iversen's treatment, in his résumé of the transfer process, takes the form largely of bank deposits.[22] But, as will be seen in the following chapter, some difference is made to the analysis of the relations between short-term capital movements and variations in purchasing power by the type of credit instrument in which the capital movement is embodied.[23]

Three main classes may readily be distinguished: foreign "money," foreign "exchange," and foreign "investments." Foreign money is simply currency or deposits the ownership of which resides in persons outside the country concerned. Foreign exchange, for present purposes, may be defined to embrace claims to foreign money proper, which may be exercised within a limited period of time, say a year. These claims may have a stated maturity or may be callable at the owner's pleasure. If they have a given maturity they may be saleable before the expiration of the credit period, by sale at a discount. Foreign investments represent titles to property or evidences of indebtedness which may readily be bought and sold in an active market in exchange for foreign money.

Foreign money is, of course, largely made up of bank deposits.[24] Exports and imports of currency take place between countries, being particularly noticeable across the borders of contiguous nations, or when foreign hand-to-hand money circulates or is hoarded in countries where the national note issue is distrusted.[25] Likewise, foreign currencies are traded

[21] James W. Angell, *The Theory of International Prices*, 1926, chap. xvi, especially secs. 2-3.

[22] *Op. cit.*, chap. xii, especially pp. 458-59, 468 ff.

[23] See J. C. Gilbert, "The Present Position of the Theory of International Trade," *Review of Economic Studies*, III (1935), 29: "Total buying power there depends upon what the short-term lenders do with their foreign exchange."

[24] See A. Vallance, "Foreign Trade and the Exchanges," in *What Everyone Wants to Know about Money*, ed. by G. D. H. Cole, 1933, p. 188.

[25] The American dollar, for example, was widely circulated in Central Europe

on the "black" exchanges in forbidden dealings with tourists and others at discounts from the official controlled rates. But in the main, especially in countries which are financially more advanced, foreign money represents preponderantly bank deposits. Inasmuch as a cable transfer is able to shift the ownership of such bank deposits almost instantaneously, we may refer to such transactions as dealings in foreign money, despite the fact that they are in reality bills of exchange drawn on foreign money.[26]

Under foreign exchange we may include all drafts and bills of exchange, whether drawn by merchants or banks, which originate and are held outside the country in which they are payable. If the bills of exchange are transmitted abroad and discounted, foreign money is substituted for them. If a foreigner then purchase the bills and hold them abroad, he must first obtain foreign money.

Foreign short-term investments include a wide variety of interest-bearing obligations and evidences of ownership. The various types of credit instrument dealt in in the money market proper, including the discount, commercial paper, call loan, and government bill markets, evidently fall into this category. In addition, stocks and bonds for which a ready market exists must be included. Some of these long-term securities are marketable in two or more capital centers. These are exceptions to the rule that foreign investments must be purchased with foreign money. If an Argentine bond is quoted in both London and New York, for example, it can be bought in one market and sold in the other, thus serving as a means of transferring funds without the necessity for recourse to the foreign exchange market proper.

Summary. This chapter has attempted to classify movements of international short-term capital from two points of view. First, after rejecting the classifications suggested by Iversen and Nurkse, largely for reasons of convenience, four analytical di-

after the war and has been continually used in Cuba and other Latin American countries. In 1936 a large part of the rise in the circulation of Bank of England notes was attributed to continental hoarding.

[26] See E. S. Furniss, *Foreign Exchange*, 1922, p. 84.

visions were made. The basis for differentiation was that of proximate motivation. The types distinguished were: (1) the equilibrating short-term capital movement, which arises directly out of an independent change in an item in the balance of payments or in response to it; (2) the speculative movement, which takes place in anticipation of changes in rates of exchange and is largely conducted by professional speculators in search of profit; (3) the income movement, which takes place when a higher income return can be earned by investing in a foreign money market; and (4) the autonomous movement, largely of the capital flight variety, which is designed to minimize anticipated losses rather than to maximize prospective gains. These lines of division, it was admitted, are not theoretically clear-cut. When the interrelations between the interest rate and the exchange rate are examined, it is seen that the second and third types are related to one another. Likewise, Iversen's point was granted—that ultimately minimizing losses is simply one aspect of maximizing gains. That reasoning, however, pursued to its conclusion, would enable no classification of capital movements to be made on the basis of motivation, except that the lender and the borrower both expect to gain from the transaction. While no theoretical precision is claimed for the system of definitions offered, yet it is believed that they may prove useful from the point of view of exposition.

Secondly, after the general relations of the foregoing types of short-term capital movements to gold flows had been sketched, a classification of capital movements was offered from the point of view of the credit instruments involved. This is preparatory to the discussion in the following chapter, concerning the relations of capital movements and the money supply. Three principal classes were recognized: (1) foreign money, consisting of deposits in foreign countries, as well as foreign currency, and cable transfers which shift instantaneously the ownership of such deposits; (2) foreign exchange, or claims to foreign money, which are not settled until the elapse of a period of time, although they may be sold at a discount; and (3) foreign investments, either in a foreign money market or in securities readily negotiable through purchase or sale in a foreign capital market.

II

INTERNATIONAL SHORT-TERM FUNDS AND THE MONEY SUPPLY

The adjustment of the balance of payments to disturbances arising from changes within one or more of its items has invariably been described with some reference to changes in the supply of money. As an example, the Thornton-Mill price-specie-flow mechanism and the neoclassic variations on it rest in large part upon some form of the quantity theory of money.[1] When gold leaves a country owing to an unfavorable balance of indebtedness, the resultant decline in the amount of money, according to this theory, tends to reduce prices. The price decline was alleged to increase exports and decrease imports and thus to correct partially the adverse balance. Conversely, in the country receiving the gold, the increase in the money supply was supposed to raise prices, thereby encouraging imports and discouraging exports and rendering further assistance in the correction of the balance of payments.

The Money Supply in International Trade Theory. The mainspring of the classical theory of international trade adjustment, then, was the quantity theory of money, in which gold movements served as the immediate factors bringing about monetary changes. In the later versions of the process of adjustment many portions of the earlier descriptive analysis were modified in order to conform more closely with the realities observed in foreign trade and the banking world. The underlying dependence of the postulated process on monetary changes was not, however, altered. Marshall, Giffen, and Sidgwick suggested that gold movements did not affect prices directly so much as through bank reserves, interest rates, and speculation.[2] Later, Taussig and Viner made note of the fact that the money supply might alter first, with gold moving after-

[1] See Angell, *op. cit.*, pp. 57, 85, 160, and elsewhere. [2] *Ibid.*, chap. v, secs. 2-4.

ward to sustain the expansion of bank deposits previously undertaken on the basis of foreign exchange reserves.[3] Finally, Angell pointed out that the bill market, through variations in the volume of bills discounted, produced direct changes in the money supply in debtor and creditor countries in response to balance of payments disequilibria.[4]

Recently an attempt has been made to rewrite the theory of international trade adjustments in terms of changes in buying power in debtor and creditor countries. A foreign loan, to take an example, increases the buying power in the borrowing country, and, if this buying power is directed toward the products of the lender country it may result in an adjustment of the balance of payments, without any gold movements or even price changes.[5] This revision of the theory of international-trade ad-

[3] See Frank W. Taussig, *International Trade*, 1927, pp. 259 ff.; Jacob Viner, *Canada's Balance of International Indebtedness, 1900-1913*, 1924, p. 79 and elsewhere. See also White, *op. cit.*, pp. 11-18, and Iversen, *op. cit.*, pp. 224-38.

[4] See Angell, *op. cit.*, chap. xvi, secs. 2-3.

[5] Bastable and Nicholson, whom Iversen credits with being the founders of what he terms the "modern school," were not so much interested in shifts of purchasing power as in denying the necessity for gold movements. As to the mechanism taking the place of gold movements, they were never clear or consistent. See C. F. Bastable, "On Some Applications of the Theory of International Trade," *Quarterly Journal of Economics*, IV (1890), 1-17; (quoted by Angell, *op. cit.*, p. 101; White, *op. cit.*, p. 18; Iversen, p. 202) and *Theory of International Trade* (4th ed., 1903, reprinted 1934), pp. 77-78. Iversen suggests (*op. cit.*, p. 206) that in the latter passage Bastable was referring to international short-term capital as the mechanism of transferring purchasing power. This interpretation, however, is hardly adequately founded.

Although the present writer is not particularly interested in the origin of theories, yet he cannot refrain from quarreling with Iversen's account of the growth of what Iversen terms the "modern" theory. His historical account follows White's brief references to forerunners (see White, *op. cit.*, pp. 18-19), bringing the doctrine from Bastable and Nicholson in the nineteenth century to Wicksell in 1917 and to Ohlin in 1927. Bresciani-Turroni, however, cites a passage in Mill (J. S. Mill, *Principles of Political Economy*, Ashley edition, p. 624) which relates changes in purchasing power to repercussions in the balance of trade (see C. Bresciani-Turroni, *Inductive Verification of the Theory of International Payments*, 1932, p. 91). Doubtless a complete historical account would be able to trace the doctrine to early mercantilists.

A serious omission on the part of Iversen has been his neglect of Hawtrey's fairly complete account of the part played by shifts in purchasing power in the mechanism of capital transfer. See *Currency and Credit, op. cit.* (1st ed., 1919, pp. 64-66, 3d ed., pp. 83-85). The majority of writers on international trade, before Ohlin placed such emphasis upon shifts in demand schedules, were partly aware of the importance of them, without consciously and systematically

justment first took the form of introducing shifts in demand schedules into the mechanism.[6] Present-day writers generally agree that the price-specie-flow mechanism, with its emphasis on price levels, does not embrace the whole process of adjustment. Changes in demand schedules which have their origin in alterations in the national income, which again can be related to changes in money or its velocity, perform a large part of the task of adjusting the balance of payments directly, without the necessity for price movements. Unequal stress is given by various authors to the role played by gold flows, short-term capital movements, credit policy, and so forth. Likewise, varying emphasis is placed upon the effectiveness of shifts in demand schedules and the indirect sequence of changes traced through sectional-price-level adjustments. Nevertheless, there is general agreement that importance must be attached to changes in incomes arising from variations in the supply of money or its velocity. These may be affected by gold movements or by changes in the net short-term foreign assets[7] at the disposal of a country.

It will thus be seen that the process of international trade adjustment, whether viewed from the classical position or from the point of view of present-day writers, depends in large degree upon changes in the money supply. Furthermore, there is common agreement that the money supply can be affected by gold flows or by means of movements of international short-term capital. This position implies recognition of the various money equations only as truisms. It does not involve the theorists concerned in the ancient debate over the validity of the quantity theory as a unilateral explanation of the value of money.

The Money Supply and Foreign Bank Deposits. It does not

making them a part of the adjustment mechanism. Today, of course, no writers can be counted in the so-called "classical" school.

[6] The theory can be stated in terms of the national money income. Changes in the national money income affect, and are affected by, the balance of international payments under all but the most extreme conditions. The few alterations necessary to expand the doctrine of demand shifts into one of the national money income and the balance of payments will be stressed below.

[7] Foreign short-term assets minus foreign short-term liabilities. This magnitude may be plus or minus. The concept will be refined in some detail below,

require an extensive knowledge of economic processes to realize that international transactions generally take place without the entrance of the currency or deposits of one country into the monetary and banking system of another. Imports, as a rule, cannot be paid for with local bank notes or with checks on local banking establishments.[8] Gold is, to be sure, an international medium of payment, but many more international payments are made in the course of a given period than can be accounted for by net movements of gold between countries or even, following White's suggestion, by gross movements.[9] In the present instance it is not necessary to rehearse the fundamentals of the foreign-exchange mechanism whereby debts due in the various places are cleared against one another. If, as the preceding section was calculated to indicate, changes in the money supply are part of this mechanism, we are necessarily led to a consideration of what is comprehended in the concept of a national money supply. The necessity for so doing is made more urgent by the fact that any description of international payments makes some assumptions, either explicitly or implicitly, about the money supply or money incomes.[10] On the basis of

[8] Angas is of the opinion that the whole problem of international payments might be settled if there were a world bank which issued internationally accepted notes and with which national banking systems kept clearing balances (L. L. B. Angas, *The Problems of the Foreign Exchanges*, 1935, pp. 3-4). This, of course, misses the mark. The problem is not so much one of acceptability or lack of acceptability of means of payment among national banking systems, but rather one of making necessary monetary adjustments as goods and services move in space, i.e., it is a problem of maintaining interspatial equilibrium. See Ohlin, *op. cit.*, Introduction, *passim*; also Hawtrey, *op. cit.*, p. 126: "The essential function of the [foreign] exchanges is not to relate debts payable in different *currencies*, but to relate debts due in different *places*." (The italics are his.) The problem of capital transfer, with its attendant necessity for an adjustment in money and real incomes in the lending and borrowing regions, may be posed for sections within a country, as well as internationally.

[9] *Op. cit.*, pp. 30 ff.

[10] See Taussig, *op. cit.*, p. 341: ". . . Let it be assumed that the monetary situation is stable . . . prices . . . are no longer subject to changes because of the increase or decrease in the volume of money. It is not the consequence of changes in the volume of money and in prices that we are now to examine, but the characteristics of international trade between countries having different monetary standards and between which no money can pass." Iversen (*op. cit.*, p. 320) attacks these assumptions on the ground that they are inconsistent within the terms of the problem; Angell (*op. cit.*, pp. 166-67) only on the ground that they do not conform to reality. See also Nurkse (*op. cit.*, pp. 131-

these assumptions a writer will refer to repercussions of money on international payments and vice versa. The value of the discussion, then, granting its logical validity, will depend on the consistency of all the assumptions and the relevance of the assumptions to the facts of the real world.

We may follow Currie in restricting the concept of money (for the United States) to currency in the hands of the public and "demand deposits, including government deposits, but excluding [domestic] inter-bank deposits."[11] Currie, however, excludes not only domestic interbank deposits, but also foreign bankers' balances. It is clear that counting domestic interbank deposits involves double counting,[12] but the issue is not as clearly drawn when foreign bankers' deposits are considered. These are of the utmost importance to the problem from the point of view of international transactions.

The deposits of foreign banks with banks in a given country should be counted as part of the money supply of that country, whereas the balances owned by banks in the given country and on deposit with foreign banks should not be included in the money supply. Several reasons support a division of this sort. In the first place, no double counting is involved in adding foreign bank deposits to the money supply. In fact, if they were not so treated a large group of deposits would exist which would not be included as money in any country, since balances in for-

32) who points out that capital transfer can take place without gold movements and without changes in money (Geldverschiebung). Here the definition of money is of paramount importance to the solution of the problem within the consistency of the assumptions. But see Ohlin (*op. cit.*, p. 377): "Let us assume that the sum total of incomes . . . is kept constant," and so forth. This assumption is made, not by way of setting forth the underlying conditions of analysis, but to describe an economy before adjustment takes place.

[11] See L. Currie, *The Supply and Control of Money in the United States*, 1934, p. 24. The Federal Reserve Board publishes a figure for "demand deposits adjusted," which is similar to Currie's "adjusted demand deposits," except for its exclusion of government deposits. (See *Federal Reserve Bulletin*, November, 1935, p. 714.) The discrepancy need not concern us. The Federal Reserve Board, in describing its series, says (*ibid.*): "The figure for demand deposits adjusted may be said to represent in a general way the cash resources of the community placed on deposit and readily available for use." See also J. W. Angell, *The Behavior of Money*, 1936, chap. i.

[12] See *Federal Reserve Bulletin*, *loc. cit.*

eign countries cannot be included in the money supply of the country where their ownership resides, inasmuch as they are not "available for use" there. Secondly, foreign bank deposits are on a par with foreign privately owned deposits[13] so far as the domestic monetary system is concerned. They may both be used for the purchase of investments or goods. When so used for purchases from domestic sellers, no change is recorded in the quantity of money and the volume of bank assets within the country evidently remains unchanged. The ownership of deposits may be said to have changed internationally, but the quantity of money has not so changed. Finally, foreign bank deposits should be included in the money supply of the country where they constitute a liability, since they differ in no important economic way from domestic deposits. Legally the control of such deposits is alienated to another country. And, as will be seen presently, this fact has an important bearing upon the uses to which they are put. But from the economic point of view there are no vital differences in the uses to which they may be put.

Thus, from the point of view of the international trade adjustment processes foreign bank deposits, which are not included as part of the American money supply, should be so included. A shift of domestic bank deposits into foreign hands does not affect the money supply in quantity, whether the foreign hands are those of a bank or of a private individual. Such a shift in the ownership of deposits between countries does have an economic effect, but that effect may be estimated more precisely by attention to another factor; and the quantity of money available for the purchase of land and past and present output

[13] No distinction is made for privately owned deposits between those domestically and those foreign owned. This is largely due to the difficulties of making the economic distinction, which is one, not of nationality, but of geography. The dollar deposits of the foreign branch of an American bank are foreign deposits, and the dollar deposits in New York of an American expatriate are foreign deposits. If used for the payment of New York legal services, there has evidently been an export of services and a shift in the ownership of deposits between domestic and foreign persons. See Roland Wilson, *Capital Imports and the Terms of Trade*, 1931, p. 28. Obviously, compilers of balance-of-payment statistics cannot pay attention to these refinements.

should be permitted to remain unchanged in the banking statistics.[14]

The Industrial and Financial Circulations. But shifts can take place in purchasing power between countries without the necessity for variations in the money supply. The national money income is the product of the money supply and its turnover in a given period of time against currently produced goods and services. If the money supply as a whole remain constant, its average "circular velocity"—the rate at which it turns over against current output—may change and affect the national income (buying power).

As an analytical aid it may prove useful to follow a device used by Keynes,[15] who divides the total quantity of money into the "industrial circulation" and the "financial circulation." The former consists of the deposits used by business in maintaining the "normal process of current output, distribution and exchange and paying the factors of production their incomes" while deposits in the latter are used in the "business of holding and exchanging existing titles to wealth." Both groups of deposits have transactions velocity, that is, they are exchanged in payment for goods, services, and existing wealth. But only deposits in the industrial circulation turn over against current output. It is the size of this group of deposits and their income velocity which determine the national money income.

It can readily be shown that foreign deposits belonging both to banks and to private individuals should be included predominantly in the financial circulation. Foreign deposits are used, to be sure, to pay for exports of goods and services. But they are probably turned over to income receivers, during a given year, at a much slower rate than domestic deposits.[16]

[14] R. F. Harrod's definition of money in this connection amounts to the same thing (see *International Economics*, 1933, pp. 96-99). He holds the amount of money in a country to be determined by the country's gold holdings plus outstanding bank loans. A change in the ownership of deposits internationally, therefore, would result in no change in the amount of money.

[15] See J. M. Keynes, *A Treatise on Money*, 1930, I, 243.

[16] It is impossible to make a comparison between the circular velocity of the domestic money supply as estimated by Currie (*Quarterly Journal of Economics*, XLVIII (1934), 354) or Angell, *The Behavior of Money* (*op. cit.*),

On this showing, it follows that a shift of deposits from domestic to foreign hands tends to have a deflationary influence, while a shift in the opposite direction, from foreign deposits to domestic deposits, tends to operate in an inflationary fashion.[17] These tendencies cannot be accepted as precise. If a foreign deposit is used to purchase securities from a stock market speculator, evidently the deposit does not immediately escape from the financial circulation. On the other hand, however, if the proceeds of a sudden excess of imports are held on deposit, it is clear that funds have passed out of the predominantly industrial circulation to the predominantly financial circulation. Conversely, a sudden rush of exports, resulting in the drawing down of foreign deposits which are paid out to exporters, will increase the money supply in the industrial circulation at the expense of the financial circulation. When long-term securities are floated and their proceeds held on deposit, the funds used to subscribe to the issue may come partly from the industrial and partly from the financial circulation. It would be impossible to determine *a priori* whether the shift had resulted in deflation or not.

A shift in deposits from domestic to foreign ownership, then, does not change the money supply, but may have a deflationary effect if it involves a change from the industrial to the financial

p. 191, and the turnover of foreign balances against goods and services. This is due to the fact that a great part of merchandise exports and service credit transactions for a given country are paid for with exchange transactions which are cleared against one another, or "swapped" (forward for spot) and never enter into balances at all. A comparison of sales of spot foreign exchange to banks and to other customers is not exactly in point, since the other customers include persons engaged in purely financial transactions and since the sales include foreign exchange that does pass through American banks' balances abroad and foreign exchange that does not. When, however, in a week chosen at random, that ended March 6, 1935, 80.3 percent of total sales of spot exchange sold by American banks and bankers were sold to other banks, not to customers (see *Statistics of Capital Movements between the United States and Foreign Countries and Purchases and Sales of Foreign Exchange in the United States*, published by the United States Treasury Department, 1936, pp. 95-96), it suggests that the greater part of transactions affecting foreign balances are financial in character.

[17] We shall employ the terms "inflation" and "deflation" to refer solely to upward and downward changes in the national money income, respectively. No value judgment attaches to the words, which become, then, simply descriptive.

circulation, resulting in a reduction in the average income velocity of the total money supply. Conversely, a shift from foreign to domestic ownership may be inflationary. It is impossible to say more than this, however, until the circumstances under which such shifts take place are examined. Before that can be done it is necessary to point out that short-term capital movements which result in gold flows do affect the money supply directly under certain circumstances.

Gold and the Money Supply. The manner by which direct monetary changes result from gold movements may be briefly indicated. It should first be mentioned, however, that we are not at present interested in indirect variations in the money supply caused by changes in the reserves of banks and their ability to make loans. This topic will be treated in the following chapter.

It is clear that if gold is imported by a private individual receiving payment from abroad in specie rather than in bills of exchange, such gold, when deposited to his account at a bank, increases the amount of the monetary supply. When gold shipments are handled by banks, however, it is not clear that private deposits with those banks are so affected. A New York bank may convert a part of its Paris balances into gold at the Bank of France and import it into the United States without apparently increasing the volume of private deposits in the United States directly, even though member-bank reserve balances rise. On the other hand, if Paris banks undertake gold shipments to this country, they build up both bankers' deposits with the member banks and member-bank reserve balances.

Without going into the various methods by which gold shipments may be financed or into the balance-sheet variations to which the different methods give rise,[18] it may be pointed out that gold shipments do increase the money supply if foreign short-term credit balances remain unchanged. If the American

[18] The gold may be American owned and financed, Paris owned and financed, or Paris owned and American financed. In the last case the Paris banks are given balances in New York immediately, thereby increasing the money supply. When the gold arrives, the only change that takes place is between "loans on gold" and "reserve balances" on the asset side of the New York bank's statement.

banks draw down their foreign balances in order to import gold, no direct change in the money supply takes place. But if they first buy foreign exchange to purchase the gold or buy foreign exchange with which to build up their balances after they have originally been used for the purchase of gold, the amount of the money supply in the hands of those selling the foreign exchange is increased. These may, of course, be exporters of goods, although they are more likely to be exporters of long- or short-term capital from the foreign country whose currency is at the gold export point. Thus gold shipments, except when they are effected through the drawing down of foreign credit balances belonging to the gold-importing banks, do affect the money supply directly. In addition, as will be seen in the following chapter, they may have indirect effects on the money supply of a more far-reaching nature.[19]

Short-Term Funds and the Money Supply. In the previous chapter a distinction was made between various types of credit instruments by use of which short-term capital is transmitted between money centers, the basis for differentiation being the diverse effects on the money supply and national income of the three main classifications: foreign money, foreign exchange, and foreign investments. We may properly examine in more detail here the intricacies of analysis alluded to there.

Were foreign payments made entirely through foreign money transactions, that is, through cable or currency transfers, changes in the net balance of remittances between countries would affect the national income. If for purposes of exposition the money payments to be made internationally be restricted to (1) merchandise transactions in the income balance and (2) short-term capital movements of the equilibrating sort, and if the rate of exchange be held fixed,[20] a balance owed to exporters in country A by importers in country B would be set-

[19] It is interesting to note that in the 1934-36 period, however, the direct effects of gold imports into the United States on the gold supply were far greater than the indirect effects. The gold so imported largely went to swell excess reserves, as reserve ratios climbed steadily upward.

[20] A country whose currency is held fixed in terms of other currencies by means of equilibrating short-term capital movements only (gold being excluded) may be described as on the "fixed-exchange standard."

tled in one of two ways. Either banks in B would draw down their normal level of deposits in A or balances of A banks in B would be built up in larger-than-customary proportions. Either mode of payment would tend to bring about changes in the national incomes of both countries.

If B's foreign balances in A banks were drawn down, owners of private deposits in B would exchange them for claims to B banks' foreign balances, which would then be paid over to A exporters. Demand deposits would be canceled in B; in A, demand accounts of domestic individuals would increase at the expense of "Due to Foreign Banks." The remittance from B to A would reduce the money supply in B and increase the average velocity of that in A by adding to the "income circulation" at the expense of the "financial circulation." The shift from foreign bankers' deposits to privately owned domestic deposits, while not affecting the quantity of the money supply, since that concept embraces both, does alter the national income.

Were the payment made through an expansion of bankers' balances owned by A in B, B importers would have had to pay their debts in foreign money, which A exporters sold to the A banks. When A banks' balances in B rose, a shift would ensue there, which if it did not change the amount of the current money supply would result in a shift of money out of the income circulation into the financial circulation, with a net deflationary effect on the national income. The average income velocity of deposits would tend to be reduced by a change in deposits from private domestic to foreign bank hands. In A, of course, the money supply is directly affected, and through it the national income. A banks buy the foreign money by furnishing the A exporters with domestic balances.

If, under the same assumptions, foreign exchange is used as the means of payment, the effect is not felt upon the national income and/or the money supply in A and B simultaneously. Assume that importers in B arrange to pay A exporters by having the latter draw on them or their banks at, say, ninety days after sight and acceptance. A exporters draw such bills, discount them with A banks, receiving demand deposits which expand the domestic money supply and exert an inflationary effect on the national income. A banks may, after acceptance, hold these bills to maturity, under which circumstance the money supply in B is not affected until the bills mature. Should the A bank, however, discount the bills immediately in the B money market, allocating the funds received to its balance with the B bank, there will occur a shift in the ownership of deposits in B but no necessary change as between the industrial and financial circulation. If a bank in B buys the bill, the money supply in B will actually be increased without, however, affecting the national income, since the change occurs only in the financial circulation. In both instances a change between the industrial and financial circulations occurs when the obligation matures, the B importer paying the holder of the bill its face amount, subtracting money from the industrial and adding it to the financial circulation. A time lag has intervened, however, between the inflationary change in A and the deflationary change in B. The time lag will probably be shortened in relation to the period of the bill's life by the fact that the B importer may be required by his bank, or may prefer for business reasons, to maintain a relatively higher idle deposit with his bank while he is in debt to it.

As for the third type of foreign short-term capital instrument, foreign investments, payment cannot be made by them under the present assumptions without liquidation and transfer through one of the channels already discussed. If B importer buys securities quoted in both A and B, sends them to the A capital market for sale there, and turns the proceeds over to A, no change will take place in the money supply of either country. There will nevertheless be a strong presumption that national incomes will be affected. In the purchase of a security in the B capital market the debtor importer takes funds out of the industrial circulation and injects them into the financial circulation; the reverse of the process occurs in A. While in time other funds in B may be transferred from the financial to the industrial circulation by an issue of new securities or by a reduction in the rate of interest, and while the change in A may likewise be reversed, the prima facie result is to affect the national income in the same fashion as if a shift in gold had taken place.

In the case of payments of the unilateral type considered in the above problem and negotiated by changes in foreign money, foreign exchange, or foreign investments, the form the short-term capital movement took affected differently the money supplies in the lending and borrowing countries. In each case, however, the national income was presumably affected, although the timing was not in all cases identical. It remains, in discussing short-term money market investments, to indicate the range of possible effects on the national income of changes in the form in which capital is held abroad at short term without there being any net short-term capital movement.

Assume that B banks decide to convert their A balances into earning assets, for example, short-term treasury bills. A rise in the national income may be produced if the lowering of the rate of interest thereby effected induces the industrial circulation to borrow funds for expenditure on goods and services. If the movement is small, however, it is likely that the result of the lowering of the rate of interest will simply be that other persons will hold the idle balances which had formerly been held by the B bank. If someone in B with a balance in A decided to speculate in the security market in A or encouraged security speculation by others by offering to lend his funds on call to finance the purchase of securities, the shift from bank deposits to money market investments might have a downward effect on the national income in A if it induced people with funds in the industrial circulation to move them to the financial circulation. On the other hand, however, if B funds on deposit in A were spent on the purchase of equity securities, persons in A may be induced to spend more money in the industrial circulation by reason of the paper profits which accrue to them by the rise in the prices of stocks. The question cannot be readily answered as to the effects of shifts of this kind, especially where equity securities are concerned.

The presumption remains, however, that the national income

is affected by international shifts in short-term capital, and that this result is not materially altered by the form that the capital movement takes. If funds are loaned from the industrial circulation in one country to the industrial circulation in the other, as when an import is paid for by short-term lending, income velocity in the two industrial circulations themselves may fairly be assumed to remain stable, and the national incomes will be therefore affected. If the funds are loaned by the financial circulation in one country to the industrial circulation in the other, the presumption remains that some deflation will take place in the borrowing country, while it is clear that inflation will take place in the lender country. If the financial circulation in one country lends to the financial circulation in another, the national incomes are still likely to be affected, as the increase in the financial circulation in one and the decrease in the other will in part be likely to spread to the industrial circulation and affect thereby the quantity of money available for expenditure on current output.

There are many variations which may be considered in an analysis of this sort, without affecting the basic underlying presumption that short-term capital movements will react, as a primary phenomenon—the secondary implications being reserved for the following chapter—on the national income in the remitting and receiving countries. J. C. Gilbert apparently stresses the superficial complications without realizing the basic element of reality in Iversen's contention when he writes:

> The increase in buying power as a concomitant of the equalizing short-term capital movement is not at all certain. There may be no increase of buying power in the borrowing country. The person who exchanges domestic currency for foreign exchange may merely place buying power in the hands of long-term borrowers which would otherwise have been placed in the hands of other borrowers. The purchaser of the foreign exchange may purchase this exchange instead of treasury or commercial bills on his domestic money market. An increase in total buying power in the borrowing country necessitates an increase in the transactions-velocity of circulation which cannot be assumed implicitly. It is possible that there will be an increase in the velocity of circulation, but it

cannot be argued as if such an increase is certain. Similarly, it can be shown that the decrease of buying power in the lending country is uncertain. Total buying power depends on what the short-term lenders do with their foreign exchange.[21]

Summary. The analysis of the present chapter is concerned only with the direct inflationary and deflationary results of equilibrating short-term capital movements under a number of simplified assumptions. It has been indicated that there is a presumption that an inflationary effect will be produced when net short-term foreign assets increase (or liabilities decrease) and that a deflationary effect will follow if net short-term foreign liabilities increase (or assets decrease). This presumption is especially strong where the change (that is, the short-term capital movement) occurs in bankers' balances (or foreign money). When capital movements take the form of foreign-exchange movements and especially when they consist of shifts of foreign investments, the presumption, although remaining, is weakened by the necessity of considering what will happen to other prospective lenders in the financial circulation and to borrowers in the industrial circulation.

In the following chapter we shall show the secondary effects of international short-term capital movements on the money supply and on the national income. This will involve consideration of the interest rate on the short-term money market and hence of such phenomena as reserve ratios, secondary reserves, credit policy, and so forth. Likewise we shall be required to amplify the foregoing discussion of the effects of changes in foreign short-term investments (income short-term capital movements) on the money supply and on the rate of national income. By increasing the number of variables we shall find that

[21] "The Present Position of the Theory of International Trade," *op. cit.*, pp. 28-29. The references to the borrower and lender are to countries serving in that capacity on long-term account. So far as the short-term capital transaction is concerned, the designations are reversed. Nurkse argues that the borrower on short-term account will suffer some deflation as the transaction velocity of all money is reduced by the acquisition of a deposit by the lender. (See pp. 137-38, *op. cit.*) He does not, however, explore the ramifications involved in a consideration of what happens if the short-term lender invests his foreign assets.

the effects upon the national income lose in determinateness, even while it be admitted that so far as the primary effects of such shifts are concerned the normal expectation is for inflation in the lending countries (those that increase their net foreign short-term assets or reduce their foreign short-term liabilities) and for deflation in the borrowing countries (which increase their net foreign short-term liabilities or reduce their net assets).

III

THE SHORT-TERM RATE OF INTEREST AND THE MONEY SUPPLY

Gold flows, it was pointed out in the previous chapter, result in direct changes in the money supply when the net amount of short-term foreign assets is kept stable. Since the rise of deposit banking and the international gold standard, however, such gold movements have also been the occasion for secondary changes in the money supply in multiples of the amount added to or subtracted from the net gold stock in question. This has been brought about by the general practice followed by banks in financially developed countries of maintaining their deposit liabilities as a fairly constant proportion of their primary reserves, whether these be gold or deposits with the central bank.

Gold, Reserve Ratios, and Money. The details of practice vary from country to country and from banking system to banking system, so that no simple statement is possible of the hypothetical degree of expansion in money as a secondary result of the addition of a given sum of gold to the bank reserves of any nation. In England, for example, banks maintain the ratio of cash (deposits with the Bank of England and currency) to deposits at roughly 11 percent,[1] while in the United States the required minimum consequent to the final increase in reserve requirements of May 1, 1937,[2] was approximately 20 percent for all member banks. These practices, the one traditional, the other required by law, have the result of enabling the banking deposits of a country to expand as a multiple of the amount added to the country's monetary gold stock, unless the central bank takes steps to offset that possible expansion by depleting the member-bank reserves; and, conversely, they require a multiple contraction in the monetary supply when a reduction in

[1] See Willis and Beckhart, *Foreign Banking Systems* (1929), pp. 1168-69.
[2] See *Federal Reserve Bulletin*, June, 1937, pp. 503 ff.

gold stocks takes place at a time when the bank reserve ratio is at its legal or traditional minimum. These results are additional to the primary changes in the money supply resulting from changes in gold holdings when net short-term foreign assets are assumed unchanged.

The Demand and Supply of Short Loans. It is not necessary to repeat the sequence of banking steps by which these secondary changes in the money supply are brought about as a result of gold movements. The description of this process has been set forth often enough.[3] It is sufficient here to point out the role played by the short-term rate of interest[4] in connection with the reserve position of the member banks and in connection with the gold position of the central bank, which, under the international gold standard, affects that member bank reserve position. The effect of the short-term rate of interest in changing the money supply and, indeed, the very concept of the short-term rate of interest require some elucidation.

For the purposes of this study the short-term rate of interest is that prevailing in the section of the money market which is lending in the largest volume. Different rates will occupy this position from time to time. On one occasion the rate of interest in the security call-loan market may rule; at another, the general rate of discount on bankers' bills, or even that on Treasury bills.[5] If the banks are loaned up to the full extent of their legal or traditional reserve ratios, however, and if they are either currently borrowing from the central bank or would have to do so in order to expand their deposit liabilities, the

[3] See Hawtrey, *op. cit.*, chap. i, *passim;* D. H. Robertson, *Money* (2d ed., 1929), chap. iii, pp. 52-64; Keynes, *op cit.*, chap. xiii, *passim;* K. Wicksell, *Lectures on Political Economy*, II, *Money* (trans. 1935), pp. 79-87.

[4] Currie (*op. cit.*, p. 7) rightly interprets a changed willingness to lend funds at the same rate of interest as identical in effect with the change in the interest rate. Durbin, likewise (E. F. M. Durbin, *The Problem of Credit Policy*, 1935, p. 198), considers variations in willingness to lend at any rate of interest a powerful weapon of credit control in the hands of the banks.

[5] In the 1936 period the rates on call-loans and bankers' acceptances prevailing in the New York market were nominal. The Treasury bill rate, then, which for general purposes of international comparison was taken as zero, constituted the short-term rate of interest.

rate at which they obtain a replenishment of their reserves is likely to constitute the effective rate in the market.[6]

A gold inflow increases member-bank reserves and produces an automatic direct expansion of money (on the assumption of unchanged net foreign short-term assets) but does not necessarily lead to a secondary expansion in the money supply. It will increase the banks' willingness to lend, and it may do so to an extent sufficient to change the currently prevailing quoted rate of interest. Such would be the case if the added reserves induced banks to compete strenuously with one another to lend funds to the most active section of the short-term market. In the case of a gold outflow the loss would affect interest rates when the member banks were in debt to the central bank if the subtracted reserves induced the central bank to raise its discount rate. But if more loans are to be made, there must be borrowers willing to take loans either at the old rate or at the new rate if an actual rate change is brought about.

The rate of profit, current and prospective,[7] is the vital factor affecting the efficacy of additional gold reserves in producing changes in the money supply through an expansion of bank loans. We may call this rate of profit the determinant of the demand price in the short-term money market. At a given rate of profit, currently realized and envisaged, varying amounts of new loans will be contracted for, or old loans renewed, at different positions of the interest rate. The willingness of banks to lend new money, which depends on their reserve position, current and prospective, determines the supply price at which these loans will be offered. The interaction of demand and supply, that is, the readiness to borrow and the willingness to lend, may

[6] In France, shortly before the 1936 franc devaluation, the Bank of France discount rate, which was available to borrowers other than bankers for specific purposes, was not the going rate. See P. Einzig, "Some Theoretical Aspects of Forward Exchanges," *Economic Journal,* XLVI (1936), 464. At this particular time, because of the heavy discount on forward francs, the going rate of short-term interest was the rate of interest paid on foreign deposits. See below, chap. xii.

[7] See J. M. Keynes, *The General Theory of Employment, Interest and Money,* 1936, p. vii: "A monetary economy . . . is essentially one in which changing views about the future are capable of influencing the quantity of employment and not merely its direction."

be said to determine the rate of interest and the amount of loans outstanding at any given rate.[8]

When the demand for loans increases and the willingness to lend remains unchanged, an expansion in loans will occur. When the demand for new loans decreases, the total volume of loans falls as old loans are paid off.[9] If the demand curve shifts to the left so that no part of it is above the X-axis to the right of the Y-axis, the money supply will contract so far as loans are concerned, inasmuch as banks do not lend at negative rates of interest. This result will be independent of the terms the banks are willing to offer on loans down to zero interest. Similarly, the willingness of the banks to lend at any rate of interest may vanish, as the curve S-S′ moves upward or changes its slope to arrive at a position well to the left of the Y-axis in the usual range of interest rates. No matter what terms are offered them for loans then, no monetary expansion can occur.

[8] Using the familiar system of right-angle coördinates, the rate of interest may be plotted along the vertical axis, being positive above and negative below the horizontal axis. The amount of new loans engaged in and matured loans renewed or canceled may be ranged along the horizontal axis, new borrowings being plotted to the right, cancellations to the left of the vertical axis. D-D′ represents the willingness of borrowers to obtain loans, which will be negative at very high rates of interest and will approach infinity at negative rates. S-S′ stands for the bank's readiness to lend and will be unlikely ever to go below the horizontal axis. Under the conditions illustrated the banks are willing neither to contract nor to expand credit, and borrowers are similarly contented at the current rate of interest. Increased anticipations of profits would shift the D-D′ curve to the right; decreased expectations or prospective losses, to the left. Increased reserves would tend to shift the S-S′ curve downward, although presumably not below the horizontal axis, while decreased reserves would tend to move it up. If a shift in either D-D′ or S-S′ occurred under the conditions illustrated, the effect of the new loans made or the old loans called would interact on both curves until they came to rest with their intersection resting on the vertical axis above the horizontal axis. There would then be no new loans being made or old loans repaid on balance, and the going rate of interest would be determinate for new loans made with the proceeds of old-loan repayments.

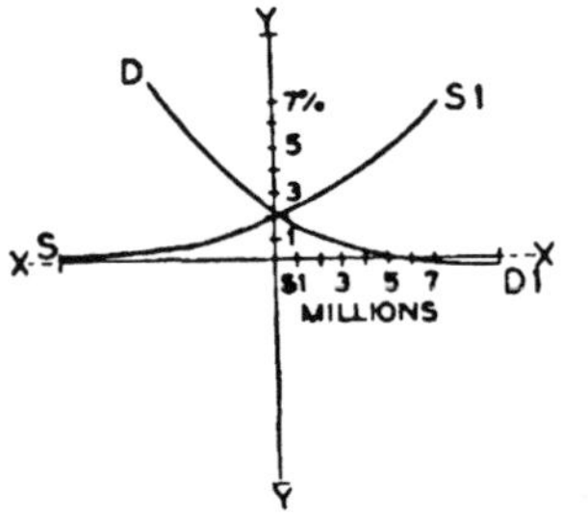

[9] The rate of profit on a given, pre-existing loan is determined both by the opportunities, actual and envisaged, for profit and by those for avoiding loss. Thus, with interest rates high in times of crisis, the demand for loans may be very great on the basis of borrowers' estimates of losses to be avoided.

Should gold reserves be added to the system and increase the banks' willingness to lend at a time when the demand curve does not cross the upper right-hand area of the system of coördinates, no new loans will be made and the primary expansion of the money supply will be followed by no necessary secondary expansion.[10] When, however, a going rate of interest for new loans exists, an increase of reserves brought about by gold flows will result in a secondary expansion of the monetary supply. If the money supply had previously been stable, the increase will be absolute. If it was in the process of being contracted, the increase will be only relative. Evidently the rapidity of such expansion and the possibility of its being pursued to the theoretical limit set up by the reserve ratio depend on the position of the demand and supply curves previous to the inflow of gold. The first steps in any absolute expansion will be followed by a revision of the willingness of banks to lend as their traditional or legal reserve ratio is approached.

The same type of reasoning may be applied to the analysis of gold outflows. Primary contraction of demand deposits takes place in any event if net short-term foreign assets are unchanged. Secondary contraction, in multiples of the amount of gold exported from the banking system's reserves, depends upon the willingness of the banks to lend or their insistence upon liquidation of maturing outstanding loans and upon the willingness of borrowers to borrow, their readiness to repay, or their need for the renewal of old loans in order to avoid losses. It is unnecessary for us to pursue the analysis through its various phases, since the argument has been sufficiently clarified by that concerned with expansion.[11]

[10] The banks may buy securities, which complicates the issue. An expansion of the money supply in this fashion, under the circumstances outlined, probably only adds to the financial circulation and thus does not affect the national income. It is only if the bank buys new securities or buys securities from others who will in turn buy new securities that the national income is affected, an increase in the industrial circulation taking place.

[11] Obviously the banks' readiness to lend depends upon many more considerations than the state of the banking system's gold reserves. Other factors affect the reserves themselves, and pressure may be brought upon the banks from the monetary authorities to lend or to refrain from lending. We shall deal with some of these factors below, pp. 43-45.

Secondary Expansion and Short-Term Capital. It is necessary now to consider the possibilities of secondary expansion and contraction resulting from short-term capital movements between countries. We may revert to the example utilized in the previous chapter, in which country B has an import surplus vis-à-vis country A, for which it pays by borrowing no short-term account. It will be remembered that while no *a priori* conclusion can be drawn as to the possibilities for primary expansion and contraction of the total money supply in A and B, respectively, yet a strong presumption exists that inflation will take place in the lending country whose net foreign assets are increased and deflation in the borrowing whose net foreign assets are reduced. This presumption is based on the primary relative changes between the industrial and the financial circulation which may be expected to follow the short-term capital movement.

The possibilities of secondary reactions in the industrial circulation and in the total money supply depend almost entirely on the practices of banking systems and on the laws or traditions under which reserve proportions are set up. In the lending country, if a gold-exchange standard is in force the foreign money or exchange acquired by the banks will be sold to the central bank. There it will be as effective in increasing the member banks' reserves and their willingness to lend as if it had been gold. The increase of foreign assets held by the central bank is tantamount to an increase in gold from the viewpoint of its legal reserve position. But similar reactions may follow even though the A country is not on the gold-exchange standard. Foreign exchange held by the member banks may be regarded as secondary reserves, over and above the primary reserves required by law.[12] Additions to these may in turn increase the member banks' willingness to lend, provided such lending does not endanger the legal reserve ratio by expanding deposits too far. The primary expansion of the money supply resulting (under the necessary assumptions) from the original short-term lending operation may lower the free reserves of the banking

[12] See J. Viner, *op. cit.*, p. 164.

system by, say, one-tenth of the amount loaned. If free reserves remain in the system the banks' eagerness to lend is increased by the addition of secondary reserves. Particularly is this the case when the secondary reserves are held in a gold-standard country, where they may be converted into gold for addition to primary reserves when necessary. Evidently under these conditions banks will not expand in the same degree as they would if actual gold were acquired. Nevertheless, the possibility of exchanging foreign assets for gold, when that is present, is sufficient to enable an expansion of multiple proportions[13] to start on the basis of the increase in short-term foreign assets.[14] These reactions depend in large measure on the practices of individual banking systems. When a gold-exchange standard exits, of course, the acquisition of short-term foreign assets results in the same degree of expansion as would have taken place if actual gold had been imported. When the banking system makes a practice of keeping outside reserves, as in the pre-war Canadian example made familiar by Viner, an increase in these secondary reserves is almost as effective as would be the case on the gold-exchange standard. In other cases the tendency may not be as strong. Yet the experience of the French in the period from 1926 to 1931 indicates that the factor must not be overlooked. The Bank of France from 1926 to 1929 acquired sterling and dollar assets, as French capital on long-term account was repatriated, and this operation gave the French banks of deposit reserves through which they were able to increase the circulation

[13] Barrett Whale (in his review of Ohlin's *Interregional and International Trade*, in *Economica*, No. 5 N. S. (1935), 114 ff.) states (p. 117): "An increase in the foreign balances held by joint-stock banks may sometimes lead to an equivalent (not a multiple) increase in their own deposits without any change in discount rates." Our analysis, both here and in chap. ii, suggests that Whale understates the possibilities of expansion. If the country's foreign assets are increased by the banks' holdings, the primary expansion is certain and the multiple expansion a distinct possibility.

[14] See Ohlin, *op. cit.*, p. 395: ". . . when gold moves it is often less a *causa efficiens* with regard to later credit policy of central banks than to restore their gold reserves to a percentage which is considered desirable or normal although in excess of the legal minimum—this percentage having already been changed through changes in the credit volume, which are directly or indirectly due to declines or increases of foreign exchange reserves in one form or another." See also Nurkse, *op. cit.*, p. 142.

and increase loans in a (low) multiple of the foreign exchange thus acquired.[15]

In the borrowing country the possibilities of secondary contraction consequent to a loss of net short-term foreign assets are not as great as those of secondary expansion in the lending country. Some contraction of a secondary nature will ensue when gold-exchange countries or nations whose banks made a practice of keeping outside reserves lose short-term foreign assets. But nothing of the sort has followed in practice when the deposits of foreign nations increased in New York or London. This was the objection to the gold-exchange standard raised by many critics in the last decade, that is, that the standard did not function bilaterally. An increase in the foreign liquid assets of a gold-exchange country permitted it to expand its monetary medium, but did not place the country whose assets were acquired under any necessity to contract. Thus the gold-exchange standard was attacked on the ground that it was inflationary from a world point of view and that it failed to facilitate the process of maintaining equilibrium in the balance of payments to the same degree that the pre-war gold standard had done.[16] In discussing domestic interregional capital movements Iversen suggests that an increase of "due to banks" in New York for the account of California banks will be likely to result in a secondary contraction in New York: "the New York bank . . . knowing that the balance of the San Francisco bank is a less reliable deposit than that belonging to the lending capitalist in New York, will probably attempt to strengthen its cash position by a credit transaction."[17] This has not been usual in international changes in short-term liabilities. In London, before

[15] See R. G. Hawtrey, *The Art of Central Banking*, 1933, pp. 16-19.

[16] See, e.g., J. Y. le Branchu, *Essai sur le Gold Exchange Standard*, 1932, p. 120; M. Palyi, "A Desirable Monetary Policy" in *International Economic Relations*, 1934, p. 238. Hawtrey's defense of the gold-exchange standard against these attacks (*The Gold Standard in Theory and Practice*, 3d ed., 1933, pp. 217-18) on the grounds that no disturbance occurs until the gold-exchange standard is abandoned and those with exchange ask for gold has little force. The gold-exchange standard in essence permits the country whose assets are being acquired to overvalue its currency gradually, so that in time the mechanism must break down. See below, chap. viii.

[17] *Op. cit.*, p. 466.

the crisis of 1931, an increase of foreign liabilities resulted in no corresponding increase in English foreign assets or gold. Eventually the Macmillan Committee estimated: "Our liabilities may be as much as double our liquid assets, reckoning these as made up of our acceptances and our surplus gold hitherto available for export."[18] The fact that the outflow of short-term capital in 1931 made the New York banks borrow heavily from the Federal Reserve system suggests that there, too, the preceding short-term international borrowing had not been immediately deflationary in its secondary effects.[19]

A well-managed gold-exchange standard possesses only the advantage that it enables a small country to save the costs of shipping the yellow metal. Presumably all else should follow as on a gold standard, particularly expansion when gold-exchange assets increase, contraction when they decrease.[20] In the other

[18] See Committee on Finance and Industry, *Report*, 1931, p. 150. The Exchange Equalization Account is attempting, in a measure, to match increases in English short-term liabilities with off-setting foreign assets (or gold). But see below, chap. xiii, for an extended discussion of the stabilization fund technique.

[19] See Iversen, *op. cit.*, p. 467, to the effect that the long-term capital export of the United States in the post-war period was facilitated by the exchange balances kept by European (and South American) countries in New York. Nurkse avers that inflation characterized the period and that the long-term capital export took place out of (artificially) created credit (*op. cit.*, pp. 204-5). He refers to Hardy (*Credit Policies of the Federal Reserve System*, 1932), Reed (*Federal Reserve Policy*, 1930), Anderson and Young (without specific citations). It would appear that if the New York borrowing on short-term account was deflationary in its secondary manifestations, it was only so in comparative, not in absolute, terms.

[20] See G. F. Luthringer, *The Gold Exchange Standard in the Philippines*, 1934, pp. 16 ff., 257. Luthringer, without distinguishing between primary contraction brought about by currency payments into the Gold Standard Fund in Manila and that in which drafts on New York were bought with deposits, criticizes the Fund's policy at one time of depositing a portion of its assets in local banks and of later investing them (pp. 16 ff., 20 ff.). He does not appear to realize, however, the various possibilities for different degrees of contractions or even expansion latent in the situation. Assume that the Gold Standard Fund in Manila acquired 1,000,000 pesos for remittance to New York. Were the payments made in currency and no further currency drawn immediately into circulation from the banks for replacement, the gold fund, by retaining the currency would effect a primary contraction of the full amount. It might, however, deposit the currency, increasing banking reserves, and permit expansion up to the point where the currency requirements would rise to draw down banking reserves. If the in-payment were made with deposits, the gold fund's retention of the deposits in the same form results in a primary contraction. If

country, however, in which the balances are kept, expansion and contraction do not necessarily take place as the converse reaction. If the foreign assets are invested or if they are balances on deposit with the member banks, no primary change takes place in the money supply of the borrowing country. A presumption exists that primary contraction will take place as funds are shifted from the industrial to the financial circulation. Secondary contraction, possible though not usual when the foreign assets are kept in the form of bank deposits, will not be brought about unless by conscious direction of the monetary authorities, who take cognizance of the fact that the borrowing increases the country's contingent liabilities to foreigners on investment account.[21]

Within the limitations set by the exceptions noted in the previous chapter the incidence of primary inflation and deflation may be said to be fairly symmetrical, even though the changes in the total money supply brought about by short-term capital movements are not. Such is not as likely to be the case with the secondary expansion and contraction. The expansion in the lending country as a secondary result of the movement is apt to be greater in extent than the contraction in the borrowing country. This is due to the fact that the expansion takes place as a result of the acquisition of assets considered on an equal footing with gold, whereas in the borrowing country the primary banking reserves are not likely to be reduced, and

---

the fund should draw down the reserves of the banks by demanding currency for its deposit, multiple contraction would take place. If it invests its deposits, no change in the money supply takes place.

Luthringer notes the possibilities of expansion if the original contraction took place in the active circulation and was then deposited: "since the cash deposited by the government could be used as reserves for further loan and deposit expansion" (p. 17), citing E. W. Kemmerer, *Modern Currency Reforms*, 1916, pp. 275-77. Such a possibility, however, appears remote, since a large contraction in the active circulation would presumably have to be made up to some extent, particularly if any move was made to expand the means of payment. See p. 191 where the coincidence of deposit and currency movements is revealed in chart form.

[21] The exchange standard country can, of course, take steps to insure that contraction will follow in the other country. It may, as did Denmark in its recent revision of the statutes of its central bank, permit the inclusion as foreign exchange reserves only of net balances with foreign central banks. See *Federal Reserve Bulletin*, July, 1936, p. 538.

hence the contraction of actual means of payment may not be as great. Hohlfeld and Iversen illustrate the point with diagrams, indicating the asymmetry in secondary expansion and contraction between the lending and borrowing countries, respectively.[22] But the point can be made clear without the necessity for graphic representation.[23]

Credit Policy. The rate of monetary expansion or contraction in the internal economy depends on the present and the anticipated rates of profit, on the one hand, and on the reserve position of the member banks, on the other. Gold movements affect the latter and hence affect the direction and rate of money change, provided always that the demand for capital has been positive at positive rates of interest. International short-term capital movements affect the reserve position, first by virtue of the direct expansion or contraction in deposits which may result from them and secondly by virtue of the practice, followed by many banking systems, of treating reserves of foreign money or claims to foreign money as primary, or at least secondary, reserves. If the foreign exchange can be sold to or bought from the central bank in exchange for deposits, foreign exchange reserves are as effective as gold in inducing secondary expansion or contraction.

But there are other influences affecting the banks' willingness to lend, apart from gold and short-term capital movements. One is central-bank credit policy, under which are subsumed the various powers of the monetary authorities, including open-market operations, moral suasion, discount rate changes, and so forth.[24] Bank reserves may be expanded or decreased through

[22] See H. H. Hohlfeld, "Die Struktur der zwischen-landischen Kapitalbewegungen," *Weltwirtschaftliche Archiv*, 1933, Bd. I, pp. 473 ff.; and Iversen, *op. cit.*, pp. 523 ff.

[23] Nurkse (*op. cit.*, p. 138) holds that on the exchange standard there is a tendency for one country to change the volume of its means of payments. His statement that the means of payment increase in the lending country, but do not change in the borrower, contradits his statement quoted above, p. 20 n., that no money change need occur when a capital movement takes the place of gold flow. See also above, p. 31 n.

[24] See Iversen, *op. cit.*, p. 514: ". . . it is realized by modern economists that the credit policy of central banks is influenced by many other considerations besides the size of their gold reserves . . ." See also pp. 320-21; Ohlin, *op. cit.*, pp. 415 ff., 544 n.; Nurkse, *op. cit.*, pp. 140-41; Harrod, *op. cit.*, p. 139.

various means open to central banks, national treasuries, and stabilization funds, without the necessity for an initiatory disturbance in the balance of payments. Furthermore, the willingness of borrowers to avail themselves of opportunities to obtain funds is dependent upon external conditions to only a slight degree. The principal factors determining the rate of profit and therefore the demand for loan funds are almost entirely associated with the business cycle.

Credit policy may be so operated as to vitiate all the effects of monetary contraction and expansion which would otherwise have resulted from the international movement of gold and short-term capital. When gold leaves the United States, for example, the Federal Reserve system can purchase government bonds to restore member bank reserves to their erstwhile level and thus avoid the necessity for any contraction whatsoever. Palyi thinks that central banks are prone to act in this way as a general rule, making the problem of international monetary adjustment more difficult. Ohlin, however, disagrees.[25] It may fairly be said, nevertheless, that many economists who are concentrating on the internal aspects of credit policy advocate exactly this type of reaction to changes in the reserve position brought about by disequilibria in the balance of payments.[26]

If a policy of stable exchanges be assumed, the central bank may be expected to aid the adjustments in the country's international position which are necessitated by gold and short-term capital movements. If the member banks are loaned up, the bank rate will be the going rate for the new loans, and changes in it will react directly upon the money market where loans are being negotiated. If the bank rate is raised, on the assumption of an unchanged demand for loans, the willingness of the banks to lend at the old rate changes. The supply price of new loans will then rise to reduce the rate of expansion, or even to induce contraction.[27] If the bank rate is lowered, under similar

[25] See M. Palyi, "Die Zahlungsbilanz der Vereinigten Staaten," *Schriften des Verein fur Socialpolitik*, 1928, quoted by Ohlin, *op. cit.*, pp. 415-16. See also Nurske, *op. cit.*, p. 141.

[26] See below, chap. xi.

[27] Nurkse, *op. cit.*, pp. 138-39, holds that the "market" rate must be raised

conditions, the opposite holds true. The rate may be changed, however, not only when actual gold reserves change or when the central bank's foreign assets diminish. The same step may also be taken if a weakness in the rate of foreign exchange develops at home or abroad indicating a prospective change in reserves, whether of gold or foreign assets.[28] Thus the contraction and expansion may be geared to foreign short-term capital movements, without the necessity for legal provisions whereby foreign exchange is included as primary reserves.

Changes in the discount rate, however, also have an effect on the expansion and contraction of the monetary supply through their reactions on the current and prospective rate of profit and hence on the demand for loanable funds. A rise in the rate may suggest an imminent crisis and induce would-be borrowers to postpone negotiating for loans. At the same time it may precipitate an increased demand for funds as those already operating with borrowed short-term capital find themselves faced with loss if they are unable to obtain extended accommodation. A lowering of the discount rate may act in the opposite way, upon occasion, to heighten entrepreneurs' anticipations of profits. In the security markets, especially, discount rate changes are often followed by variations in the rate of long-term interest with resultant alterations in the prices of fixed-interest obligations.[29]

Short-Term Lending and Inflation. We may now return to our illustration of a simplified balance of payments, under which B has an excess of imports from A, for which it pays by short-term borrowing. On this occasion we will permit equilibrating, speculative, and income short-term capital movements;

---

above the "natural" rate of interest to induce deflation. The application of these terms to the short-term money market appears to be a little strained. Is the natural rate that which equates the supply of temporary savings to the need for working capital?

Ohlin, *op. cit.*, p. 413, in considering the expansion of credit as the result of an inflow of gold, indicates that it will take place "if the discount rate and the willingness to give credit are unchanged." This omits the rate of profit and the willingness to borrow. Likewise, it seems to be more logical to relate the willingness to lend to the banking system's reserves, rather than to consider it independently.

[28] See Ohlin, *op. cit.*, p. 413.

[29] See Hawtrey, *Currency and Credit, op. cit.*, chap. ix, *passim.*

assume a credit policy in both countries oriented to maintain stability of the exchanges within limits comparable to gold points, but without gold movements taking place; and allow interest-rate changes due to central-bank manipulation, on the further assumption that member banks in both A and B are possessed of only small amounts of surplus reserves. We need not enter here into a discussion of the degree of inflation and deflation required in A and B, respectively, to restore exactly the equilibrium of the balance of payments. That question will arise more appropriately in the treatment of the transfer mechanism in Part II below. It will suffice if we confine our analysis to the possibilities of inflation under the limited assumptions set forth, whether the degree of dynamic monetary adjustment falls short of, precisely meets, or exceeds the exigencies of the given situation it is required to correct.

The original short-term borrowing under our assumptions will be likely to be in the form of an equilibrating capital movement, for example, A banks receiving for discount a net balance of sight bills drawn by A exporters on B importers. The A banks may hold such bills or sell them to the speculative public or discount them in B and hold cash or money market investments there. If A is on the fixed-exchange standard proper, they may also discount them with the central bank. Under our assumptions they cannot sell them to A importers, because their requirements for B exchange have already been satisfied.

The incidence of primary expansion on the money supply depends on whether A member banks or the A central bank, on the one hand, or the A money market, on the other, eventually holds the loan. In either event, however, we may assume that primary inflation takes place, as the industrial circulation increases at the expense of the financial circulation. For secondary expansion to ensue, an A bank must consider the foreign assets acquired as secondary ("outside") reserves, which increase its willingness to lend; or, if it discounts them with the central bank, its willingness to lend will be enhanced by the increase in its primary reserve. If the public (the money market) eventually carries the loans, the possibilities of secondary expansion are reduced but still present.

If the A bank sells the equilibrating short-term assets thus acquired, it will force lower the rate of exchange on B. Exchange speculators may then buy bills as a speculative operation, with the result that they substitute their credit for that of the A bank. No primary expansion of the total money supply occurs, as that which has already taken place is canceled when the exchange dealers give up bank deposits with which to buy the foreign exchange, unless the dealers operate on borrowed money. In this last instance the bank lending funds to them is essentially lending money abroad, although it avoids an exchange risk. The rate of exchange on B will be restored to its previous level if A banks sell all their exchange to A speculators, but the average price paid by the latter is lower than this level. Similarly, the speculators hope that when B achieves an export surplus and is ready to repay the A credits, they will be able to sell this exchange at an average level above that at which the A-B rate stood before the original B import surplus.

The A central bank may be constrained to lower its discount rate and thus increase the possibilities of secondary expansion, on the one hand, and a movement of income short-term funds to B on the other. Two circumstances might contribute to such a decision. If the foreign assets acquired by A member banks are sold to or discounted with them, their heightened reserve position, assuming foreign exchange to count as legal reserve for the central bank, might conduce to a lowering of bank rate. Should foreign assets not be considered reserves and should the A bank on that account, not itself wishing to hold the exchange, sell it in the open market, the fact of weakness of the B exchange rate on A, foreshadowing an increase in actual reserves (an inward gold movement), might induce the A central bank to lower its bank rate. In either event the rate reduction would stimulate a movement of income short-term funds to B. This would restore the rate of exchange and hence obliterate the symptom that prompted the rate reduction, under one set of circumstances. Or, alternatively, the market would have to purchase its foreign exchange from the central bank itself and thus deprive it of its newly gained reserves. The movement of funds by speculators or international investors (in short-term money markets) would affect the money supply in A only if they buy the exchange from the A member banks or central bank rather than trade foreign exchange among themselves. In either of the latter cases the money supply, which was expanded as a primary result by the acquisition of the exchange by the banks, is contracted unless the dealers or investors purchase the foreign assets, not with their own deposits, but with borrowed funds.

The discussion of the effects on the money supply and inflation in A, when speculative and income capital movements and the interest rate are removed from the seclusion of *ceteris paribus*, may be summed up as follows:

1. If the B import surplus is financed by book credit or by bills drawn and held by A exporters, there is no change in the total money supply of A or in the industrial circulation, and there is no primary or secondary inflation.

2. If A banks finance the surplus by increasing their foreign deposits for the duration of the disequilibrium in the balance of payments (a speculative transaction) or their foreign investments (an income movement),[30] primary expansion takes place in the total and industrial circulation, and primary inflation ensues. Secondary inflation will result if the A banks consider their foreign assets as secondary reserves and are more willing to satisfy the demand of domestic customers for loans as a result of having acquired them.

3. If A banks sell their foreign exchange to dealers before interest rates move, the resultant speculative movement, replacing the equilibrating movement, will decrease the total money supply after the original increase. It will, however, leave undis-

[30] The transaction may be considered an "equilibrating" movement only so long as an A bank has a chance to decide whether it wants to retain or dispose of the foreign assets acquired by discounting the A exporter's surplus bills. Should it retain them because of a seasonal need for increased B deposits, the movement changes from an equilibrating to a speculative one. Should it keep them because of a higher rate of interest to be earned on them, the movement is one of the income order.

turbed the primary increase in the industrial circulation and the resultant primary inflation. If the dealers borrowed in order to buy the exchange, even the total supply of money remains unchanged. No secondary expansion results unless the central bank acts to lower the rate of discount as a consequence of the strength of A currency in the exchanges.

4. If the central bank acquires the exchange and is on the fixed-exchange standard, primary and secondary expansion of the money supply follow. So long as the central bank does not change its discount rate this result will occur because of the increase in A's primary bank reserves. If the central bank in A does lower its discount rate, the money supply is increased, on the one hand, as marginal borrowers at the old rate are satisfied; but, on the other, income movements of capital to B begin, forcing the central bank to sell the foreign exchange it has acquired and thereby to reduce the previously enhanced bank reserves.

Short-Term Borrowing and Deflation. Despite the wide range of possibilities with respect to changes in the total money supply, the industrial circulation within the total money supply and the national income in A, the problem in B cannot be attacked symmetrically. It is perhaps unnecessary to do more than to sum up the various situations which might arise, since the details of each operation are sufficiently clear in the light of the exposition of the previous section.

1. If the import surplus is financed by book credit or by bills drawn and held by A exporters, there is no primary or secondary money change in B, either for the total money supply or for the industrial circulation. Income velocity will probably be affected as importers build up balances to meet maturing obligations.

2. If the foreign lender holds bank deposits, no change in the total money supply occurs. A reduction in transactions velocity takes place, however, and a reduction in circular velocity occurs if the importer transfers the bank deposits which the A lender holds. If such bank deposits are held with the B central bank, secondary deflation results, due to losses of reserves by

the B banks. This necessitates, under our assumptions, a multiple contraction in deposit liabilities. If the deposits are held with the B member banks, some secondary contraction may ensue if the B banks deem foreign deposits less stable than domestic.

3. If the foreign lender holds bank deposits or money-market investments, a secondary contraction may result if the B central bank raises the rate of discount as the B rate of exchange weakens.

4. If the loan takes the form of an investment in the B money market, the total money supply is not affected, though a prima-facie case for primary deflation exists, because funds have been shifted from the industrial to the financial circulation. No secondary deflation results, barring a change in the central bank rate of discount.

5. Although not within the limits of the assumptions of the problem at hand, it is important to mention that the import surplus may have been paid for, not by a new loan from A to B, but by a reduction in net loans from B to A. This would occur if B were on a fixed-exchange standard pegged to A. In this instance the likelihood of deflation in B as a secondary phenomenon is greater. When the B central bank foreign exchange reserves are reduced, it is obvious that such deflation results. The same applies in case the B member banks maintain outside reserves, on the assumption that they maintain their deposit liabilities as a fixed multiple of their primary and secondary reserves.

Part II

THE TRANSFER MECHANISM

IV

SETTING THE PROBLEM

Economic discussion of the mechanism through which equilibrium in the balance of international payments is attained and preserved has largely devoted itself in recent years to the transfer process. This has been the case partly because of the great importance of the problem in the real world.[1] The choice, however, has been made in largest part for expositional purposes. A unilateral payment made from one country to another brings into play the whole range of factors concerned in the adjustment process. Where a tariff has been newly imposed or where a change in international demand or in costs of production of internationally traded goods occurs, the technique of the transfer balancing process can be readily applied.[2] A new tariff imposed by country A upon the products of country B, for example, disturbs the balance of merchandise trade of both A and B, requiring B to export more goods at lower costs or A to export less goods to B. In the same fashion a long-term capital loan raised by A in B calls for heightened exports from B and reduced exports from A or both. The analogy cannot be pursued too far, in the present instance, since conditions of supply and demand will alter the equilibrium position differently in the two cases. On the whole, however, the transfer process holds its favor as a topic for analysis by international trade and exchange theorists, largely because it affords a clear and unequivocal case in which the general principles of international trade and monetary equilibrium may be expounded.

Purchasing Power and Real Transfers. International capital transfer has two aspects: there is first of all the transfer of purchasing-power ownership and, secondly, there is the goods or

[1] As in the case of the hotly debated reparations discussion. See Iversen, *op. cit.*, chap. vii.

[2] See Nurkse, *op. cit.*, p. 8.

"real" transfer. Actually the two aspects are closely interrelated. As an analytical aid, however, it is useful to consider them separately in order to show their relation to intranational borrowing and, indeed, to the whole monetary problem of capital formation. If a citizen of A lends money to a compatriot, the borrower is presumably content to receive payment in the same monetary unit that the lender has available. The purchasing power is thus readily transferable within a single monetary system. The difficulties of the "real" transfer remain, however, if the goods and services which the borrower purchases with his newly acquired funds differ from those the lender would have bought had he not parted with his accumulated buying power.[3] In international dealings the inhabitant of A is in few cases satisfied to receive a loan in the currency of the lender in B. A purchasing-power transfer from B currency to A currency must therefore take place. To make the purchasing-power transfer possible between monetary systems, a real transfer of goods and services between the localities concerned is necessary. Or, regarded from the other standpoint, a real transfer in goods, which must precede, accompany, or follow the transfer of purchasing power if the loan is to be carried through, takes place inevitably as a result of the decreased purchases in the one country and increased purchases in the other.

That the real transfer should take place at approximately the same time as the purchasing-power transfer thus follows both from the nature of the foreign-exchange market itself and from the characteristics of money borrowing. In the former case it is evident that unless payment is to be made in a universally accepted medium of exchange, such as gold, the lending country needs foreign money, or claims to it, to present to the individual borrowers abroad. To obtain this it must have previously sold,

[3] It is not our intention here to enter upon a discussion of monetary theory proper beyond pointing out that these shifts in demand do ordinarily take place as a result of domestic loans. Economics knows very little about these shifts in demand and their effects, whether the shifts take place between various types of consumers' goods or between producers' and consumers' goods. How much less it knows, therefore, about international shifts in demand, in which the possibilities are many times multiplied because of the increased number of variables!

currently sell, or at some future date be prepared to sell goods to possessors of foreign money in excess of goods it buys from them. For this surplus it has received or will receive claims on foreign money which it may turn over to the foreign borrowers in satisfaction of its loan contract.

If gold is available to make the purchasing-power transfer required by the loan, the real transfer follows from the nature of the money transaction. After the gold flow the borrowing country A is possessed of a larger proportion of the combined monetary base of the two countries than before. Hence it can purchase a larger proportion of their combined output. Under modern banking arrangements credit expansion in the country receiving gold and credit contraction in the country losing it will enable this result to be achieved. A may, on the basis of its expanded credit, buy products it normally would have exported to B, or may simply buy more B products than formerly, or both. In any event, it will normally be found, after sufficient time has elapsed to re-establish an equilibrium in the trade between the two countries, that A has developed a relative import surplus, B a relative export surplus. B receives the greater part of its gold back in payment for the excess goods shipped to A. While the purchasing-power transfer was brought about immediately through gold shipments, yet eventually it was accomplished by a real transfer of capital[4] in goods and services.[5]

The Stages of Adjustment. Our present concern with the transfer process is a limited one. We are primarily concerned with the description of the sequence of steps by which the real transfer is completed, under different assumptions regarding the credit mechanism, and the part played by gold, the rate of for-

[4] Not necessarily capital goods. See Iversen, *op. cit.*, p. 21; Nurkse, *op. cit.*, p. 13.

[5] It often lends clarity to discussions of international trade problems, to think of the two or more countries concerned as one, their individual demands as joint demands, their production of goods of the same type as composite supply, etc. The best example of this type of analysis is to be found in Haberler, *op. cit.*, pp. 8 ff. See also, F. A. Hayek, *Prices and Production*, 1st ed., 1931, p. 94: "The increase or decrease of the quantity of money within any one geographical area serves a function just as definite as the increase or decrease of the money incomes of particular individuals, namely, the function of enabling the inhabitants to draw a larger or smaller share of the total output of the whole world."

eign exchange, and short-term capital movements. The possibilities regarding the terms of trade,[6] concomitant factor movements,[7] and the effects of the change in factor equipment in the two countries resulting from the international transfer of capital[8] fall outside the scope of our immediate sphere of interest. We are concerned in discussing the mechanics of transfer and the various factors bound up therewith and the extent of the various adjustments necessary. The degree of inflation required in the borrowing country and of deflation in the lending are intimately related to numerous nonmonetary factors. A discussion of these factors and of their relationship to the extent of the monetary change made necessary under given circumstances is therefore in point. Especially is this the case since it is concerning this aspect of the problem that the literature is the most confused.

The required degrees of inflation in the borrowing country and of deflation in the lending country depend, in theoretical discussion, upon the assumptions made about the loans and the changes in international demand consequent to them. These assumptions have to be made at three stages of monetary change: (1) at the receipt of the loan by the A borrower; (2) at the increase of incomes in A resulting from the spending of part or all of the proceeds of the loan there; (3) at the increase in incomes in A resulting from any secondary expansion in the money supply.[9] Three parallel deflationary stages may be dis-

[6] See Taussig, *International Trade, op. cit.*, pp. 113 ff. We shall use the term "terms of trade" to refer to the "net terms of trade," that is, the relation between the export and import price levels.

[7] See Ohlin, *op. cit.*, p. 404; Nurkse, *op. cit.*, p. 20 and pp. 31 ff.

[8] See *ibid.*, chap. xvii, *passim*.

[9] See Iversen, *op. cit.*, p. 466 n.: "Ohlin distinguishes between three stages: of the 'primary' increase in buying power—equal to the amount of the loan—the part spent on domestic goods remains in circulation and constitutes an inflation of credit [*sic*], which serves to call forth a 'secondary' increase in buying power as it passes from hand to hand and creates money incomes to an amount much larger than the original loan. To this is finally added the 'tertiary' increase in buying power which is due to the more liberal credit policy which the increasing outside reserve tends to call forth." See Ohlin, *op. cit.*, pp. 412-13. We have hitherto referred to primary and secondary expansion (and contraction) in incomes, the former being the result of the receipt of the loan, the latter being the result of the monetary response to movements of gold or short-term capital. Hereafter, however, we shall use the three stages suggested by Ohlin. His "in-

tinguished in B. The present analysis, however, may be confined to the inflation in the borrowing country A, since theoretically the deflation in B is the converse.

When the A borrowers have successfully floated a loan in B and received B currency as its proceeds, we may consider that there has been an expansion in "incomes" in A equal to the amount of the loan. At this first stage, should the loan be spent directly on imports from B no adjustment through gold shipments, fluctuations of the rate of exchange, or short-term capital movements is called for. If the lenders, by their act of saving, abstain from the consumption of the same B goods that the A borrowers buy, no prices are affected and the terms of trade between the countries remain unaltered. If the lenders in B give up the consumption of home-market goods,[10] the demand for B's exports will have increased absolutely. Thereupon, their prices will rise relative to import prices, and the terms of trade will shift in favor of the lender rather than the borrower, or contrary to the usual classical presumption.[11] Actually, all, part, or none of the loan may be spent by the A borrowers directly in B. White gives reasons for believing that agricultural countries, the most frequent borrowers of large amounts in normal times, spend a larger proportion of foreign loans directly on imports that can be inferred from the ratio of foreign to domestic trade. In the case of foreign governmental loans for budgetary purposes, he admits, the proportion thus spent will

crease in buying power" is synonymous with the expression "an expansion in the national money income."

[10] See Harrod's distinction among A, B, and C goods (*op. cit.*, pp. 59 ff.). A goods are those which are continually traded internationally. B goods' prices occasionally alter sufficiently to enable them to move between countries. C goods are home-market goods which cannot be sold abroad because of their immobility or their high costs of transportation. White's remarks (in his review of Ohlin and Haberler, *Quarterly Journal of Economics*, XLVIII (1934), 734) to the effect that so much inertia exists in international trade channels, because of the high costs of selling any but standardized commodities, suggest that B goods are not of great importance quantitatively. We shall use the term "foreign-trade goods" to apply to A and B goods, the term, home-market goods, for C.

[11] This special case is mentioned by Nurkse, *op. cit.*, p. 166, and by Iversen, *op. cit.*, pp. 472 ff., though in somewhat different terms of analysis. Iversen believes the possibility of this sort of change in the terms of trade is large (p. 488). Not so Nurkse, *op. cit.*, p. 108, or Gilbert, *op. cit.*, pp. 30 ff.

be greatly reduced. He suggests, nevertheless, that "the probability that a goodly proportion of the loan will be spent immediately on imports is by no means a small one."[12] Whatever share is so spent reduces the need for the foreign-exchange adjustment mechanism to operate, and the necessity for changes in money incomes brought about by shipments of gold, or movements of exchange rates or international short-term capital.[13]

At the second stage, that part of the loan not spent for B foreign-trade goods will be transferred to A. This may be brought about by a gold flow, by movements of short-term capital in the opposite direction, or through a shift in the rate of exchange. For present purposes we may assume that the A member banks extend to the A borrowers a credit, with the foreign proceeds of the loan as security. This increase in incomes, now in A money, will be spent by the A borrowers and received there as incomes. When so received, it will be spent by the recipients. Some proportion of the increase in incomes resulting from the turnover of the part of the primary increase in buying power transferred to A will be spent on foreign-trade goods, either in B exports or on goods normally exported by A to B. This proportion depends upon the flexibility of demand for foreign-trade goods, that is, upon the manner in which total money income is divided between home-market and foreign-trade goods when total real income is changed, or upon the "income elasticity" for foreign-trade goods.[14] If the flexibility of demand is unitary, the demand for foreign-trade goods will increase in the same proportion as the total money income. If it is greater than unity, a larger proportion of the increased total money income will be spent on foreign-trade goods than was so spent before the change in money income. If it is less than unity, a smaller proportion of total money income will go for foreign-trade goods.

[12] See White, *op. cit.*, p. 21.

[13] See Nurkse, *op. cit.*, p. 74.

[14] For a discussion of this point, see "Flexibility of Demand in International Trade," by the present writer, in *Quarterly Journal of Economics*, LI (1937), 352-61.

Evidently the flexibility of demand for foreign-trade goods may be such that all the increase in incomes is devoted to them. This is not the limiting case. Or it may be, on the other hand, that the flexibility of demand for home-market goods is so great that the absolute amount of money income spent upon foreign-trade goods remains unchanged, or is even reduced, following the rise in incomes at the second stage. Again, generalizations about demand flexibility for foreign-trade goods are of doubtful value, but the opinion may be hazarded that in agricultural countries such demand is relatively flexible, whereas in industrial countries, it is more apt to be inflexible.[15] In the case of a loan from an industrial country to an agricultural country, therefore, flexibility of demand would tend to operate in such a fashion as to bring about the real transfer with a reduced necessity for thoroughgoing changes in monetary income.

It may be in order to discuss, parenthetically, the terms of trade in the light of what has just been said about changes in demand. The price changes which follow from these shifts in demand could not be predicted categorically, even though one had complete information concerning the degree of flexibility of demand for foreign-trade goods in both the inflating and deflating countries. Other problems must be simultaneously considered, including those of joint demand, composite supply, the law of one price,[16] and the elasticity of substitution. When the A demand schedule shifts to the right for a given product but is offset by an equal shift to the left of the B schedule, no changes in price arise from the demand side. If it is an A product, however, inflation may be expected in time to raise the supply price, as competition in A calls for increased money incomes for the factors of production. This will raise the price, if the joint demand be still considered given. The amount then imported by B will depend upon the elasticity of demand in B for the product at the new position of the demand schedule. If

[15] *Ibid.*, p. 360.

[16] See Brisman, S., "Reflections on Foreign Exchange Theory," in *Economic Essays in Honour of Gustav Cassel*, 1933, p. 70. The later writers did not ignore the law of one price to the extent that earlier economists did. See, e.g., Viner, *op. cit.*, p. 228.

the commodity is produced in B, deflation there in time may be expected to lower the supply price and hence the price in A, so that the amount imported will depend upon the elasticity of A's demand at the new position. Proceeding still on the assumption that the original shifts in demand schedules in A and B (which are determined first by the degree of income change and secondly by the flexibility of demand for foreign-trade goods) balance one another, the real transfer will be aided if the A demand schedules for foreign-trade goods are relatively inelastic and the B schedules relatively elastic. The price changes, under these assumptions, will depend upon fairly long-run supply-price reactions and will move the terms of trade in favor of the borrower and against the lender.

Where unequal portions of a particular commodity are consumed by A and B, the analysis becomes more complex. If A normally exports one-third of a commodity and consumes two-thirds locally, it may be assumed further that a 25 percent inflation of incomes at the second or third stage, or at both stages, increases the A demand with unitary flexibility, or 25 percent. In B a similar deflation of money incomes at the second or third stages may be assumed to have decreased the demand for the product by 25 percent, the product being demanded with unitary flexibility. After the change in incomes the joint A and B demand will be $2/3\ (1 + 1/4) + 1/3\ (1 - 1/4)$, or $10/12 + 3/12$, or $1\ 1/12$. If B had formerly consumed two-thirds of the commodity, while A consumed one-third, the total joint demand would have fallen as a result of the inflation in A and the deflation in B (by the same simple arithmetic computation) to $11/12$. In the former case the price would have risen as a result of the impact of the changes in demand and the actual quantity exported by A to B or by B to A would have depended upon the A or B elasticity of demand at the new positions. A supply-price change can be expected eventually to affect this reaction, accentuating the rise if the commodity is produced in A, counteracting it if it is a B product. In the first instance, however, the terms of trade shift in favor of the country producing the article. In the second illustration the price declines at the impact of the demand changes, and the terms of trade shift against the country producing the commodity. In time a supply-price reaction may be expected to accentuate or offset the price change due to the demand shift, the direction of the supplementary change being dictated by the country producing the article.

From this digression a few general rules may be drawn about the direction taken by the terms of trade in the transfer process when the rate of exchange is held stable. So far as the supply reaction is concerned, the terms of trade will tend to shift in favor of the inflating and against the deflating country. With respect to demand, it may be suggested (1) that the terms of trade tend to shift against the country whose demand is the more flexible for foreign-trade goods; (2) that the terms of trade will tend to turn in favor of the borrower if its foreign trade is only a small proportion of its total trade, or against it if its foreign trade is important in comparison with domestic trade, and vice versa for the lender; (3) that the country which undergoes the larger monetary change with respect to money incomes runs the greater chance of having the terms of trade turn against it; and (4), other things being equal, an elastic demand for foreign-trade goods in the borrowing country and an inelastic demand in the lender will tend to turn the terms of trade against the latter and in favor of the former; while the opposite holds true if the conditions are reversed.[17]

At the third stage the banking system in A may be assumed to expand loans on the basis of increased gold or foreign ex-

[17] This digression has been made necessary by the vagueness of the literature on the subject. The classical reasoning is concerned solely with the supply reactions. On the demand side, Iversen stresses demand elasticity (*op. cit.*, p. 317); Gilbert, the "direction of total demand" (*op. cit.*, p. 24); and Nurkse, the extent of the gold movement or the change in the rate of exchange, which are themselves determined by the proportions in which the added buying power in the borrowing country is spent (*op. cit.*, chap. ii, especially secs. 1-2). The principal cause of difficulty is that demand flexibility after the "first stage" is entirely disregarded. When it is taken into consideration that the loan can be transferred to the borrower in gold, used by the original borrowers for the expenditure on domestic goods and services but by the income recipients for foreign-trade goods, the direction to be taken by the terms of trade become *a priori* indeterminant, unless full information is available on at least the four variables listed above.

change reserves. The reaction of the inflation arising from the secondary changes in the money supply on the balance of trade will follow along the lines just analyzed for the second stage. Demand flexibility for foreign-trade goods, demand elasticities, the proportions of foreign-trade goods consumed and produced in the two countries, and the extent of the inflation in the borrowing and deflation in the lending country will all affect the speed at which the real transfer takes place.

The Extent of the Adjustment. We may summarize the foregoing discussion concerning the extent of the monetary adjustment in incomes necessary to bring about the real transfer of capital, when the rate of exchange is held fixed, as follows:

(1) At the first stage, when the borrowers in A obtain funds in B the real transfer can be accomplished, altogether or in part, by the direct expenditure of such funds in B goods for importation to A.[18] The part of the loan which is so expended reduces the need for further adjustment *pro tanto.* The part not so expended makes necessary a money transfer to A, with resultant monetary adjustments at the second and third stages.

(2) At the second stage, the part of the loan brought to A for expenditure there increases incomes, unless hoarded, to an extent dependent upon the income velocity of money. The rise in incomes thus brought about will be likely to increase the amount expended by inhabitants of A on foreign-trade goods, including both imports from B and potential exports to B. The relation between the increase in incomes thus brought about and the increased demand for foreign-trade goods depends upon the flexibility of demand for the latter. As the total demand for a given foreign-trade good changes, relative elasticities of demand, increasing or decreasing costs, and so forth, enter to affect the degree of adjustment accomplished at the second stage. On the assumption that the demand for foreign-trade

[18] Nurkse cites an amusing hypothetical case in which actual imports are unnecessary because the A borrowers go to B to live as the guests of the lenders, thus setting free their personal attendants, etc., in A to work on the construction of capital equipment (*op. cit.*, p. 20). The modern counterpart, of course, is tourist travel. If, at the second and third stages the increase in money incomes induces the consumption of tourist utilities in B, the adjustment is made thus easier.

goods is of unit flexibility in both borrowing (inflating) and lending (deflating) countries, it may be said that a greater part of the adjustment will be taken up if A's demand is elastic for B's goods and inelastic for its own goods, while B's demand is elastic for its own goods and inelastic for those of A.

(3) The increase in incomes at the third stage, arising from a liberalization of credit policy as foreign reserves are acquired in the form of gold or balances abroad, affects the adjustment in the same manner as the change in incomes at the second stage. More inflation is required in the borrowing country if its demand for foreign-trade goods is inflexible; more and more deflation is required in the deflating country if its demand for foreign-trade goods is inflexible. Elasticities of demand also play their part.

The Necessity for the Third Stage. How much adjustment is taken up at each stage in an actual case of international borrowing is, of course, impossible to determine *a priori*. It is difficult even to guess what a typical pattern would be. It may be assumed for our purposes, however, that the requirements of the adjustment extend through to the third stage. How much of the real transfer remains to be undertaken at that time is a question that does not arise, inasmuch as the second and third stages, in point of time sequence, will be undertaken simultaneously. They may still, however, be kept theoretically distinct. Were adequate data available, and could all possible interfering factors be abstracted, the amount of the adjustment accomplished at the first stage might be measured either by the net change in gold holdings plus net foreign short-term assets or by the amount of the loan expended directly abroad. The second and third stages could not be treated separately in any aggregate of statistical data, however. The primary increase in incomes, which is associated directly with the secondary expansion, is possible only through the international movement of gold or short-term capital on which the tertiary income increase is based.

For these reasons and because of the slimness of the analytical possibility that the real transfer can be accomplished by reactions at two stages only, it appears evident that as a rule inflation at stage three is necessary to complete the capital movement from the lender to the borrower in the form of goods and services. As a first approximation it may likewise be granted that deflation at three stages is necessary in the lending country if the adjustment is to be made easily.

When inflation in one country or deflation in the other does not take place at the third stage, owing to offsetting credit policies pursued by the central banking authorities, a real transfer is still possible. What is then required is a larger monetary change in the other country.

Flexibility of Demand with Paper Exchanges. The foregoing portions of this chapter have assumed that monetary change has been necessary after the first stage, owing to the fact of stable exchanges. These monetary changes, presumably, are brought about either through gold movements or through short-term capital movements between countries. On the unregulated paper standard, however, when gold flows are not necessarily present and when capital movements may not aid in the adjustment, the real transfer may have to be effected by changes in the rate of foreign exchange through their effect on sectional price levels.

It may be granted that if the A borrowers spend the proceeds of their loan in B, the real transfer will take place directly and smoothly. Similarly, it may be granted that if as the B rate of exchange starts to decline A speculators purchase B exchange in hopes of profits, the buying-power transfer will take place at the second stage and money incomes will be increased in A and reduced in B. If this is the case, the analysis may proceed in the same fashion as that above, because the rate of exchange has been held stable.

But it may be assumed for purposes of exposition that the A borrowers choose to transfer all of the loan proceeds to A and, further, that no speculative short-term capital movements come forth to sustain the price of B exchange. In this case the A currency appreciates while the B currency depreciates. The relative prices of foreign-trade goods are altered in the two countries, the total disparity between the prices of any given commodity—costs of transfer being abstracted[19]—being the percentage of depreciation. It is not possible to foretell whether prices of foreign-trade goods will rise in B while they hold steady in A, fall in A while they remain stable in B, or rise somewhat in B and fall somewhat in A.[20] For present purposes it is unnecessary to analyze the various conditions of demand and supply which will determine exactly what price relationships will be reached after the exchange depreciation. We may, for purposes of exposition, simply assume that foreign-trade goods have risen in price in B and fallen in A.

In these circumstances the relations between foreign-trade goods prices and home-market prices will have altered in both A and B. In A foreign-trade goods will be relatively inexpensive compared to home-market goods, while in B the reverse will be true. This will lead to a shift in demand from home-market goods to foreign-trade goods in A, and one away from foreign-trade goods in B, resulting in the transfer of the capital in goods and services.

The relations between home-market and foreign-trade goods may be analyzed in terms of flexibility of demand. The usual single demand curve is drawn on the assumption of small price changes which do not markedly affect real income. Furthermore, each demand curve presupposes a whole set of other demand curves drawn for other commodities. When a large change in price occurs in one commodity, requiring a signifi-

[19] The expression "costs of transfer" is one devised by Ohlin (*op. cit.*, p. 142) to include costs of freight, handling, insurance, duty, etc.

[20] Most writers apparently assume that foreign-trade goods prices will both rise in B and fall in A by the full extent of the depreciation. See, e.g., Keynes, *Treatise on Money*, I, 358: "Now when the rate of foreign exchange is altered, the prices of all foreign trade goods are changed forthwith in terms of the local money." But see Taussig, *op. cit.*, p. 353: "Observe further . . . that the goods exported from the United States to Great Britain, though dearer in Great Britain, are unchanged in price *in the United States*. Similarly, the goods exported from Great Britain, though cheaper in the United States, are the same price *in Great Britain* [his italics]." This would be the case, of course, only under special conditions of demand and supply. It may well be possible, as Gilbert points out (*op. cit.*, p. 29), that the terms of trade will not be changed at all by currency depreciation, both exports and imports rising in consonance with one another in the depreciating country and falling in the appreciating country.

cant change in the amount of money income spent upon it, all the demand curves of the system must be redrawn to take account of the change in real income, even though money incomes remain unchanged. When the prices of a whole range of goods change with relation to the others, the entire system of demand curves must be redrawn.

In A, where foreign-trade goods are cheaper in relation to home-market goods after the depreciation, it follows that more of the total money income will be spent for them. How much more, depends upon the flexibility of demand. The converse holds true in B.

Evidently the adjustment will be facilitated if the demand for foreign-trade goods is flexible in both A and B. In A the relative cheapness of foreign-trade goods will bring it about that the increase in real income is devoted largely to them. In B, with the demand for foreign-trade goods flexible, the reduction in real income will take place largely in them. The less flexible the demand for foreign-trade goods in A or B, or both, the more will the rate of exchange have to depreciate, if the real transfer of capital is to be carried through successfully.[21]

Summary. This chapter has been devoted to outlining certain of the aspects of the transfer problem. This is preliminary to a description in the remainder of Part II of the role of short-term capital movements in capital transfers under different institutional conditions. No complete exposition of the many and intricate factors involved was attempted, and in particular the whole range of problems connected with the reaction of costs of foreign-trade and home-market goods during and consequent to the transfer of capital in real form was disregarded. The analysis was confined to the factors that determine the extent of the monetary adjustment necessary to bring about the transfer of a given amount of capital, and dwelt, in consequence, almost entirely upon the characteristics of demand shifts.

The extent of the change in money incomes under the gold standard (or where exchange rates are held stable) was seen to depend upon the amount of the foreign loan expended directly

[21] See "Flexibility of Demand in International Trade," *op. cit.*, pp. 357-58.

by the borrowers in the lending country and consequently upon the flexibility of demand for foreign-trade goods as incomes change in terms of money. The elasticity of demand for foreign-trade goods, it was indicated, is a lesser but important factor.

Where currency relations are not fixed, it was pointed out, the degree of the adjustment to be taken up by changes in the relations between demands for foreign-trade goods and home-market goods could be lessened. If the borrowers spend a portion of their funds in the lending country or if equalizing short-term capital movements take place to bring about changes in relative buying power, the degree of necessary exchange-rate fluctuation is reduced. In the absence of these factors, however, the rate of exchange of the lending country depreciates as its money is sold to obtain that of the borrower. This alters the prices of foreign-trade goods between the two countries and changes the relationship of home-market to foreign-trade goods in each country. Demand flexibility again enters the problem at this stage, since the price changes of a wide range of goods necessitate the redrawing of the entire system of demand curves. In the lending country, where foreign-trade goods have risen in price relative to home-market goods, the demand for foreign goods shifts to the left; in the borrowing country, where the prices of foreign-trade goods have fallen relatively, the demand for them increases.

V

THE LIMITING CASE: TRANSFER UNDER THE PAPER STANDARD WITH FIXED EXCHANGES

It is popularly assumed that equilibrium in the balance of international payments is maintained either by movements of gold or by shifts in the rate of foreign exchange. It has been seen in the foregoing chapters, however, that this view oversimplifies the foreign-exchange mechanism. It leaves out of consideration short-term movements of capital between countries. These may aid in bringing about equilibrium in the balance of international payments in the narrower sense, that is, they may serve to make the supply of foreign exchange equal to the demand for it at a given price at one time. Are they sufficiently effective as an agency in the balance, however, to restore equilibrium in prices and incomes when no gold movements take place and when the rate of exchange is held stable? The question may be rephrased: What are the conditions necessary to the successful operation of the fixed-exchange standard?

The Fixed-Exchange Standard. Most international fixed-exchange standards operate with gold as one of the commodities traded between the countries concerned.[1] Such is the case, for

[1] See Iversen, *op. cit.*, p. 313: "Between paper standard countries, *gold moves, not as money, but as a commodity* [his italics]." This fact and the possibility of short-term capital movements between paper-standard countries lead Iversen to make the statements: ". . . the transfer mechanism is essentially the same between paper countries and gold countries" (*ibid.*, p. 469); and "The chief difference between gold and paper conditions, as far as the immediate mechanism is concerned, is rather that the *order* in which the different means of adjustment begin to operate is different [his italics]." (*Ibid.*, p. 315.) We have demonstrated above, however, that if transfer takes place when neither gold nor short-term capital moves between countries, the means of adjustment do differ markedly from the gold-standard mechanism. In the one case money incomes change absolutely between the two countries; in the other, the relative proportion of a fixed money income spent on home-market and foreign-trade goods alters. See further below, pp. 89-96.

example, in India, Australia, and New Zealand. India has been a consumer of gold, but lately she has been exporting it in large amounts. Australia and New Zealand produce gold, but not enough in each year to care for their domestic requirements. In the case of the Philippine gold-exchange standard, the Anglo-Egyptian exchange system, and the present sterling-area currency arrangements, however, gold does not move between countries in important amounts. The parities of the exchanges concerned are nevertheless maintained.

Within a given country the fixed-exchange system operates interregionally.[2] Monetary adjustment to intranational capital movements is effected, when a central bank operates, through monetary change (inflation and deflation) brought about by shifts in reserves and in interbank balances. While gold movements may take place within a country, as they did in the United States before the establishment of the Federal Reserve system and do now through the Gold Settlement Fund of the Federal Reserve banks,[3] the greater part of the adjustment is brought about through short-term capital movements which can be traced through changes in interbank deposits. Under the national banking system interdistrict clearing took place through movements of notes, of gold to a limited extent, and of interbank balances, in which latter form half of the required reserves could be held by many types of banks.[4] At the present

[2] The fixed-exchange system in this instance is not to be confused with the par-collection system. See W. E. Spahr, *The Clearing and Collection of Checks*, 1926, pp. 113 ff., and chap. vii, especially pp. 241 ff. Par collection involves the absorption of the definite cost of collecting items—payments for stationery, printing, stamps, etc.—by the banking system rather than by the customers of the system. The charges imposed by banks upon customers before the spread of the par-collection system did not correspond to a rate of exchange. The charge was fixed and did not vary with the supply and demand for drafts on other parts of the country.

[3] See H. P. Willis, *The Federal Reserve System*, 1923, pp. 775 ff., and Spahr, *op. cit.*, pp. 291 ff., on the establishment and principles of the Gold Settlement Fund. Cassel (*Theory of Social Economy*, 5th German ed., trans. 1932, p. 657) indicates that an interesting study of the interspatial trade mechanism could be worked out on the basis of the records of the Gold Settlement Fund. It would also be necessary, of course, to take account of interbank balances, which bear a good portion of the burden of the interregional adjustment, required by capital and trade changes between, for example, Federal Reserve districts.

[4] See C. F. Dunbar, *The Theory and History of Banking*, 5th ed., 1929, p. 250.

time, even with the system of intradistrict clearing through reserve balances at the individual reserve banks and of interdistrict clearings through the Gold Settlement Fund, many banks maintain reserves under state laws or in addition to state and national required reserves in the form of balances in larger localities.

An interregional fixed-exchange system differs from an international one, of course, as Iversen emphasizes.[5] The sovereignty of a nation with relation to its currency is not impaired by its membership in an international fixed-exchange agreement. A region, however, as part of a larger sovereign currency system, has no choice but to use the standard money unit which it exchanges at par with the rest of the country. That is to say, an individual Federal Reserve district is required to maintain a fixed rate of exchange for the dollar, without exercising any choice in the matter.

From the point of view of economic as opposed to legal and political distinctions, however, there is a broad similarity. Especially is this the case under circumstances in which the monetary adjustments are carried out through the medium of changes in bankers' and reserve balances, without dependence upon a gold settlement fund. If a Pittsburgh steel mill floats a long-term bond issue in New York for expenditures at its plant, it first acquires title to New York balances. These it sells to its local bank, which receives as an asset to offset its new deposit liabilities bankers' balances in New York. On the basis of this liquid asset it may expand credit to its customers, thus bringing about a secondary expansion in buying power in the Pittsburgh area. In New York a primary contraction takes place as investors place funds in the bond issue and as New York banks experience a decline in private deposits and again in "due to Pittsburgh Banks." Secondary contraction may follow, inasmuch as the New York banks are aware that the "due to banks" deposits are inherently unstable and may be drawn down by the Pittsburgh banking institution if the latter demands reserve balances.[6]

[5] *Op. cit.*, p. 6.

[6] See Iversen, *op. cit.*, chap. xii, pp. 458 ff., where a more extensive account of a domestic capital movement is given for New York and California.

Monetary Adjustment on the Fixed-Exchange Standard. Let us now trace through the effects of an international movement of capital between countries operating on a "fixed-exchange" standard. No opportunities are present for the borrower either to obtain gold in the lending country or to ship gold abroad to build up foreign reserve balances. If an absolutely rigid rate of exchange be maintained, where no fluctuations of the rate of exchange, however narrow, are permitted, the central bank or the member banks must be prepared to buy and sell exchange on other countries in unlimited quantities. "Outside reserves," that is, those held abroad, will then fluctuate with changes in the income and capital balances of indebtedness. If their foreign balances are not sufficient to satisfy the demands for foreign exchange, the banks must either borrow abroad or abandon the exchange parity. If a range of fluctuation be permitted which is comparable to the gold points on the gold standard, it is only necessary that the central bank or the member banks be prepared to sell foreign exchange at what would correspond to the gold export point and to buy it at the gold import point.

Our usual example may now be considered. A borrows from B at long term, and the A borrowers determine to spend the full amount of the loan in A on home-market goods and services. When a central bank operates the fixed-exchange system, it may be expected that the borrowers will first exchange their foreign funds for deposits with the local member banks. These in turn exchange the foreign balances for increased reserves with the A central bank. Primary expansion takes place in A as the foreign exchange is sold by the A borrowers to the member banks. Secondary expansion ensues as a consequence of the improved reserve position of the latter, provided a going rate of interest is in effect. Moreover, the rate of interest may fall as a result of the increased reserves. By holding foreign money in B currency among its assets the A central bank has made an equilibrating loan abroad.

If the rate of interest falls, while the rate of exchange is held stable, income short-term capital movements may be induced from A to B. Those who prefer to lend in B rather than in A, however, must obtain their exchange from the A central bank, thus drawing down its reserves. The movement will only proceed, therefore, until its continuance would endanger the permanence of the reduction in the rate of interest. At some balancing point international investors will desist from adding to their foreign short-term loans, inasmuch as further loans abroad would eliminate the interest-rate differential between A and B and destroy their *raison d'être*.

The A central bank and the other A owners of short-term assets in B may hold these assets in the form of balances with the B central bank, with the B member banks, or as liquid loans in the B short-term money market. If deposits are held, a primary deflation of buying power is brought about, since the deposits have left B hands and are held idle by foreigners. If deposits with the B central bank are held, secondary deflation results since the reserves of the B member banks are thereby reduced. Even when the deposits are held with the B member banks there is some likelihood of secondary deflation if the banks regard foreign deposits as inherently unstable and if they therefore endeavor to improve their reserve position by contracting loans.

The portion of the foreign assets that is held in the form of investments in the short-term money market requires somewhat extended analysis. In Chapter II, where an import surplus was financed through a foreign short-term loan to the money market, it was pointed out that a presumption existed that primary deflation would take place in the importing country as funds were subtracted from the industrial monetary circulation and added to the financial monetary circulation.[7] Even in the case of acceptances or of loans to the industrial circulation, if the industrial circulation was not directly reduced its turnover might be expected to decline. Importers, as their debts neared maturity, would be likely to hold larger average balances with their banks to meet their increased liabilities. In case the equilibrating loan offsets, not an increase in imports, but an increase in loans, however, the likelihood of deflation is not as

[7] See above, pp. 31-32.

obvious. The capitalist whose loan to A is offset by short-term money market investments would presumably not have employed his funds directly and immediately in the purchase of current output.

Evidently the short-term rate of interest will here tend to fall relative to the rate in the capital market. This may be deflationary under certain circumstances. If the long-term lender in B otherwise expends his money capital for capital goods in B through direct investment or through the purchase of new domestic securities and if the inward short-term capital movement, through its effect on the short-term rate of interest, induces a change in the liquidity preference of former holders of short-term investments so that they now prefer to hold balances, the operation is deflationary. If, on the other hand, the additional investment in the short-term money market enables other holders to respond to the change in comparative interest rates and to divert the funds formerly held in short-term obligations into new long-term securities, no deflation takes place. Which of these alternatives or their many variants will eventuate can only be determined when the shape of the demand curves for long- and short-term capital are given. It is apparent, however, that when short-term income capital movements offset a long-term capital loan in the opposite direction, the presumption of deflation is not as strong as it was in the case in which they functioned to equalize an import surplus.

From the point of view of the fixed-exchange standard, then, inflation is very likely to be produced in the borrowing country (on long-term account, which is the lender at short-term). Deflation in the lending country does not necessarily follow when the offsetting short-term capital movement is of the income type or when it is held by the central bank in the form of investments in the foreign short-term money market. The real transfer of capital can still be accomplished if deflation does not take place in B. All that is required is more drastic inflation in A.[8]

It is thus evident that if the borrowing country prefers to

[8] See Nurkse, *op. cit.*, pp. 137-38.

avoid the necessity for a considerable inflation, in which it would take unilaterally the full burden of the adjustment, it should hold its foreign assets as balances with the foreign central bank. Its ability to do this is limited, of course, by the extent to which the proceeds of an equalizing short-term capital movement are held by the central bank or by member banks, not by international investors.[9] This, however, does not appear to be the regular practice. Sweden, Australia, New Zealand, and other countries now on the exchange standard fixed to the pound sterling hold their London assets largely, so far as can be determined, in the form of bills on which they earn a low rate of interest.[10]

Speculative and Income Movements. When the rate of exchange on the fixed-exchange standard is not held absolutely rigid but is permitted to fluctuate within limits comparable to the gold points on the gold standard, the role of the central banks may be lessened in importance by the introduction of speculative movements of short-term capital. As the A borrowers of long-term capital begin to convert their B funds into A money, the rate of exchange on A rises, while that on B falls. In A speculators will buy additional amounts of B currency, thus providing the supply of A balances necessary to enable some part of the money transfer to take place. If the central bank in A lowers its discount rate or if the bank rate in B is conversely raised as the original alteration in the exchange rate takes place, income movements may accompany the speculative shifts of short-term funds. It may be that the rate on B never reaches the point at which the central bank is forced to buy foreign exchange (at what would be the gold import point). Under this circumstance secondary expansion in buying power and incomes can come about only if the rate of interest has

[9] In agricultural countries, which previous to the collapse of international long-term borrowing in 1928 constituted the most important class of borrowers, the central bank or member banks would be the most likely holders of foreign short-term assets. The reason for this is the fact that the foreign exchange and short-term money markets in such agricultural countries are not apt to be as fully developed as those of larger and industrial countries.

[10] But see the recent revision of the statutes of the National Bank of Denmark, cited above, p. 42 n.

fallen in A or if the member banks have taken part in the arbitrage and income capital movements. In the latter case the member banks would have to increase their willingness to lend at home on the basis of their enhanced "outside" reserves, despite the fact that their legal reserve position has presumably not been bettered.

It is unlikely, however, if the original capital movement was a large one, that the demand for foreign exchange on the part of dealers and investors will be sufficiently elastic to absorb all the exchange necessary to complete the income transfer. The probability remains that the central bank will acquire a good portion of it and that in so doing it will provide the legal reserves necessary to the banking system whereby the secondary expansion of buying power—inflation at the third stage of adjustment—will take place.

Summary. We may summarize the possibilities of completing the real transfer of international long-term capital through the sole medium of short-term capital movements,[11] that is, when gold flows and movements in the exchange rate are eliminated by hypothesis, in the following terms:

(1) When the central bank in A considers outside reserves the equivalent of gold and holds such assets in the form of deposits with the foreign central bank, primary and secondary inflation and deflation of incomes will take place in both countries, adjusting the real transfer and the money transfer of that portion of the foreign borrowing which is not expended directly in the lending country. This reaction depends upon the condition that all the foreign exchange not thus expended is sold to the central bank.

(2) When speculative and income short-term capital move-

[11] Nurkse remarks (*op. cit.*, p. 73) that short-term capital movements induced by international long-term borrowing serve only to reduce the amount of capital actually transferred. Compare with this, however, his statement (*ibid.*, pp. 60-61) that gold flows in the transfer mechanism are not part of the real payment, because they are reversed after their mission in changing the means of payment and effecting the real transfer is accomplished. In the same fashion it follows that short-term capital movements are media of payment and not part of a real payment or an offsetting item in any fundamental sense. See also below, pp. 96-97.

ments are allowed for in A the incidence of secondary inflation depends upon the amount of foreign exchange retained by the central bank and, if none is retained, on the course followed by the rate of interest. If the discount rate is lowered because of the strength of the A exchange rate or because of enhanced foreign exchange reserves, secondary inflation will take place. Likewise, when the member banks have taken part in the speculative and income short-term movements and when they consider the foreign exchange required as additions to reserves, credit can be expanded. The primary increase in incomes depends upon whether dealers hold the foreign exchange, and, if so, whether they borrowed in order to finance their holdings. The inflation of incomes at the second stage will follow inevitably if the A borrowers add funds to the industrial circulation, no matter whether other funds are subtracted from the financial circulation or not.

(3) In B, a primary deflation of incomes takes place if the short-term assets acquired by A are held in the form of bankers' deposits. Secondary deflation depends upon the possibility that these funds are held with the B central bank, that the B member banks will contract loans because of the "instability" of foreign deposits, or that the B central bank raises the rate of discount. If the short-term assets are held by A in the form of investments in the B short-term money market, deflation of incomes *may* take place. This will be the case if the fall in the short-term rate of interest relative to the long-term rate reduces the cost of holding cash, increases the liquidity-preference of marginal local investors, and reduces the industrial money supply.[12] Potential long-term investments in new securities have

[12] The possibility that the funds would be invested in the security markets for stocks has been tacitly avoided. Here, too, however, the likelihood is that foreign purchases of securities are to an extent deflationary. The point is a moot one. But if it is true that foreign purchases of stocks give balances to sellers that are more apt to be held for reinvestment than spent on current output, an *a priori* case for deflation may be made out. Other points must be considered as well. If the foreign buying of stocks induces all holders of other stocks to spend "paper profits" more freely, then it may be inflationary. It may be assumed, however, that new securities cannot come on the market rapidly enough to result in holding security prices steady and siphoning off the funds directly into the industrial circulation.

to be postponed and the available funds are added to the idle balances of those who can afford to gratify their preference for cash rather than investments, when the reward for doing otherwise has been reduced.

It must be remembered, however, that no movement of income or speculative funds from A will take place except on the assumption that the relative rates of interest between the two countries change or that the rate of exchange shifts within prescribed limits. The movement of the rate of exchange may induce a change in the bank rate by the central bank authorities. Any probable change in the rate of discount, upward in B or downward in A, will assist in bringing about a disparity in the direction of changes in their national money incomes, and will hence aid in the completion of the real transfer.

On the basis of the foregoing summary it may be concluded that the real transfer necessitated by the international movement of long-term capital can be accomplished on the fixed-exchange standard through the medium of short-term capital movements. In the limiting case, when shifts in the exchange rate and movements of gold are not operating, short-term funds are capable of achieving the desired results by themselves.

Possibility of Unilateral Adjustment. Before turning to the transfer mechanism on the gold standard and under irredeemable paper currencies, it is necessary to consider briefly the monetary consequences of the real transfer after it has been accomplished. We shall abstract in this discussion from all consideration of changed scarcity of factors of production in the borrowing and lending countries, with resultant changes in factor prices and costs of production of output.

We may limit ourselves to a simple case. The A-B rate of foreign exchange is held rigid by a fixed-exchange standard maintained by the A central bank through its holdings of foreign assets in B. A borrowers obtain a loan in B, sell their B funds to the A central bank (directly or indirectly), and expend the proceeds in A funds on commodities and services in A. Primary inflation of incomes takes place, and incomes also increase at the second stage of the transfer as factors of production are paid. The A banking system, upon the basis of a heightened reserve ratio, expands loans and the money supply. Secondary expansion of the money supply and income inflation at the third stage in the adjustment sequence then follow. The increase of incomes at the second and third stages may be assumed to increase the demand for foreign-trade goods in the amount of the loan, reducing A goods available for export and increasing imports from B. In time an import surplus will be created to the sum of the loan, and the real transfer of capital from B to A will have been brought about.

All this can be accomplished, given sufficient expansion at the third stage and a sufficient flexibility of demand for foreign-trade goods, solely by the action of the banking system in A. If the A central bank holds short-term investments in the B money market which have the effect, because of the shapes of the demand curves for long- and short-term capital, of inducing previous investors to buy new securities or to make direct investments in capital equipment in an amount equal to the original decrease in income, no necessary decrease in total money incomes will follow in B. The inflation in A would bring about the real transfer alone.

This real transfer, however, reverses the monetary changes which made it possible. As an import surplus develops in A, under conditions in which A and B divide the burden of the adjustment equally, the foreign assets held by A are expended to pay for the increased inflow of goods. The disbursement of these foreign assets, on which the A inflation has been founded, leads to a reversal in the expansion. Primary and secondary contraction of buying power take place, and the import surplus is reduced to the point occupied before the transfer began. In B, where contraction had originally taken place, expansion is brought about. The release of foreign balances held by the A short-term lenders results in a primary expansion of income, and the increased reserves of the B central bank or the liquidation of the foreign liabilities of member banks permit of a secondary expansion of the money income where contraction had previously been in effect.

In the case in which the full adjustment is brought about by inflation in A alone and deflation in B does not simultaneously occur, the situation is somewhat different. The adjustment is not likely to reverse itself and to restore the preloan equilibrium between the two countries except under highly improbable assumptions. In A the existence of the import surplus requires the encashment of foreign assets and the release of their proceeds. The inflation built upon the enhanced reserve position is followed by deflation, when the reserve position is restored to the *status quo ante*. The real transfer of capital from B to A results in a return of the monetary and banking situation in A to its previous position.

In B no deflation had taken place during the real transfer. Imports had been reduced and exports increased, however, and the short-term assets held by A were disbursed to pay the B exporters. As a result of the real transfer, inflation follows when no deflation preceded—unless one of two remote possibilities occurs. B exporters may elect to hold the short-term securities which the A banking system formerly owned. But this may be ruled out by hypothesis, since the B exporters are entrepreneurs, not investors. Or, as a consequence of the rise in the short-term rate of interest relative to the long-term rate, new capital expenditure may be postponed and savings held in the form of liquid assets. This latter possibility seems unlikely to be of sufficient magnitude to offset the increase in the industrial circulation resulting from the original expenditure of A's foreign assets. This expansion will raise the effective demand for capital and will presumably tend to reduce the difference between the short- and long-term rates of interest. The fact that inflation is cumulative will tend to increase the desire of the entrepreneurs to borrow, even if the willingness to lend is unchanged when permanent and working capital are considered together.

Thus it is likely that the symmetry of the return to conditions in existence before the capital transfer will be broken by the possibility that the real transfer is accomplished by inflation in the borrowing country alone. In time, of course, the adjustment will be brought about, if the same exchange rate be maintained, as a result of the overvaluation of the B currency.[13] The fact that the long-term capital does not, or is not as likely to, flow back into the short-term capital market as short-term funds are apt to spill over into long-term capital market, requires that after the real transfer is completed, the equilibrium between the two countries will have to be re-established.

Merits of the Fixed-Exchange Standard. The fixed-exchange standard, operating solely by means of international short-term capital movements, is fully capable of bringing about the real transfer in goods and services necessitated by the money loan. This is the more likely to occur if central bank officials in the borrowing country expedite matters by furthering credit expansion at home and by keeping their foreign assets in the form of deposits with the central bank of the lending country. It has been held that the fixed-exchange standard is superior to the gold standard or to freely fluctuating exchanges because, for obscure reasons, the classical theory of the exchanges is thereby disproved.[14] It may more plausibly be argued that if it be desired to maintain stability in rates of exchanges the fixed-exchange standard is cheaper than and as effective as the gold standard. The cheapness derives, not from the possibility of investing short-term foreign balances and earning interest thereby, which reduces the effectiveness of the bilateral adjustment, but from the elimination of the costs of transfer of gold. It functions, in short, in the same way as a gold standard under which gold is earmarked, rather than shipped, or under which all the gold is stored in a world settlement fund and international balances in gold are settled by bookkeeping transactions.

[13] See below, chap. viii.

[14] See W. A. Shaw and A. Wigglesworth, *Principles of Currency, Credit and Exchange with Special Reference to Methods of Financial Reconstruction in the United States and Great Britain,* 1934, pp. 81 ff., and especially pp. 98-100. The authors' demonstration that the fixed-exchange standard (called by them the par-exchange standard) eliminates the necessity for sectional price adjustments in restoring and maintaining equilibrium in the balance of payments is unintelligible to me.

VI

THE ROLE OF SHORT-TERM FUNDS IN THE TRANSFER MECHANISM UNDER GOLD AND PAPER STANDARDS

We have devoted complete chapters to the background of the transfer case and to the instance in which the real transfer is brought about concomitantly with or subsequent to the purchasing-power transfer by means of short-term international capital movements alone. On this account it will suffice to give a less extended treatment of the role of short-term capital movements in the transfer mechanism under the gold standard and under conditions in which the rate of foreign exchange is free to fluctuate without official intervention.[1] We may begin by considering what part is likely to be played by changes in net short-term foreign assets when an international long-term loan is made under the gold standard.

Importance of Gold Flows. Nurkse's discussion of the transfer mechanism under the gold standard places a preponderant emphasis on gold movements, owing to his failure to recognize completely the fact that short-term capital movements can replace gold as the basis for monetary expansion and contraction.[2] Iversen, on the other hand, tends rather to minimize the influence of gold, which, he suggests, is only one medium of international payment along with equalizing short-term loans.[3] Both these writers are aware, of course, that the role of gold can vary

[1] See P. Einzig, *Foreign Exchange Control,* 1934, p. 13. By intervention is meant the purposeful purchase or sale of foreign exchange by monetary authorities, including, of course, both stabilization funds and central banks. The fixed-exchange standard discussed in the previous chapter thus involves a maximum of intervention.

[2] See Nurkse, *op. cit.*, pp. 56-57; "Zu einer Goldbewegung muss es in allen Fällen, wo nicht ganz minimale Kapitalbewegungen in Rede stehen, immer kommen." See also, *ibid.*, p. 133.

[3] *Op. cit.*, chap. xiii, sec. 1.

from the case in which the loan is made entirely in gold[4] to that in which a gold flow takes place in the opposite direction from that of the long-term loan, that is, from the borrower to the lender.[5] The circumstances surrounding the particular loan, the development of the banking systems of the borrowing and lending countries, the state of international demand, of production, and so forth, all aid in the determination of the role of gold in particular instances. It is our purpose, however, merely to describe what may be thought of as a typical relationship between gold and international short-term funds in the transfer process. The percentage of the loan transferred by international gold flows in any individual case does not appear to be uniform even within wide limits.

In the Canadian borrowings, analyzed by Viner, the evidence is inconclusive. Net imports of gold for the fourteen-year period examined were $118,211,000,[6] as compared with a net capital import of $2,369,250,000.[7] Gross gold movements cannot be computed, inasmuch as the net figures were arrived at indirectly, from the data for gold production and from gains in gold stocks, as well as from the Dominion customs statistics.[8] In France the net export of capital between 1880 and 1913 has been estimated at 30,255,000,000 francs,[9] while gold flowed into

[4] See L. H. Jenks, *The Migration of British Capital before 1875*, 1927, pp. 31, 66, where there is a mention of the English gold loan to the Second Bank of the United States. Similarly, the Dawes loan to Germany in 1924 was transferred largely in gold. See Bresciani-Turroni, *op. cit.*, pp. 27-29.

[5] Gold may flow from A to B when the flexibility of demand for B's goods on the part of A is such that an amount greater than that of the loan is expended for them. See Nurkse, *op. cit.*, p. 132. Such a case may be readily envisaged, as, for example, where a company borrows abroad to obtain the final increment to the funds it intends to spend for imports. Or, a slight increase in money incomes may lead to a large gain in tourist travel. White (*op. cit.*, p. 8 n.) suggests that if interest rates change sufficiently between A and B, a movement of income short-term capital in the opposite direction to that of the long-term loan may induce a gold flow toward the lending nation. But see below, pp. 85 ff.

[6] *Op. cit.*, p. 34.

[7] *Ibid.*, p. 106.

[8] *Ibid.*, Table II, pp. 30-31. Revealed exports of gold totaled $84,081,000, with imports of $113,177,000, for a recorded net import of $29,096,000—or approximately one-quarter of the amount arrived at by the indirect method. Evidently gross movements of gold can only be compared with gross movements of long-term capital in the effort to determine the part played by gold movements in the transfer of buying power.

[9] See White, *op. cit.*, p. 51.

France to the extent of 6,422,000,000 francs net.[10] On the basis of his investigations of the French experience in this period, White suggests that the role played alternately by net gold flows, gross gold flows, and movements of international short-term capital in bringing about the real transfer is indeterminate.[11] Certainly the British pre-war experience, recently examined by Beach and analyzed below, bears out this contention.[12]

Investigation calculated to ascertain statistically the comparative importance of the two media of international payment would be exceedingly difficult, in cases in which the answer is not already obvious.[13] The weight of the other factors in the balance of payments in causing the disturbances can rarely be satisfactorily allowed for. So far as the loan itself is concerned, unequal amounts of the loan may be expended in the lending country; varying degrees of inflation and deflation occur at the second and third stages (which will alter the amount of purchasing power needed to be directly transferred); and international loans are not unique nor independent items in the balance of payments. In many cases they are called forth to consolidate a previous real transfer of capital.[14]

[10] *Ibid.*, p. 122.

[11] *Ibid.*, pp. 147-50. White believes that short-term capital movements at no time played as important a part in the French balance of payments as gold, because of the institutional background of the French banking system.

[12] See below, pp. 135 ff.

[13] For example, in Australia, New Zealand, or Egypt.

[14] This possibility is seldom considered analytically by those who undertake to verify the theory of international trade by appeals to statistical data. The element of truth in the statement of Keynes: "Historically, the volume of foreign investments has tended to adjust itself, at least to a certain extent, to the balance of trade, rather than the other way round . . ." ("The German Transfer Problem," *Economic Journal*, XXXIX, 1929) has often been disregarded as economists attempt statistically to establish the opposite.

Theorists over-simplify when they describe the adjustment mechanism in terms of "unique" capital movements alone. Nurkse, e.g., objects to the "journalistic" propensity present among writers to establish causal connections among items in the balance of payments. He is guilty of the same failing, however, when he says that long-term capital movements play "ein durchaus selbstandige Rolle" (p. 79). An extreme case of the opposite (Keynsian) statement is furnished by Malpas (*Les Mouvements internationaux des capitaux*, 1934, p. 401): "Les mouvements à long terme ont une limite naturelle qui est le sole net crediteur de la balance des comptes [his italics removed]." Nurkse (*op. cit.*, p. 80) and Malpas (*op. cit.*, pp. 40, 414) are both aware of the error of assum-

Transfer under Gold. It has been mentioned previously that gold movements bring about primary changes in the money supply only when net short-term foreign assets can be assumed unchanged.[15] In the particular case about to be considered a gold import accompanied by a reduction in net foreign assets at short-term would produce no primary change in the money supply. Similarly, an export of gold accompanied by an increase in net short-term foreign assets leaves the money supply unaffected. These gold movements result, not from changes in the other items in the balance of payments, but rather from changes in bankers' decisions about where reserves will be kept. On that account they will be excluded from the present discussion by hypothesis. We shall assume that all gold movements do bring about corresponding alterations in the total means of payment.

When A borrows from B and both countries are on the gold standard, the direct result under our usual assumptions is an equilibrating short-term capital movement from A to B, while the A borrowers arrange for the monetary transfer of their funds from B currency to A currency.[16] The conversion of these balances into domestic money by the A borrowers results in sales of B exchange against that of A. The A-B rate moves toward the gold import point in A, the export point in B. As the B currency declines in terms of A, speculative foreign-exchange dealers will tend to purchase B foreign exchange with the intention of selling it at a later date, when the rate rises again.[17]

---

ing one item in the balance of payments to be either wholly independent or wholly dependent. But they both indulge in it.

Similarly, most expositions of the transfer mechanism, including our own, assume that the capital movement is independent. This is perfectly proper as an expositional device. When inductive studies are undertaken, however, it must be recognized that the long-term capital movement can either bring about or be brought about by the import surplus. See C. K. Hobson, *The Export of Capital*, 1914, pp. 5 ff.

[15] See above, pp. 25-26.

[16] Nurkse (*op. cit.*, pp. 57-58) omits this step, inasmuch as he is accustomed to conceiving of the long-term loan as being written in A currency. The lenders presumably buy A currency as subscriptions to the loan are received by the underwriters. As a result the exchange rates move immediately.

[17] Not necessarily to the mint par of exchange. Between the upper and lower gold points there is no "normal level." Nurkse is in error when he suggests that the mint parity constitutes such (*ibid.*, p. 57).

A importers, likewise, may increase their purchases of B currency to provide funds for future imports at cheaper than usual rates.[18] Should the short-term rate of interest shift, either upward in B or downward in A, or both, as a result of central bank action influenced by the change in the exchange rate, investors in international short-term money markets may sell liquid obligations in A and buy similar assets in B. Thus at the same time equilibrating, speculative, and income short-term capital movements may take place as the A borrowers sell part of their B funds to dealers, part to investors, and retain part.[19]

That some part of the B foreign exchange sold by the A borrowers will be bought by dealers, importers, and investors in A can be deduced from the realistic assumption that the demand for foreign exchange in A is not altogether inelastic.[20] That sufficient short-term funds to result in a flow of gold from A to B will not be induced ordinarily (a possibility mentioned by White) follows from the nature of the motivation for each type of capital movement. Speculative movements of capital will be brought to a halt after the rate of foreign exchange rises above the average rate at which the exchange was purchased on the decline. Thereafter such movements will tend to be reversed as speculators take their profits. If the rate of interest is changed by central bank policy because of strength or weakness in the rate of exchange arising from the transfer of the long-term loan, the fact of the reversal in the course of exchange quotations will tend to induce a return of the rate of interest to its pre-loan position. This will, of course, react unfavorably on continued movements of income short-term capital. Thus it seems doubtful, unless credit policy is determined by extraneous

[18] This is to be interpreted as a speculative short-term capital movement having no necessary relationship to immediate and direct increases in imports. It is probable that changes in the rate of exchange on the gold standard do not affect the trade balance. Ohlin (*op. cit.*, p. 392) and Nurkse (*op. cit.*, p. 56) agree that the demand for foreign goods is hardly so elastic.

[19] The amount of foreign exchange retained by A borrowers (or their local bank) in order to obtain a better price for it in terms of A currency may be regarded as a speculative movement of short-term funds rather than an equilibrating loan, after they have had time to formulate their policy. See above, p. 48 n.

[20] See Iversen, *op. cit.*, p. 317.

factors, that short-term capital movements from the country borrowing at long term to the lender can produce a parallel movement of gold.[21]

While the rate of exchange is falling and before it reaches the lower gold point, short-term capital movements will hence take place from A to B in a finite amount above zero and probably short of the amount of the long-term loan. When the remainder of the foreign exchange is thrown on the market by the A borrowers, gold will move from B to A.

Gold vs. Short-Term Capital. It has been pointed out in the previous chapter that short-term capital movements can of themselves accomplish the real transfer of capital as well as be the means of making the monetary transfer, without the aid of changes in the rate of exchange or gold flows. This holds true so long as credit policy in A is operated to this end. If deflation in B is undertaken, so much the better.[22] In those instances in which gold and short-term capital movements coöperate as media of international payment, the likelihood that credit policy will react to changes in net short-term foreign assets as effectively as it did on the fixed-exchange standard is somewhat reduced. The credit policy of the central bank on a gold standard will be more likely to be affected by gold. There may be a tendency for central banks and member banks to increase their willingness to lend on the basis of newly acquired foreign assets or to strive for added liquidity when foreign liabilities mount; it will not be likely to be as marked, however, as when an exchange standard is consciously being maintained.

The primary increases and decreases in incomes will appear

[21] Nurkse maintains (rightly) that income movements of capital at short term in response to a rise in the rate of interest in B can only partially reverse the deflationary movement there (if invested such a way that they make purchasing power available to local borrowers in the amount of the long-term loan), because of the fact that a negatively inclined demand curve for loans will only use less credit at a higher rate of interest. See *op. cit.*, pp. 140 n., 28. In our terminology the short-term income movement in response to a rise in the rate of interest may offset the primary reduction in income, given certain assumptions about the shape of the demand curves for long- and short-term capital. It will not, however, affect the secondary deflation *in toto*.

[22] It is doubtful, as a matter of practical fact, whether the transfer would or could take place by means solely of deflation in B.

as on the fixed-exchange standard. If interest rates are geared to the movement in the rate of exchange between the gold points—in anticipation of actual gold flows—secondary inflation and deflation may be as effective when short-term capital moves as when gold moves. But the presumption must run the other way. Here a distinction must be made between the pre-war and post-war gold standards. Sir George Paish has said that in the pre-war era England supplied the world on an average of 200,000,000 pounds of new capital yearly, while her gold reserve stood at approximately 10,000,000 pounds. When the total reserve of the Bank of England (including gold and the assets behind the fiduciary issue) fell to 20,000,000 pounds, the rate of discount was raised, whereas when the total reserve rose to 30,000,000 pounds the rate was reduced.[23] That is, the bank rate, which was prevalently the short-term rate of interest in the money market during the period was geared to net gold movements.[24] In the post-war era, however, even gold has lost its position as the major factor in determining bank-rate policy;[25] and the bank rate is less frequently the prevailing rate in the short-term money market.[26]

Thus, when gold and foreign short-term capital both play a part in restoring the equilibrium of the balance of payments after a movement of long-term capital, it is probable that credit policy pays greater attention to the former than the latter. This has been more widely true in the post-war, than in the pre-war, period. In the thirty-year era ending with 1913 the world was essentially on a sterling standard, and the Bank of England sought to defend its gold reserves against actual and anticipated

[23] See Sir George A. Paish, "Commercial Policy and the Gold Standard," in *Proceedings of the Academy of Political Science,* XVI (1934), 84.

[24] And also, of course, to changes in the domestic circulation. The fact that the bank rate prevailed more widely in the short-term market for liquid funds then than now may be explained by the fact that the banking system operated with very little slack. See Beach, *op. cit.,* p. 173.

[25] See B. H. Beckhart, *Discount Policy of the Federal Reserve System,* 1924, *passim.*

[26] In the 1920's, it is generally agreed, the prospective speculative gains to be made in stocks quoted on the New York exchange largely determined the demand for short-term capital in New York and hence affected greatly the rate of interest.

changes. The latter could be to some extent foreseen from movements in the rate of exchange between the gold points, which were likely to be occasioned by short-term capital movements. In the post-war period the bank rate has not been used with the previous frequency nor in response to such comparatively small changes in either gold reserves or the rate of exchange. As a result the secondary changes in incomes necessitated by the appearance of a dislocation in the balance of payments due to (for example) a capital transfer have not met with as extensive or as immediate response in the form of secondary buying-power alterations as formerly.

The effectiveness of actual or prospective changes in gold reserves in bringing about the secondary response in incomes on the pre-war gold standard suggests one reason why international capital movements took place before the war without the necessity for large gold movements, either net or gross.[27] This was the case at a time when few persons sufficiently understood the nature of short-term capital shifts to make the practice general in industrially mature countries of deflating when net short-term foreign assets fell and of inflating when they rose.[28]

In the post-war period other factors entered to alter the relative roles of gold and short-term capital in the exchange mechanism. While it is likely that central banks have learned a great deal about the possible effects of short-term capital movements and are beginning to understand the necessity for deflation when foreign short-term liabilities rise,[29] yet the welter of complicating circumstances affecting both gold flows and short-term funds has made it impossible to verify statistically such theoretical advances as have been made. Autonomous movements of

[27] Other reasons were, of course, the large percentage of loans expended directly for foreign-trade goods, the great flexibility of demand for foreign-trade goods on the part of the underdeveloped borrowing countries, the relative absence of present-day forces resisting deflation, and the fact that the loans, being continuous, were adjusted to continuous export and import surpluses and thus obviated the necessity for severe periodic adjustments.

[28] See, e.g., Walter Bagehot, *Lombard Street* (1917 ed.), chap. xii, esp. pp. 291 ff.

[29] See, e.g., the Macmillan Report, *op. cit.*, paragraph 354.

short-term capital, the semi-dependent role of long-term capital movements (arising partly as a result of changes in demand rather than of independent foreign loans), the rise of the gold-exchange standard, reparation payments, and so forth, have so disturbed the scene—which had never been clear for lack of adequate statistical data—that the precepts derived from arm-chair theorizing could not readily be applied in practice. Moreover, deflation as a corrective for disequilibria in the balance of payments is now avoided where possible because of the new resistance of prices and the rewards of factors of production to downward pressure.[30]

If it now be recognized that short-term balances are capable of correcting dislocations in the balance of international accounts, as well as of causing disturbances in them, provided monetary policy is geared to their changes, it follows that on some future gold standard short-term capital movements will assume a greater role than that played by them in the 1920's. This should certainly be the case where the disequilibria are of the minor sort that arise under normal conditions.

Long-Term Lending on the Paper Standard. The role of short-term capital movements in the transfer mechanism under the assumption of freely moving exchanges (autonomous movements still being abstracted) can be similarly outlined. In practice, however, the problem is quite different from that generally treated in theoretical expositions. Actually, it is borrowing countries, not lenders, which are the most likely to suffer depreciation of their foreign exchanges. This is partly due to two circumstances. In the first place, the payment of interest and sinking-fund charges after a period of extended borrowing presents a continuous problem in transfer, especially if the lending country has ceased to lend for some reason.[31] Secondly, a young borrowing country, when met with the necessity of transferring interest and amortization payments abroad, is generally likely to be faced with a shrinking and inelastic demand for its ex-

[30] See A. D. Gayer, *Monetary Policy and Economic Stabilization*, 1935, chap. iii.

[31] This anticipates some of the discussion in chap. x, below, especially pp. 160-63.

ports.[32] This factor makes it difficult for a debtor agricultural country to expand exports by domestic deflation, since price reductions cannot greatly increase the value of the larger quantities of goods sold abroad.

Depreciation is not apt to accompany original international lending, because there are apt to be few borrowers from countries on unmanaged paper currencies. The reason for this reluctance is not to be found in the losses which Nurkse deems inevitable on loans made between unmanaged-paper-standard countries.[33] Whether such losses will befall the borrowers themselves is most uncertain, and they surely cannot fall on the borrowing country as a whole.[34] Uncertainty is the paralyzing element.[35] The lenders are perfectly willing to engage in contracts for loans, so long as they will be transacted in their own currency; but the borrowers are not generally disposed to agree to pay after the maturity of the loan what would be for them

[32] See Laurence Smith, "The Suspension of the Gold Standard in Raw Material Exporting Countries," *American Economic Review*, XXV (1934), 431.

[33] Nurkse, *op. cit.*, pp. 71 ff. Nurkse's argument runs as follows: the purchasing-power transfer depreciates the lender's currency (as the supply of it increases when the loan is used to bid for the borrowers'). If the loan is denominated in the lender's currency, the borrowers find, after the purchasing-power transfer is made, that they have received fewer units of their own currency than they had anticipated on the basis of the exchange rate in effect when the loan was contracted. (Nurkse errs in assuming that it is the final rate that determines how much of their own currency was received. Evidently it is rather the average rate at which transfers were made.) If the rate of exchange returns after the real transfer has been effected, the repayment of the loan entails a depreciation of the borrower's currency and the accumulation of a larger amount of it in order to pay off the face value of the loan. If the loan is denominated in the borrower's currency, the loss falls on the lender, who lends more of his own currency and receives back less than the amount which would have been loaned if the exchanges had been stable.

[34] These losses cannot fall on a country as a whole, as Nurkse intimates in his discussion of the French experience (*ibid.*, pp. 74-75), since no money moves between countries. The losses of the borrowers or lenders are offset by gains to exporters, importers, and those with foreign assets or liabilities in the corresponding country.

[35] An interesting instance of a loan clause attempting to limit this uncertainty is found in a refunding loan obtained by the city of Zurich (Switzerland) in London, in 1935. The loan contract contained an exchange-guarantee clause whereby, at maturity, the city cannot be required to pay more than 18 Swiss francs per pound sterling and cannot pay less than 12 francs. See *European Financial Notes*, U. S. Department of Commerce, Division of International Finance, No. 206, November 24, 1935, p. 16.

an uncertain sum. Similarly the borrowers would be willing to borrow if the loan were stated in terms of their own currency, but the lenders object to a proposal saddling the uncertainty upon them.

This uncertainty is not measurable because of the wide range of political and economic variables affecting the international value of a given monetary unit some years in the future, when it is not linked to gold. Even when loans are made between gold-standard countries, there is some uncertainty that the gold standard will be maintained. But when the currency of either lender or borrower is left free to fluctuate in accordance with a multitude of factors or is even managed with reference to short-run objectives which may or may not be stated, while no long-run policy exists, the uncertainty is palpably greater. As a result, the underwriting of international long-term loans during periods of unregulated exchanges is apt to be brought to a standstill.

Transfer on the Paper Standard. Despite the lack of conformity of the example to the facts of real world, it is still possible to use the transfer mechanism under unmanaged paper conditions to demonstrate the relationships existing among the various media of international payment. We may again return to our usual example. The A-B rate of exchange is free to fluctuate without intervention. At the outset, however, assume that it holds steady from day to day, the demand for B rate of exchange being equal to the supply. Entrepreneurs in A undertake to borrow funds from B capitalists with the intention of spending them entirely in A. When the loan has been floated in B, the A borrowers will sell their newly acquired B funds to banks in A in exchange for A currency. While the B funds are held in B, an opposite and equilibrating short-term capital movement balances the long-term loan, and the rate of foreign exchange remains unaltered. Primary inflation of incomes has occurred in A, and primary deflation of incomes occurs in B so long as the funds are held in idle bank balances. A member banks may stimulate secondary increases in incomes, as their willingness to lend expands on the basis of their newly acquired foreign assets; and similarly B member banks may attempt secondary deflation because of the increase in foreign (unstable) liabilities. If the balances have been transferred to the central bank in either case, the likelihood for secondary changes in money incomes is greater. If the B funds are held in the form of short-term money-market investments, the probabilities for a primary and secondary deflation in B depend upon the shape of the demand curves for permanent and for working capital.

As the B funds are sold for A exchange, the B rate of exchange undergoes depreciation. What will be the reaction of speculative and income movements of short-term capital, autonomous capital flows still being ruled out by hypothesis?

The inducement for A dealers and banks to build up their stocks of B funds again will depend upon the extent of the movement anticipated by them. If they believe that the depreciation will be a temporary affair, they will purchase blocks of B funds for future resale. If the movement has the appearance of an extended one, however, they will not only be likely to forego purchasing additional B funds, but may even reduce their current balances abroad with the intention of rebuilding them at the low point in the depreciation. Importers will stop buying exchange to pay for their foreign purchases while the rate is still declining. If it were known in advance what the probable course of the rate of exchange was to be without any speculative movements taking place, speculative sales of B funds would be liable to drive the B rate of exchange rapidly to the lowest point it would have otherwise reached. Thereafter the sellers would slowly buy back foreign funds while the A borrowers transfer their loan into A currency.

Income movements will be slow to come forth on the unmanaged inconvertible-paper standard. The A central bank may lower its discount rate, and the B central bank raise its rate; but the differential in potential returns on a given amount of capital stated in A currency is not likely to be sufficient to compensate for exchange risks. No international investor will buy a depreciating currency on an uncovered basis merely because he can earn a higher rate of interest on investments in it. And when exchange rates fluctuate widely or are expected to fluctuate, the forward quotation in the exchanges renders the rate of interest which may be earned on money-market investments ineffective as a regulator of the movement of spot funds.[36]

Further, it does not follow with as great a degree of certainty under freely fluctuating exchanges as on the gold standard that interest rates will be manipulated in response to changes in the balance of international payments. One of the principal arguments put forth in behalf of paper exchanges is that they permit the rate of interest to be managed with reference to the needs of the domestic economy rather than with reference to actual or potential changes in the gold supply.[37] When the paper standard is in operation, central banking authorities are relieved of the necessity of changing interest rates to protect the banking system's reserves from international drains. They may very well refrain from encouraging movements of income short-term capital on this account.

The above reasoning suggests that short-term capital movements may play a very much smaller role in aiding capital transfer on a paper standard *which is not controlled* than on the gold standard.[38] So long as control is being exercised with a view to holding the rate of exchange steady (within limits), speculative and income movements are evoked. If, however, there is no intervention in the foreign-exchange market by central authorities, it is difficult to see why short-term capital movements in the direction required by the transfer mechanism should be induced.

If speculative movements take place in the same direction as the flow of long-term capital, the exchange rate will obviously fluctuate more rather than less than it otherwise would. The

[36] See below, chap. xii.

[37] See, e.g., H. D. Henderson, "The Case against Returning to Gold," *Lloyds' Bank Review*, June, 1935, pp. 340-41.

[38] See Iversen, *op. cit.*, p. 314: "It might perhaps be argued that such equalizing capital flows are less readily called forth under a paper standard, but surely they play an important role here too." The importance of their role appears to be dictated by the amount of knowledge that speculators and investors have regarding the extent of possible exchange rate fluctuation. In the normal case, when a certainty about the extent of future depreciation is out of the question, it is likely that short-term capital movements will disturb rather than abet the adjustment of the real transfer.

same applies to autonomous movements of capital which may be frightened out of the lending country by the fact of currency depreciation. Depreciation in a currency is, at the outset, self-inflammatory, since owners of capital seek to protect their funds by moving them abroad. If confidence is maintained that the depreciation will be ephemeral, short-term capital may move to the lending country and reduce the degree of depreciation otherwise necessary. If uncertainty exists as to the future course of the rate of exchange, however, the degree of depreciation is likely to be increased.[39]

When short-term capital movements take place from A to B, they reduce the range of currency depreciation, but tend to alter incomes in the direction required by the transfer mechanism. If the currency depreciates somewhat, the prices of foreign-trade and home-market goods are altered in relation to one another, changing real incomes and calling flexibility of demand into play to rearrange the amount of money income spent on home-market and foreign-trade goods. Both the change in money incomes (downward in B and upward in A) and the relative change in prices of foreign-trade goods (upward in B and downward in A) tend to work in the same direction, inducing B to buy less foreign-trade goods and A more.

If short-term capital moves from B to A, relative money incomes will change in A and B in the opposite direction from that required by the transfer mechanism. But the rate of foreign exchange will be altered in a greater degree, changing real incomes insofar as they are affected by foreign-trade goods. The real transfer may be able to take place if the tendency for flexibility of demand to operate as a result of the relative price changes is sufficiently strong.

Evidently the adjustment in either case will be speediest if the demand for foreign-trade goods is flexible in both countries, since A will then buy greatly increased quantities of such goods and B greatly reduced amounts. Similarly, the adjustment will be aided if the demand for foreign-trade goods is elastic in A

[39] See Iversen, *op. cit.*, p. 314, and Gilbert, *op. cit.*, p. 28 n.

and inelastic in B. The reaction of the supply factors may similarly affect the speed of the adjustment.

Summary. The part played by short-term capital movements in the transfer process under paper-standard conditions constitutes largely a theoretical problem, remote from reality, despite the fact that it has engaged the attention of many economists. The examples of this type afforded by the experience of the last seventy-five years are principally those where the lending country has been on the gold standard and the borrowing country on paper.[40] Instances in which the lending country has been on an unmanaged paper standard are not common in practice. Lending countries generally stop lending when they abandon gold, unless they manage their rate of exchange by other methods.

The general type of short-term capital movement probable in the hypothetical case of international lending under paper conditions is the equilibrating movement. The A borrowers will doubtless be tempted to convert their B balances into A buying power as slowly as possible in order to avoid losses from precipitous depreciation in the rate of B exchange. So far as other types of short-term capital movements are concerned, however, the direction they will take is probably indeterminate on an *a priori* basis. It is doubtful because of the uncertainties surrounding almost every currency depreciation, whether such capital movements will occur from A to B to the extent that would have been the case under the gold standard. If the rate of exchange is pegged, of course, we arrive back at the fixed-exchange standard, where the short-term capital movements of the equilibrating, arbitrage, and autonomous varieties, singly or in coöperation, accomplish the real transfer of capital by them-

[40] See John H. Williams, *Argentine International Trade under Inconvertible Paper: 1889-1900*, 1920, and Frank D. Graham, "International Trade under Depreciated Paper. The United States, 1862-79," *Quarterly Journal of Economics*, XXXVI (1922). These are reviewed by Iversen, *op. cit.*, chap. xi. Dr. Heckscher's account of the Swedish export of capital ("Sweden's Monetary History, 1914-1925," in *Sweden, Norway, and Iceland in the World War*, 1930, pp. 127-278) reveals that part of this took place while the krona was appreciating. This was not the case of an independent export of capital, however, but one where a shift of securities and foreign assets took place in payment for Swedish exports already purchased for the conduct of the war.

selves and without the aid of gold flows or exchange-rate fluctuation.

Real Nature of Short-Term Capital Flows. A word may be added as an epilogue to Part II. A number of writers have expressed the opinion that international movements of short-term capital are not instruments of transfer but serve merely to reduce the necessity for a real transfer of capital insofar as they offset the long-term loan.[41] In the hypothetical cases examined in this and the previous two chapters, the short-term capital movements served to facilitate the transfer of capital in goods and services rather than to eliminate the necessity for it. Because of their tendency to promote deflation and inflation in the borrowing and lending countries on short-term account, respectively, short-term capital movements deserve to be classified with gold as a means of international adjustment.

It may be admitted that there are instances on record in which "real" movements of short-term capital (in Iversen's sense) offset a movement of long-term capital. These on occasion have been of the income type,[42] as can be seen when the special cyclical patterns of rates of interest are considered. This type of movement will be discussed at length in Chapter IX, below. In the present instance we have been assuming that the only disturbances to which the banking system has had to adjust itself have been those arising from the balance of payments. Short-term capital movements under such circumstances perform an active function as a corrective, as well as acting as a stopgap.

The fact that gold, short-term capital movements and exchange-rate fluctuations are all means of international adjust-

[41] See Nurkse, *op. cit.*, p. 73; White, *op. cit.*, p. 9; also Gilbert, *op. cit.*, p. 28: "He (Iversen) argues that the equalizing capital movement serves to postpone the ultimate commodity transfer, but it also effects a monetary transfer which facilitates the transfer in goods." If Gilbert agrees that gold movements equally postpone the ultimate commodity transfer, the above statement is correct. If he would not so agree, however, the word "postpone" does not convey either Iversen's or the correct view.

[42] As, e.g., the movement of funds from abroad into the short-term money market of the United States, especially into the call-loan and stock markets, which, in 1927-28, offset in large part the long-term loans being floated in New York for foreign account.

ment (although with varying degrees of effectiveness dependent upon the particular capital transfer and its attendant circumstances) can be further demonstrated by examination of their reactions to the completion of the real transfer after a unilateral, discontinuous long-term loan. After the real transfer is completed, gold will return, net short-term foreign assets will revert to their former position, and the rate of exchange on the lending country will appreciate, other things being equal. The import surplus which the real transfer has evoked in the borrowing country must be paid for with gold or with short-term capital acquired from the lending country. Except for changes in the productive equipment of the two countries, the *status quo ante* is restored. These short-term capital movements, then, are not accidental offsets to the long-term loan. They are called forth by the very reaction of the banking system and the rate of exchange to the long-term loan, and they are eliminated when their usefulness is over.

Part III

SOURCES OF MOVEMENTS OF SHORT-TERM FUNDS

VII
FOREIGN-EXCHANGE EQUILIBRIUM

Foreign-exchange theory has been the center of a more or less turbulent storm of controversy among economists for the last twenty years, especially among the German writers who have been trying to furnish explanations of the phenomena associated with the inflation of the 1921-24 period.[1] The purchasing-power-parity theory, its variant, the cost-parity doctrine, the "balance-of-payments" theories, the psychological theory, and innumerable compromises among them have been put forward by various authors purporting to reveal the correct interpretation of the relations between the domestic economy, the balance of payments, and the rate of exchange.

Much of this controversy now seems to represent only sound and fury signifying little. Capable writers of all schools admit that the various factors stressed by individual writers are able to exert influence over the actual or equilibrium rates of exchange. The differences among them lie not so much in the elements which enter into the determination of rates of exchange as in the emphasis placed upon these elements. When it is admitted—as the responsible spokesmen for all groups are doubtless willing to admit—that in certain circumstances, with specific institutional factors operative, any one influence can be temporarily dominant in its effects on the rate of exchange, the grounds for dispute largely fall away.

Equilibrium Defined. All theories of foreign exchange which attempt to go beyond a description of the various factors in the balance of payments to a classification of the causal interrela-

[1] Dr. H. S. Ellis has brought together a tremendous quantity of the German argumentation, with cross references to similar discussion currently carried on in England and the United States, in Part III of his *German Monetary Theory, 1905-1933*, 1934, pp. 203-95. We shall rely in large part on Dr. Ellis's admirable summary of this discussion, injecting a few more strands of thought from later writers who did not fall within the compass of his period or attention.

tions among these factors, have need of a concept of foreign-exchange equilibrium. The foreign-exchange rate is in equilibrium when it exerts no influence on the domestic economy and the domestic economy exerts no influence upon it. This equilibrium may be regarded from two points of view: first, that of money costs, money prices, and money incomes; secondly, that of the foreign-exchange market itself. From each point of view the equilibrium discussed must be related to a given point of time.

To take the foreign-exchange-market equilibrium first, it is clear that if all the semidependent items—merchandise trade, service items, and long-term capital—are of such size that the demand for foreign exchange of a certain country equals the supply of it, the rate which equates this demand and supply is the equilibrium rate. If the level of rates be fixed, disequilibrium will be indicated by a net movement in gold and short-term capital. If the rate is free to vary, the presence either of short-term capital movements or of changes in the rate of exchange will reveal disequilibria.

Disequilibrium, however, is a relative concept. If the level of foreign exchange is fixed, in-payments to a country may not balance out-payments each day, each month, or even each year. For the shorter period, then, the movement of liquid funds and/or gold would show that equilibrium had not been attained. If the movement is tending to reverse itself and to restore the *status quo*, however, the short-run disequilibrium may not be incompatible with a long-run equilibrium. The example may be cited of seasonal fluctuations in merchandise trade. Were one to look at the trade figures for the United States, one would notice a relative import surplus during the first six months and generally an export surplus for the last six months. Taken by themselves the first six months of the year would show overvaluation of the currency, so far as merchandise trade was concerned. Conversely, however, the last six months would indicate that the currency was undervalued. So far as the year is concerned, it is necessary to regard the positions at the beginning and at the end in order to make valid comparisons. For most purposes the year is the best period to take for foreign-exchange market estimates of rate equilibrium. If the foreign-exchange rate has remained stable within a fixed range for a whole year without requiring a net movement of short-term capital and gold in either direction, the rate may be said to be in equilibrium. If the country concerned has gained gold and foreign short-term assets on balance, the rate of exchange may be said to be undervalued with respect to a year; if, on the other hand, it has lost gold and foreign short-term assets on balance, it may be said to be overvalued.

With relation to money prices, costs, and incomes, foreign-exchange equilibrium can be similarly defined. If the costs and prices of foreign-trade goods and services for export by a country are such that, given the state of foreign demand and given foreign costs and prices, a sufficient supply of foreign exchange is made available to pay for the foreign-trade goods and services that it wants to buy, the rate of exchange may be said to be in equilibrium. The domestic and foreign demand for money capital should also be balanced with the merchandise and service items. If the rate of exchange is such, given the state of money prices and costs and of demand at home and abroad, that the receipts from exports of goods and services do not suffice to meet payments for foreign goods and services, the currency is overvalued; while if the receipts are exceeded by the payments, the currency is undervalued. Here it is more evident that equilibrium, undervaluation, and overvaluation are all concepts that must be related to a time period. No one expects imports and exports to balance each hour, each day, each week, or each month. Prices and costs may change seasonally, yet the changes may be compatible with equilibrium over a longer period.

When money costs are considered, it is possible to conceive of foreign-exchange equilibrium in this sense somewhat differently. The money costs of an economic community bear a rough relationship to the national money income. Given the national money income for a definite period of time and given the country's resources available for the export of goods and services, its demand for foreign goods and services and similar data for the countries with which it trades, then there is an equilibrium rate of foreign exchange which can be maintained without exerting any pressure on the level of the national money income. A change in the national money income, in resources, in the demand for foreign-trade goods, or in the foreign-exchange rate itself will require a shift in one or more other items if foreign-exchange equilibrium is to be regained.

All these methods of approaching the subject of foreign-exchange equilibrium are related. The foreign-exchange market merely reflects the operation of the underlying factors in the domestic money economy in relation to other economies, with the addition, however, of certain disturbing elements peculiar to the market itself. As will be seen in the remainder of this chapter, no one method of getting at a statistical demonstration of the existence of equilibrium, undervaluation, or overvaluation of the foreign-exchange rate is fool proof. Within broad limits, however, all three comparisons—of net gold and foreign short-term assets, of money costs and prices, and of national money incomes—throw some light on the problem, although no one of them affords a complete answer to it. We may perhaps clarify the issues involved by reference to the theories of causation which have grown up to explain changes in rates of foreign exchange.

Theories of Foreign Exchange. Dr. Ellis divides the theories of foreign exchange into (1) the *inflation theory*, which believes as far as changes in the rates of exchange are concerned "that causation runs from prices to the rate of exchange"; (2) the *balance-of-payments theory*, "which would either treat the rate of exchange as an independent phenomenon or ascribes to the balance or rate of exchange causal effectiveness on prices"; and (3) *synthesizing theories*, "admitting both lines of causation or . . . tracing internal and external depreciation alike to a common cause."[2]

The inflation theorists generally subscribe to the purchasing-power-parity doctrine. Within the broad group, however, there are some, for example, Cassel, who believe that changes in in-

[2] *Ibid.*, p. 203.

ternal prices will affect the rate of exchange, and others, such as Pigou, who hold that, in addition, changes in the rate of exchange can affect internal prices.

Ellis subdivides the balance-of-payments theories into three groups. The first, or truistic, is content merely to state the fact that the rate of exchange is affected by the demand for and supply of foreign currencies. As such it is not a theory of foreign exchange, since it fails to take into account basic interrelationships. Even as a description of the foreign-exchange ratemaking process, it does not go very far. The second maintains that the rate of exchange is independent of prices, neither determining them nor being affected by them. This is clearly wrong.[3] If the alteration of prices can affect the quantities of goods sold in foreign trade, it can affect the supply of foreign exchange and thus the rate. Conversely, if the rate of foreign exchange alters, it will affect the prices of foreign-trade goods[4] and thus the general price level. The third group believes that the balance of payments[5] determines the rate of foreign exchange and the complexion of prices, either by inducing long-term capital movements and, through their effects on the terms of trade, by bringing about changes in the monetary policy and thus affecting prices and costs, or in some other fashion. The synthesizing theories, Ellis states, maintain either "not only that causation extends from prices to rate and conversely, but also that the balance of payments factors, including variations in reciprocal demand and capital movements, are as important moments in the problem as monetary inflation"[6] (or deflation) or that changes in exchange and prices have common causes affecting them simultaneously.

It is difficult to see how the first type of synthesizing theory differs from the second type of inflation theory. If the latter holds that exchange rates can affect prices, as well as prices rates, it must grant that factors other than prices play a part in the determination of rates of exchange. If it did not, then the only influence left to affect the rates, and hence prices, would be

[3] *Ibid.*, p. 268. [4] See above, pp. 64 ff.

[5] Exclusive of gold and short-term capital movements. [6] *Ibid.*, p. 206.

changes in prices themselves. Thus the bilateral inflation theory (in Ellis's terminology) does not differ fundamentally from the first synthesizing type of theory, which stresses the interaction of all factors impinging upon prices and rates of exchange. Furthermore, the second type of synthesizing theory, which stresses the proposition that rates and prices are affected by third and common causes, would presumably not deny, in the case of an outside factor affecting only one, that the other would be affected by repercussions.[7] So interpreted, it ceases to constitute a separate theory.

We are left, then, with three strands: the unilateral inflation theory, holding that prices are affected by domestic monetary factors and thus react on the rate of exchange; the balance-of-payments theory, which can be summed up by saying that other factors besides monetary inflation and deflation can alter the rate of exchange directly and in turn react on prices;[8] and the bilateral theory, which holds both propositions to be true. Which of these theories serves to explain the course of the exchange quotations of the mark in the period of the German post-war inflation is not under discussion at present. Our interest is to demonstrate that as general explanations of the behavior of exchange rates in relation to the domestic economy and the balance of payments, all three are correct, the first two being merely incomplete.

Merchandise trade may be cited to indicate this. If the mone-

[7] See *ibid.*, p. 268 n.

[8] Perhaps the best example of this type—and one which Ellis does not mention—is the French "psychological" theory of the foreign exchanges. The fact that the franc is weak when the Chamber of Deputies is sitting or when an unbalanced budget is announced is due to the fact that the French public fears uncontrolled inflation and begins to export capital. In part, of course, it is due to the fact that foreign-exchange dealers in other parts of the world expect such a reaction and accentuate it by selling the franc short at such times. The French psychological theory of the exchanges, connecting the budget with the rate of exchange can be reduced to the simple proposition that the rate of exchange can be directly affected by capital flight. See A. Aftalion, *Monnaie, prix et change*, 1924, pp. 290 ff.; B. Nogaro, *La Monnaie*, 1924, pp. 289-99; C. Rist, *La Deflation en pratique*, 1924, pp. 120-21; and Malpas, *op. cit.*, pp. 498 ff. If pressed, however, these economists would probably be willing to admit that, on occasion, the causation has run from domestic inflation to the rate of exchange (as in the 1918-21 period) and that when the rate of exchange has moved first, it can react on domestic prices and costs.

tary means of payment in a country are increased and turn over against currently produced goods and services with the same or greater rapidity, the national money income will be increased, and, when a point of reasonably full employment has been reached, the costs of production, that is, the prices of factors of production, will be raised. The rise in the national money income will increase the country's imports to an extent dependent upon the flexibility of demand for foreign goods and services. Exports will be reduced, partly as a result of the increased demand for them at home, which will raise prices from the demand side, and partly as a consequence of the increase in costs, which will tend to raise supply prices. The merchandise balance of trade will then turn relatively unfavorable, and, at the same rate of exchange, require a movement of gold or short-term capital, unless some offsetting change takes place among the other items.

Conversely, if a capital flight occurs, driving down the rate of exchange after a fixed parity to (let us say) gold has had to be abandoned, the prices of foreign-trade goods will be altered, as we have shown above.

In given circumstances, either of these explanations may be correct. Indeed, at a given point of time, both may be correct. In the United States in the period from May to July, 1933, the rate of foreign exchange dropped precipitously, and the prices of commodities and securities rose. Which one was responsible for the other cannot be clearly decided. There was at the same time a flight of capital into domestic commodities and equities, and a flight of capital abroad. Those buying stocks and raw materials may have regarded the foreign-exchange depreciation as proof of a new external value of money which would eventually be met internally; and those exporting capital may have considered the sharp rise in internal prices as an indication that the dollar was worth less. But the subsequent collapse in equity and commodity prices and the concomitant recovery in the rate of exchange revealed the purely speculative character of both phenomena.

We may conclude then that a theory of foreign exchange

cannot be unilateral if it is to be complete, except possibly as an explanation of particular instances of exchange rate movements. It is true that a comprehensive theory can admit the interaction of all the various factors mentioned, while stressing the importance of one set. The inflation theorists, who emphasize the importance of money prices and costs, stress the factors that lie behind the income balance of payments (with gold excluded). The balance-of-payments theorists stress the items in the capital balance. It should also be noted, however, that the rate of exchange can be varied by direct means through changing the price of gold, or by monetary action in changing the pegged rate by means of short-term capital movements. In such cases the income balance and the long-term capital balance, together with the factors which underlie them, will be affected by the change in the exchange rate.

Prices, Costs, and Exchange Rates. We may next devote more detailed attention to the inflation theory and to its central proposition, the purchasing-power-parity theorem, in order to determine how far the trade balance may be said to affect the rate of exchange. To discuss the purchasing-power-parity theory at length would be gratuitous in view of the extended treatment it has received in the past.[9] It will suffice therefore to outline what remains of the doctrine after the rigorous and exacting analysis to which it has been subjected.

A recent presentation by Haberler[10] gives the theory in its most acceptable modern form. When other things are equal, the relative degree of price change between any two countries will reflect the degree to which the theoretical equilibrium rate of exchange has moved. Couched in mathematical symbols, the theory can be compressed into an equation. Where W_1 and W_2 indicate the rate of foreign exchange at the base period and the later period, respectively, and P equals the general price level in the appropriate country, A or B, at the appropriate time period, with k referring to the degree to which the actual rate

[9] See Ohlin, *op. cit.*, pp. 544-50; Ellis, *op. cit.*, *pp.* 264-68; Heckshcr, *op. cit.*, pp. 158 ff., esp. pp. 161-62; Angas, *op. cit.*, pp. 73 ff.

[10] *Der internationale Handel, op. cit.*, pp. 34 ff.

of exchange differs from the purchasing-power-parity level, then $W_1 : W_2 = \frac{P_A^1}{P_B^1 \cdot k_1} : \frac{P_A^2}{P_B^2 \cdot k_2}$ When other things are equal, $k_1 = k_2$ and the equation becomes $W_1 : W_2 = \frac{P_A^1}{P_B^1} : \frac{P_A^2}{P_B^2}$. If, therefore, other things are equal, the exchange rate differs no more from the equilibrium level at the date of comparison than it did at the base period, and the degree of relative price change can be taken to indicate the change in the equilibrium rate of exchange.

It will be noticed first of all that the theory has been so adroitly qualified by the introduction of the symbol *k* that it does not say very much. It does, however, refer to general price levels, not merely to export and import prices. If the theory is not to be entirely tautological and devoid of causative implications, this must be the case.[11] The all-important *k* represents the nonmonetary influence on the income and capital balances of payments which may affect the rate. Haberler lists these factors as those affecting (1) costs of transfer, (2) changes in (real) costs of production, (3) changes in international demand.[12] But there should also be included in *k* international capital movements[13] and the service items in the income balance for which the Casselian doctrine makes no provision.[14] All these factors which should be included in *k* may be called the "substantive course of trade," following the phrase of Professor Taussig.

It has been objected, however, that the purchasing-power-parity theory is in error in concentrating its attention on commodity prices. There is first of all the reasoning put forward by Mises (in contradiction to the purchasing-power-parity theory

[11] But see Ellis, *op. cit.*, p. 212. It may be admitted that if $k_1 = k_2$, all factors tending to make export and import prices diverge from the prices of home-market goods have been assumed away. In this form the use of general price levels is unassailable, if not particularly useful.

[12] Haberler, *op. cit.*, pp. 35-36.

[13] See the following section below.

[14] See Ellis, *op. cit.*, p. 264. It may be granted that many service items, particularly interest and sinking fund charges, do not vary substantially from year to year as a general rule. Others, however, do. See F. W. Ogilvie, *The Tourist Movement: An Economic Study*, 1933, especially Tables pp. 98-99, 125 and 131. Tourist travel varies in both secular and cyclical fashion.

that he himself affirms). This holds that the same physical goods, when located in different countries, must be considered by the economist to be different goods, because of the different "place utilities" attaching to them.[15] This difficulty can be overcome, however, by regarding costs of transfer as equivalent to the value differentials between physically similar goods situated in different places. Their prices may then be compared, costs of transfer being abstracted from them or assumed constant.

But, more fundamentally, it has been argued that the purchasing-power-parity doctrine fails to take account of the Law of One Price.[16] Relative prices for foreign-trade goods cannot differ from one another by more than the costs of transfer in one market. If the rate of exchange be fixed, inflation in one country relative to others will succeed in altering export and import prices (costs of transfer being assumed unchanged) only in the degree to which it alters world prices. The weight of this objection has led to an attempt to formulate the "cost-parity" theory. Developing this in mathematical terms, Brisman states that when *Re* is the rate of exchange for gold currencies in the paper-standard country, *Icp* stands for internal costs of production and *Gcp* for gold costs of production, the formula for foreign-exchange-rate equilibrium is $Re = \frac{Icp}{Gcp}$. That for undervaluation, it follows, is $Re < \frac{Icp}{Gcp}$ and that for overvaluation is $Re > \frac{Icp}{Gcp}$.[17] No scholarly attempt has been made to fit statistical indices to these or to similar formulae couched in terms of costs, and most theorists unite in doubting that the task can be done.[18] One must necessarily agree with the forceful arguments advanced against Sir Henry Strakosch's use of cost-

[15] See L. von Mises, *The Theory of Money and Credit* (English ed., 1935), p. 176. Ellis also makes the point, *op. cit.*, pp. 243-44.

[16] See Brisman, "Some Reflections on the Theory of Foreign Exchange," *op. cit.*, pp. 69-74.

[17] *Ibid.*, p. 73. [18] *Ibid.*, p. 74.

of-living indices as the measure of costs of production.[19] No necessary relation exists between the two series in the short run.

Conceptually the cost-parity doctrine is superior to the purchasing-power-parity doctrine. If exchange rates be fixed, the prices of internationally-traded goods in two countries will be equal to one another at different points of time, on the assumption of unchanged costs of transfer. When general price levels are compared, a discrepancy in parities in time may indicate a change in the substantive course of trade or may reveal a change in the equilibrium rate of exchange. The comparison of costs of production, it is true, reveals discrepancies due only to these two causes. But if sharp changes are recorded in costs of production, they will indicate change in the equilibrium rate of exchange sooner than general price levels if the foreign-exchange rate is maintained fixed. The general price level, which is influenced in varying degree by foreign-trade goods prices, will lag behind because of the fact that it is to an extent determined by factors outside the country. To take the example of an inflationary movement in a country with fixed exchanges, the pressure on export prices from the supply side will be indicated by a cost-of-production index before it is reflected in prices, if the exporters continue to sell in world markets by taking reduced profits or actual losses.

The cost-parity theory may be loosely set up in terms of the national money income. Given world money income and the rate of exchange, together with the factors of demand and supply underlying the substantive course of trade, there is one level of the national money income which will make the actual foreign-exchange rate equal to the equilibrium level. A higher national money income will leave the same foreign-exchange quotation overvalued; a lower level will leave the exchange rate undervalued. As will be seen in the following chapter, undervaluation and overvaluation will exert pressure at the same time on the exchange and on the national money income. If the exchange rate is held fixed, come what may, the equilibrium

[19] See Professor B. P. Adarkar's letter to the London *Economist*, July 20, 1935, p. 127.

position can be regained only by a movement of the national money income. If the exchange rate is free to vary, however, equilibrium may be regained partly through a movement in the rate of exchange and partly by a change in the national money income.

The Substantive Course of Trade. We have pointed out in previous chapters that capital movements in their effects upon rates of exchange, gold flows, and short-term capital movements are similar to changes in costs of transfer, changes in real costs of production of foreign-trade goods and services, and changes in international demand. In the purchasing-power-parity theorem, the effects of changes in any one of these factors, which may be grouped together under the convenient designation of the "substantive course of trade," are included in k which represents the deviation of the actual rate of exchange from the equilibrium rate at any one time. It should be noted, however, that the equilibrium rate from which the actual rate differed was the equilibrium rate of a particular moment, not necessarily the long-run equilibrium.

Perhaps the point may be made clear by taking a concrete example. Let us assume that the English lose their taste for Danish butter. If this were to occur, the Danish kroner would be immediately overvalued if the foreign exchange rate did not fluctuate. This would be revealed in the foreign-exchange market by the necessity of drawing upon sterling foreign exchange reserves, or of exporting gold to maintain the rate. So far as prices and costs were concerned, the price of Danish butter would fall, and the incomes of the dairy exporters would similarly decline.

Whether the equilibrium rate which would balance the demand for foreign exchange during the year with the supply in the new state of international demand is that indicated at the incidence of the change in demand or not, however, is a much more complex question. If the rate of exchange were allowed to depreciate, certain imports would be cut off and certain other exports would presumably be stimulated. The shape of the cost curves for butter and other products and the shape of the demand curves for other Danish export goods would have to be considered. If the national money income is allowed to decline in order to restore equilibrium in the foreign exchanges, similar questions must be raised. The reduction in the demand for imports will affect the value of goods imported into Denmark to a degree determined immediately by the flexibility and elasticity of demand. The reduction in the costs of export goods will affect exports to a degree determined by foreign demand schedules for them. What the equilibrium rate of exchange will eventually be in relation to the national money income which will result from the change in foreign demand is *a priori* indeterminate. The most that can be said is that in the short run the exchange is overvalued if it is held constant after the reduction in English demand. The proof of this can be found in the foreign-exchange market only, since the substantive course of trade has changed. But the disequilibrium immediately revealed is a necessary part of the process of restoring long-run equilibrium under the changed conditions.

This can be made more explicit by a further reference to the transfer process. When a new capital transfer takes place, the exchange rate in the lending country becomes overvalued so far as the day-to-day equilibrium of the exchange market is concerned. This is indicated by the loss in gold and/or net short-term foreign assets if the rate of exchange is held fixed. This disequilibrium, however, is a part of the process of attaining the long-run equilibrium which will be restored after the real transfer has been accomplished. On the paper standard the depreciation of the lending country's currency to a point below that at which it will come to rest after the completion of the real transfer is a similar indication of a day-to-day disequilibrium in the foreign-exchange market and in the relations between the rate of exchange and money prices and costs, which is aiding in the restoration of long-run equilibrium.

The Measurement of Equilibrium. When it comes to measuring the extent of departures from foreign-exchange equilibrium, little of a definite nature can be said. The purchasing-power-parity method of comparing general prices and the method of comparing cost indices or even the national money income afford only rough measures of changes in the equilibrium rate of exchange, since it is impossible to weigh the necessary change required by alterations in the substantive course of trade. Even the foreign-exchange market criterion cannot be used without qualifications. If gold plus net short-term foreign assets (or minus net short-term foreign liabilities) change, one can only be sure that the day-to-day exchange rate equilibrium is disturbed. If a longer point of view be taken, the day-to-day disturbance may be part of a necessary corrective process which is tending to keep the rate of exchange in equilibrium in the long run.

Informed judgment must supersede rule-of-thumb measures in this respect. A loss of gold or of net short-term foreign assets, when the country concerned is making new loans abroad, may be regarded with equanimity so long as it can be accounted for entirely by the change in the substantive course of trade. As the next chapter will show, it is fully possible to establish rates of exchange which bear drastically incorrect relationships to money costs and price levels or to the national money income. In cases in which the rate is maintained without further readjustment, this means that money prices and costs will tend to be brought into line to correct the disequilibrium. Upon occasion, however, and especially if the rate of exchange is established at a highly overvalued level, the maintenance of the rate of exchange may involve certain social costs which make it preferable to adjust the market rate of exchange to the equilibrium rate, rather than to permit the forces of inflation and deflation to bring about the converse process.

Summary. Equilibrium in the foreign-exchange rate can be defined with reference to the interrelationships between the domestic economy, the balance of payments, and the rate of exchange, or in connection with the exchange market itself. In the first case, equilibrium can be defined as the rate of exchange at which the balance of payments is maintained "in balance" without the domestic economy tending to alter the rate of exchange or vice versa. In the second case, equilibrium can be defined as the absence of movements of gold plus short-term capital. These two conceptions of equilibrium are interrelated. If money costs (or the national income) are relatively high in relation to the rate of exchange, for example, their effect is to increase imports relative to exports and to cause a loss of gold and/or short-term capital assets.

Equilibrium must be related to a specific period of time. Gold and short-term foreign assets may be lost in the spring of the year and gained in the fall. If the early loss is made up by the later gain, it may be said that the rate of exchange has been in disequilibrium during the spring and again in the fall, but that it has been in equilibrium for the year as a whole. Further than that, it may be true in certain cases that disequilibrium in the foreign exchanges in the short-run is a necessary condition of long-run equilibrium.

This last statement may be demonstrated by reference to the adjustment process in international trade. If changes occur in the factors lying immediately behind the balance of payments—changes in the demand for foreign-trade goods, in their real costs of production, in the costs of transferring goods internationally, or in the direction and extent of long-term capital movements—other items in the balance of payments and the prices of factors of production (the national money income) as well must be readjusted if the rate of exchange is to be maintained; otherwise the rate of exchange must move to a new equilibrium position. The disequilibrium immediately arising is a part of the process of readjustment and is therefore compatible with long-run equilibrium, even though it involves short-run disequilibrium. In the one case gold will flow or net short-term foreign assets be altered to aid in the accomplishment of the adjustment process. When new long-term capital transfers are considered, the process by which the real transfer is brought about is one of continuous short-run disequilibrium, which is necessary if long-run equilibrium is to be regained.

So far as a theory of foreign exchange is considered to be an explanation of the way in which causation runs between prices, costs, and the exchange rate, no unilateral theory can be made into a comprehensive theory. At specific times the influences of prices on exchange rates may predominate; at other times the causation will run in the opposite direction. But as a universal explanation of behavior it must be granted that variations in the rate of exchange which have their immediate cause in changes in the substantive course of trade can affect costs and prices, and that changes in money costs and prices arising from the action of the internal monetary system can equally affect the rate of exchange.

VIII

UNDERVALUATION, OVERVALUATION, AND INTERNATIONAL SHORT-TERM FUNDS

A more elaborate treatment of the relative roles of short-term capital and gold when the rate of exchange varies on either side of the equilibrium position is in order, not because the theoretical outlines of the analysis differ particularly from those of the transfer mechanism, but because of the practical importance of the subject. The post-war currency history is replete with examples of over- and undervalued currencies, in which the fact of disparity from equilibrium or its potential effects were not understood in comprehensive terms.[1] Lately, to be sure, more interest has been taken in these aspects of exchange problems, particularly in discussions of currency stabilization, but the role of short-term capital movements has not always received sufficient attention.[2]

The Practical Problem. On a gold standard when no short-term capital movements are taking place, the problem would be

[1] While economists today are generally aware of the fact that the French stabilization of the franc in the 1926-28 period seriously undervalued the currency (see, among others, J. Viner, "International Aspects of the Gold Standard," in *Gold and Monetary Stabilization*, Q. Wright, ed., 1932, pp. 21-22), yet it is curious that no mention of any such possibility was made at the time by the two American economists separately engaged in studying the French currency question. See J. H. Rogers, *The Process of Inflation in France*, 1928, and E. L. Dulles, *The French Franc: 1924-1928*, 1929. Dr. Rogers did suggest that from the *financial* point of view, a three-cent franc would have been easier to maintain than a four-cent franc (*op. cit.*, p. 352). At the time J. M. Keynes was recommending a franc of four cents or less in order to avoid deflation and to achieve an internal price rise. (See *Essays in Peruasion*, 1932, pp. 105-17.) But he does not consider the effects of French undervaluation aside from this narrow point of view.

[2] As recently as October, 1935, J. M. Keynes in an essay ("The Future of the Foreign Exchanges," *Lloyds' Bank Review*, October, 1935, p. 528) wrote that the equilibrium rate of exchange should be taken to be that which would place no strain on central banks. He further indicated that by this he meant a rate which would keep gold flows at a minimum. It should be clear, however, that changes in net short-term foreign assets (or liabilities) should also be regarded.

sufficiently clear. An undervalued currency would gain gold; an overvalued currency would lose it. On a paper standard the rate of exchange, if unmanaged, would fluctuate about the equilibrium position in accordance with movements of autonomous capital in one or another direction. Where a pegged standard exists, the stabilization fund or central bank maintaining the rate of foreign exchange at an overvalued level would lose foreign short-term assets but would gain them at an undervalued rate. In order to present the problem in its full complexity we may restrict the present discussion to the case of a gold standard in which short-term capital movements do take place. When movements only of gold or only of short-term liquid funds occur, no confusion of thought can develop as to the course of events and their meaning.

For present purposes the disparities between the actual rate of exchange and the equilibrium level, computed however crudely from costs and prices, not from observation of the behavior of the foreign-exchange market, may be restricted to those arising from changes in the relations between money costs and the rate of foreign exchange, with the substantive course of trade assumed unchanged. This is partly because we have already treated alterations in the rate of long-term capital flow, in costs of transfer, and in international demand and supply conditions in Part II. It is also due in part to the fact that the disequilibria arising from changes in the substantive course of trade do not usually require adjustments imposing severe strains upon other factors in the economy.[3]

The practical problem of exchange equilibrium arises because of the fact that the forces involved do not operate automatically and without friction. Overvaluation would be of little moment if it brought about painless and rapid deflation of costs and prices. The well-known tendency of costs to lag behind prices, however, means that an overvalued currency entails business depression when deflation does take place and entails

[3] This statement will be qualified at length in chap. x below, under the discussion of abnormal capital movements. Another qualification should likewise be made in the case of wide changes in tariffs.

a potential crisis and breakdown if the deflation is postponed by borrowing heavily from abroad on short term. The fact that governments have the power to fix any rate of exchange whatever as the official one by decreeing the gold value of the standard money or by pegging means that the forces of inflation and deflation are from time to time released when the government ties the value of its currency to gold or to other monetary units at a rate chosen for reasons of convenience, tradition, or mistaken notions of economic policy.

Examples of Undervaluation. The outstanding examples of undervaluation in the post-war era are those of the French stabilization of 1926-28 and of the United States in 1933 and 1934. The present discussion will treat them in broad outline, in order to fill out some of the gaps in our theoretical analysis, but will refrain from going deeply into the detailed statistical analysis of the two experiences which would be required to "prove" the undervaluation. A consensus of opinion would doubtless grant the fact of undervaluation without demanding such proof.

In the case of France, the budgetary inflation of the war and reconstruction periods had rendered a restoration of the pre-war level of the franc in relation to gold out of the question. Moreover, in the 1923-26 period a severe capital flight developed as the French *rentier* became afraid lest the budgetary inflation get out of hand. The heavy expenses of reconstructing the devastated areas and the panic of confidence which accompanied the reoccupation of the Ruhr region, developed a situation which for a time looked as though it would follow the lines of the German hyperinflation and dispossess the property-owning classes of their wealth. The fact that the pound sterling was appreciating in terms of gold through 1924 and 1925 made London a peculiarly convenient place of safekeeping for expatriated French capital.

These huge offerings of francs for foreign currencies, recurring with particular emphasis at the times of budgetary difficulties, drove the franc to low levels. In July, 1926, the franc reached its lowest point of 2.5 cents against the dollar which may be compared with the pre-war parity of 19.3 cents.[4] At this juncture the Poincaré cabinet was formed, the budget was put in balance by strenuous measures, and the Bank of France was empowered to buy and sell foreign exchange and gold abroad. The advent to power of a strong premier and his Draconian tactics overcame the crisis in confidence. At a gradually accelerating rate capital was repatriated from abroad, and the foreign-exchange quotation for the franc rose. In December, 1926, the Bank of France stabilized the franc on a *de facto* basis, holding the rate at approximately 3.92 cents. Further capital repatriation was carried out through purchases of gold and foreign exchange made by the Bank abroad.

In the American case, the undervaluation was brought about by more strenuous methods. Shortly after the bank holiday of March 3, 1933, foreign-exchange regulations were put into effect by executive order, limiting all transactions to those of a commercial nature. The order was designed to eliminate speculative dealings and presumably the export of domestic capital from the United States.

After April 19, however, when the gold standard had been officially abandoned, a concerted speculative attack on the dollar began, against which these restrictions were apparently without effect. The inflation scare of May, June, and the first part of July witnessed concomitant flights of capital abroad and into the market for stocks and lower-grade bonds. The entirely unreal character of the inflation was revealed when the security market collapsed of its own weight in mid-July. Thereupon the dollar appreciated *vis-à-vis* the gold franc, the August average going to 5.375 cents per franc as opposed to 5.458 in July. By this time, however, the Government had apparently committed itself to a policy of further dollar depreciation. On September 8 it announced the establishment of a buying price for newly mined domestic gold, the price being determined daily on the basis of the London open-market gold quotation and the sterling exchange rate. This step was taken as a renewed signal of infla-

[4] All foreign-exchange rates here quoted are from the *Federal Reserve Bulletin* for the appropriate dates.

tion, and capital started again to move out of the United States, driving the sterling price up and with it the dollar gold price, which rose from $29.62 an ounce on September 9 to a high of $32.28. The movement was short lived, however. The fact that the price applied only to newly mined domestic gold, of which a relatively small quantity was available, prevented dollars from being offered for gold abroad. The speculative flurry of capital exports died down until the gold price in New York had receded to $29.00 on October 16. At this juncture (on October 23) President Roosevelt announced that the Treasury, through the offices of the Reconstruction Finance Corporation, would buy gold abroad at a price to be determined presumably with reference to some index of American raw-material prices. The American gold price was reset at $31.36 and advanced by gradual stages, although the foreign-exchange quotation for the franc did not keep exact pace with the rising gold valuation. On January 15, after the Reconstruction Finance Corporation had purchased $132,000,000 of gold in a period of two and one-half months, the President asked Congress for permission to set a value for the dollar (in terms of the American gold price) not higher than 60 percent of its former valuation.[5] On February 1, 1934, after the passage of the Gold Reserve Act of 1934 on the previous day, the President set the price of gold at $35.00 an ounce, making the dollar worth 59.06 percent of its former bullion value. Thus, after first discouraging the export of private domestic capital, then fostering it, and finally exporting governmental capital in exchange for gold at an advancing price, the American Government succeeded in establishing the rate of the dollar in the foreign-exchange market at a seriously undervalued level.

The Belgian government, possibly profiting from the lessons of the American experience, depreciated its currency to an undervalued level without any preliminaries. In April, 1935, gold was nationalized and withdrawn from circulation, and the

[5] The lower limit to which the dollar could be reduced had been set at 50 percent of its former value by the terms of the Thomas Amendment to the Farm Relief Act of May 12, 1933.

value of the *belga* in terms of gold was reduced 28 percent at one stroke. A modified gold standard protected by a stabilization fund (later abandoned) was put into effect twenty-four hours after the gold standard set up in 1926 had been abandoned.

Undervaluation, Gold, and Short-Term Funds. By no matter what paths or expedients the level of foreign exchange is altered so as to depreciate it to an undervalued level,[6] the effects of the undervaluation take one of two main courses, arriving, so far as the banking system is concerned,[7] at approximately the same results. If the devaluation has been brought about by an abnormal export of capital, such capital will be apt to return, provided that the stabilization coincides with or induces a revival of confidence. When short-term capital movements to other countries do not compensate for the returning funds, the capital must re-enter the country entirely in the form of gold. The central bank may, of course, elect to buy foreign exchange and relieve the pressure on the gold supplies of other countries. When the gold price is suddenly changed, gold will be imported by the banking system (at handsome profits for a time) to bring it about that the rate of foreign exchange conforms to that indicated by the parity gold price. Thus the fact of the

[6] Theoretically, there is no reason why the undervaluation should not be achieved by internal deflation. If a country's costs and prices are in equilibrium with those of the rest of the world, a reduction in them would leave an unchanged currency rate undervalued. While deflation is attempted from time to time in order to restore equilibrium to an overvalued currency (see D. B. Copland, *Australia and the World Crisis*, 1933, p. 2, and the Laval decrees of July, 1935, *New York Times*, July 16, 1935, p. 25, col. 5), yet it is doubtful whether such strenuous measures have ever been used to gain a foreign-trade advantage. On this account, it is probable that undervaluation is in practice achieved only by movements in the rate of exchange.

[7] The stimulus to prices differs, of course, depending upon the course of world prices. Changing the relation of the currency to world currencies necessarily changes the relations between world and domestic prices of internationally traded goods. Whether domestic prices will rise, as in the case of the 1926 French stabilization, or gold prices be further depressed, as occurred as a result of the English 1931 abandonment of gold, will depend upon the state of the business cycle internationally, as well as on the importance of the depreciating country in the various world markets for the individual products it buys and sells. See D. Cassady, Jr., and A. R. Upgren, "International Trade and the Devaluation of the Dollar," *Quarterly Journal of Economics*, L (1936), 416-26, especially p. 416 n.

devaluation, whether achieved by changing the gold price or by stabilizing the currency at a level reached by the export of large amounts of domestic capital, brings about an immediate inflow of gold, provided the capital returns,[8] unless a short-term capital export takes place.[9]

Undervaluation achieved by depreciation of the rate of exchange to a point below the equilibrium level is thus accompanied by, or more usually followed by, an import of gold. If the central bank is empowered to buy foreign currencies, and elects to do so, an export of capital at short term may replace part of the gold inflow. This short-term capital export enables other countries, from which gold would have been drawn, to maintain their bullion reserves and perhaps to postpone a deflationary policy.[10]

[8] Where confidence is regained slowly, this capital is repatriated over a longer period of time. Such, very likely, was true of the United States in the 1934-35 period.

[9] It is unlikely that short-term capital will flow out of the country in very large amounts *on private account*. If foreign interest rates rise or domestic rates fall, or both, there will be of course some capitalists who prefer to retain their funds abroad. These rates of interest as a general rule, however, will not alter until a considerable portion of capital has already been repatriated. Again, much of the exported capital was probably acquired from business working capital for which it is needed as business confidence revives.

It is improbable that dealers will be able to lend more abroad at short term, since they were, in all likelihood, the heaviest exporters of capital during the prestabilization crisis. Thus money capital will be available to move only in one direction—toward the stabilizing country. This tendency is strengthened by capitalists' and dealers' desires to realize on profits from the depreciation, profits which might be jeopardized if the country of their refuge were to embargo gold or impose a moratorium on short-term debts.

The foregoing remarks apply with less force when an overnight devaluation takes place. But it is likely in this case that the professional exchange dealers have been short of the currency and will cover after devaluation.

Thus, if short-term capital is to move outward to compensate for the inflow of long- and short-term capital on private account, the movement is likely to be undertaken by an official institution, such as a central bank or a stabilization fund. After the disastrous experience of the Bank of France, however, central banks and stabilization funds have been wary of large uncovered purchases of foreign exchange. On this account, even the official funds have been dealing almost entirely in gold since 1933.

[10] Such deflation might otherwise be postponed if the banking system abroad has excess reserves or if the central banking authorities undertake to maintain the level of bank reserves through open-market policy. The drain of foreign funds from New York in the fall of 1931 led the member banks to discount bills and the reserve system to buy bills and government securities. The rate at which the latter purchases of governments and bills took place, however, did

But the undervaluation of the currency has further repercussions on the gold and short-term capital items. In the income balance of payments, a credit surplus tends to develop for the depreciated country, with the result of inducing a further inward movement of gold or an outward movement of short-term funds. In the merchandise balance the prices of foreign-trade goods rise relative to world prices. Until the costs of exports rise equally, exports will receive a bounty. Import prices have risen relatively in terms of the local currency, which tends to reduce the total value of imports. As costs rise, the national money income increases and imports will be expanded again. While costs lag behind prices, a relative increase in exports will tend to develop.

In the other items in the income balance, the tendency for a credit surplus to be fostered is perhaps not as pronounced. A devalued currency, of course, attracts tourists. When devaluation has raised internal costs (the national money income), tourists will go from the depreciating country abroad in large numbers; but previous to this time and during the lag of costs behind foreign-trade prices, something of a relative credit surplus tends to be developed in this account.

The credit surplus for the income balance attracts further gold, in the absence of an export of capital, until costs have risen to the extent necessary to restore equilibrium. In the undervalued country inflation can take place on the basis of the imported gold or exported short-term capital, at a rate dependent upon banking and credit policy. The inflation on the basis of short-term loans abroad will take place under the most favorable circumstances, if the foreign exchange is held by the central bank. The same reasons for believing that the banking system, not independent dealers and private capitalists, will conduct the lending arising from the credit surplus in the

---

not enable the member bank reserve account to reach its August, 1931, level until November, 1932. (See Currie, *The Supply and Control of Money in the United States*, pp. 108, 140-41.) It should be remembered, likewise, that another specie drain occurred in April, 1932, and that hoarding of bank notes aided in the reduction of reserves.

income balance obtain as in the case of loans produced by the fact of stabilization at a depreciated level.[11]

Whether the equilibrating item in the balance of payments called into action by the fact of undervaluation be gold or short-term capital does not greatly affect the ability of the undervalued country to expand. Part of this is due to the fact that it is likely that the central bank in acquiring foreign exchange will build up reserve balances on which the member banks can increase loans.[12] Part is due to the fact that undervaluation is generally resorted to at a time when the inflation psychology exists or can be stimulated by the fact of undervaluation itself.

In connection with an overvalued currency, however, it may make considerable difference whether the foreign-exchange market indications of overvaluation take the form of gold outflows or of mounting foreign-exchange liabilities. Dwindling foreign short-term assets in the form of outside bank reserves, on the other hand, are almost exactly the same as gold exports in the response they draw. These problems will receive attention after a brief description of the theoretical case of overvaluation, as illustrated by the broad outlines of the recent English and Australian experiences.

Overvaluation Examples. It is unnecessary here to devote much space to an account of England's return to the gold standard in 1925 at an overvalued level. The basic facts are generally agreed to by economists, and the chronological details of the stabilization have been set forth in many excellent accounts.[13]

[11] See above, p. 123 n.

[12] There may be, as there was in France, a statute in the central bank charter forbidding it to count foreign exchange as legal reserve in the computation of its own ratio. If member-bank reserve balances with the central bank were then to expand on the basis of foreign-exchange sales, the reserve ratio would decline. Should it approach the legal or customary minimum, however, the central bank could readily convert foreign-exchange reserves into gold and forestall pressure against expansion arising from the necessity to maintain the minimum reserve in gold as a percentage of its deposit liabilities.

[13] See, e.g., W. A. Brown, *England and the New Gold Standard*, 1929, *passim*; T. E. Gregory, *The First Year of the Gold Standard*, 1926, pp. 39-94; T. E. Gregory, *The Gold Standard and Its Future*, chap. iii; J. Viner, "International Aspects of the Gold Standard," *op. cit.*, pp. 23-24.

One telescoped paragraph will therefore suffice to indicate how the overvaluation of the pound sterling was brought about.

During 1924 and 1925 the dollar rate of exchange fell rapidly in London. American speculators had foreseen an attempt to restore the pound sterling to its pre-war gold ratio, and French capital poured into England to escape the toils of budgetary inflation at home. Costs and prices, which had risen drastically during the wartime inflation, had fallen but had not regained anything like their 1913 levels. While similar inflations had taken place in various degrees in the other countries of the world, those countries which had either regained or maintained pre-war parity with gold had relatively lower levels of costs and prices. The overvaluation of the pound, brought about by a speculative inflow of capital from overseas, was maintained by short-term borrowing as the practice grew abroad of maintaining foreign exchange reserves in gold standard countries, in England and the United States particularly. Wages in certain industries, especially in coal mining, were reduced, but the strength of the labor opposition evinced in the 1926 general strike prevented this lowering of money costs from becoming sufficiently widespread. Three additional factors made the position of sterling even more precarious after the resumption of gold payments. The first was the undervaluation of a number of the currencies of continental countries, in particular the French franc. So long as the Bank of France bought exchange on London and New York, however, establishing a standing claim on the Bank of England's slender gold resources, the danger from this source, while persistent, was not immediate. Secondly, the English export industries had suffered from an adverse shift in international demand, resulting from German reparations in kind (particularly those of coal to France and Italy), the rise of Japanese manufacturing power, the growing self-sufficiency of the Dominions, and so forth. In coal and textiles the depression which characterized British export industry as a whole was especially marked. Third, the overvalued state of the German mark (which might have been overvalued at any level if one takes into account the burden of reparations) posed a problem. After long-term loans to Germany had come to a halt in 1928, short-term loans were sought and granted to the Berlin money market. The rate of interest paid was considerably higher than that in London, and for three and one-half years before 1931 the British, themselves debtors on short-term account, bought German paper. The traditional English predilection for "salt-water" bills was relaxed considerably, and the finance paper of Germany bought by England, as indeed that bought elsewhere, was later, in time of crisis, to prove unrealizable.

It has been pointed out that undervaluation is generally achieved through a change in the rate of exchange, not as a rule through readjustments of cost relationships at a fixed level of foreign exchange. In the case of overvaluation, either course may be followed. Overvaluation may be produced by a rise in costs and prices at a fixed rate of exchange or by a rise in the rate of exchange while costs and internal prices remain unaltered. In England it is likely that even if the rate of exchange had not been raised in 1924-25, the pound would have been somewhat overvalued as a result of the operation of the factors mentioned in the preceding paragraph.

The Australian pound in 1928-30 remained in a fixed relationship to the gold pound sterling, but the failure of costs to respond in the direction and degree called for by the cessation of international lending and the collapse of the prices for wheat and wool left the currency seriously overvalued. Perhaps our limitation of the present discussion to cases of under- and overvaluation arising from monetary or exchange adjustments should preclude an analysis of the Australian case, where the substantive course of trade was the principal cause of the difficulty. It is, however, of sufficient general interest as an example of the depression difficulties of "young countries" to merit cursory attention here.[14]

The fact that foreign countries had been making loans to Australia at long term up to 1928 required for the smooth

[14] Further treatment of the transfer problem for young countries will be furnished below in chap. x.

completion of the real transfer a persistent overvaluation of the Australian pound. When this lending was stopped, undervaluation from the point of cost and price structures was required, in order that the Australian economy might transfer abroad monies due on interest and sinking-fund payments. If the inflow of capital previous to 1928 had been on a smaller scale and had been commensurate with the growth of Australian ability either to increase exports or to eliminate the necessity for imports, and if the reduction of loans in 1928 had not been so abrupt, it is possible that the necessary undervaluation might have been achieved at a fixed rate of exchange—at least until the demand for raw materials and foodstuffs fell off in the world depression. But Australia had borrowed at an over-optimistic rate, so that the overvaluation as expressed in increased costs (especially wages)[15] was relatively severe at the time when undervaluation was suddenly made necessary. The serious inflation which had taken place on the basis of foreign loans made the accomplishment of the deflation which was necessary to repay them all the more severe.

Overvaluation, Gold and Short-Term Funds. In the case of England the overvaluation of the pound sterling was revealed not only by losses of gold on balance for the years 1925 and 1927-31, inclusive, but also by a high level of foreign net short-term liabilities.[16] The greater part of these were about equally divided between deposits and sterling bills held for foreign

[15] The tremendous political strength of labor in the Commonwealth made the deflationary possibility the more remote insofar as it involved the necessity for wage reductions. All attempts at lowering wages up to the actual crisis were ineffective.

[16] The Macmillan Committee data (*op. cit.*, Appendix, Table 9, p. 299) extend only from 1927 to March, 1931. On the whole they indicate a fairly evenly maintained level of net liabilities for Great Britain, the figures being £279,000,000 for December, 1927, and £274,000,000 for December, 1930 (£254,000,000 for March, 1931). Thus, while one would expect to find mounting liabilities, the Macmillan report indicates that they had been comparatively constant. Both Gregory and Keynes, however, take sharp issue with these data. See Gregory, *op. cit.*, p. 52 n.; and Keynes, "Reflections on Sterling Exchange," *Lloyd's Bank Monthly*, April, 1932. Keynes roughly estimates that gross liabilities in June, 1931, ran between six and eight hundred million pounds sterling, with comparable assets less than one-third this sum (*ibid.*, p. 149). See also his estimate of £600,000,000 for the end of 1926 in "The British Balance of Trade, 1925-1927," *Economic Journal*, XXXVII (1927), 562.

account. The Macmillan Committee did not reveal the division of liabilities between the London clearing banks and the Bank of England, but the presumption should be that by far the greater portion of them were the obligations of the clearing banks.[17] Thus these short-term loans were not greatly deflationary. Foreign deposits with the joint-stock banks probably have a low income velocity, thus bringing about primary deflation when they are increased. Secondary deflation, however, apparently did not take place directly, as it would have done if the clearing banks had held higher cash reserves because of their large proportion of foreign balances. The evidence indicates that the reserve ratio of the London banks was steadily reduced from 1925 to 1930.[18] Some deflation was brought about, nevertheless, by the relatively high levels of short-term interest rates. The portion of short-term debt held in the form of sterling bills for foreign account, foreign deposits with acceptance banks, or advances by foreigners to the discount market did not require or entail deflation except insofar as foreign liabilities were regarded as more volatile than domestic or as this part enabled other would-be lenders to the money market to hold idle balances. It is sufficient to say, therefore, that the fact that the British overvaluation brought about an increase in short-term liabilities rather than a drain of gold led British banking authorities up to the time of the publication of the Macmillan report, at least, to entertain a false sense of security with respect to the current international trade and finance position.

In Australia the overvalued position of the currency was revealed when the world prices of wheat and wool fell and when the rate of international capital import fell in 1928 with the rise in the rate of interest in the London and New York capital markets.[19] Imports continued heavy until March, 1930. At that

[17] "Other accounts" in the Banking Department of the Bank of England varied between a high of £42,000,000 and a low of £32,500,000 from 1929 to May, 1931 (Macmillan report, *op. cit.*, Appendix II, pp. 302-3). The bulk of deposits at this level was doubtless made up of private English balances.

[18] See Macmillan report, paragraph 77, p. 35.

[19] To what extent these two factors were related will be discussed in the following chapter.

time the currency had begun to depreciate seriously, and a tariff, together with the rationing of exchange for importers, had been imposed.

The fall in exports led first of all to a drawing down of Australia's sterling reserve balances in London, or a reduction in her net short-term lending. This was followed by an issue of Commonwealth Treasury bills in London and arrangements for overdrafts with the London clearing banks. Gold was sporadically exported until after the Commonwealth had been granted the power to mobilize gold reserves in 1929. At that point a heavy drain of gold took place, to be brought to a halt by the depreciation of the currency after the turn of the year.

It is probably unnecessary to devote any considerable attention to a discussion of the chain of circumstances which cause an overvalued country to lose gold or to run into debt on short-term account. It is the exact converse of that already described in connection with undervaluation. Exports are depressed by the fact that costs are high relative to world prices. Imports suffer to some extent, due to the depression and resultant unemployment in the exporting industries, which reduce the national income and hence the demand for world products; but they are relatively higher than exports because of the fact that the incomes of the employed factors are maintained, since the prices of factors of production have not materially fallen.

It is of interest and importance in this connection, however, to indicate some of the conditions determining whether gold or short-term funds will move as a result of overvaluation. In the case of Australia the question whether gold reserves would be exported, funds would be borrowed abroad, or foreign reserves would be drawn down was largely academic. The comparatively sudden and catastrophic nature of the reversal of the balance of payments made it necessary that all three methods be pursued to patch up a day-to-day equilibrium in the balance. In the case of England the importance of the question has already been mentioned. So long as there was a short-term foreign debt which was maintained or increased rather than gold flowing from the vaults of the Bank of England, the problem of adjusting the currency to the cost structure or vice versa could be postponed. The ability of the British to attract foreign funds depended upon a number of considerations.

The institutional factors in the situation were numerous. In the first place the traditional hegemony of the London short-term money market and the sterling bill in pre-war years led many continental nations, as well as constituent parts of the Empire, to maintain external balances in the form of London balances or sterling bills. Secondly, the Law of August, 1926, in France, under which the stabilization of the franc took place, permitted the Bank of France to purchase foreign exchange. In practice this meant balances or investments in the short-term money markets of New York and London only.

In addition, the Bank of England discount rate was maintained at a comparatively high level throughout the period. The rate of the Federal Reserve Bank of New York from 1925-31 exceeded it for only two months in 1929; that of the Bank of France fell below it at the end of 1927 and remained below it through the 1931 crisis. Of the important money centers, only Germany manifested a continuously higher level of short-term money rates; but in this case part of the differential was in the nature of a premium for risk to counteract the growing disposition to regard loans to Germany unfavorably.[20]

[20] The bank rates of the various central banks give a rough approximation of short-term money rates in the four countries mentioned. They were, with the date of their changes, as follows:

Bank of England	*From*	*Federal Reserve Bank (N. Y.)*	*From*	*Bank of France*	*From*	*Reichsbank*	*From*
5	12- 3-25	3½	7-27-25	6	7- 9-25	9	2-26-25
		4	1- 7-26	7½	7-31-26	8	1-12-26
		3½	4-23-26	6½	12-16-26	7	3-27-26
		4	8-12-26	5½	2- 3-	6½	6- 7-26
						6	7- 6-26
4½	4-21-27	3½	8- 5-27	5½	2- 3-27	5	1-11-27
				5	4-14-27	6	6-10-27
				4	12-29-27	7	10- 4-27
		4	2- 3-28				
		4½	5-18-28	3½	1-19-28		
		5	7-12-28				
5½	2- 7-29	6	8- 9-29			6½	1-12-29
6½	9-26-29	5	11- 1-29			7½	4-25-29
6	10-31-29	4½	11-15-29			7	11- 2-29

This firmness of money rates in England, while preventing England from enjoying the same degree of expansion as did the United States, enabled the money market to attract sufficient short-term loans to retain the greatest portion of the Bank of England's gold. The weight of the debt, however, made the entire financial position peculiarly vulnerable to the events of 1931. It is not necessary to repeat here the history of those events. It is sufficient to re-emphasize the part played by short-term capital in sustaining the rate of sterling in its overvalued condition during the six years of stabilization.

Summary. Deviations of the market from the equilibrium rate of exchange are reflected in (and caused by) changes in cost and price parities, but are more surely revealed by net movements of gold plus short-term capital. When moderate changes in international demand, in costs of transfer, in real costs of production or in capital movements at long term bring about the deviation from equilibrium, the under- or overvaluation is an important part of the process of re-establishing equilibrium. This is true both of the fixed-exchange standard, of the gold standard, or of freely fluctuating paper exchanges. In the latter case the short-run fluctuations of the paper rate, in the absence of further movements of capital, bring about the under- or overvaluation necessary to the settling of the exchange rate at the future equilibrium level.

If the exposition be limited to the case of fixed exchanges—and it should be emphasized that the unrestricted paper-exchange mechanism is the same, if exchange-rate fluctuations are

Bank of England	*From*	*Federal Reserve Bank (N. Y.)*	*From*	*Bank of France*	*From*	*Reichsbank*	*From*
5½	11-21-29						
5	12-12-29						
4½	2- 6-30	4	2- 7-30	3	1-30-30	6	2- 5-30
4	3- 6-30	3½	3-14-30	2½	5- 2-30	5	3-25-30
3½	3-20-30	3	5- 2-30			4½	5-20-30
3	5- 1-30	2½	6-20-30			4	6-21-30
		2	12-24-30			5	10- 9-30
2½	5-14-31	1½	5- 8-31	2	1- 3-31	7	6-13-31
3½	7-23-31			2½	10-10-31	10	7-16-31
4½	7-30-31					15	8- 1-31
6	9-21-31					10	8-15-31
						8	9- 2-31

substituted for movements of short-term capital and gold[21]—the deviation from equilibrium is a necessary part of the process of adjustment in the balance of payments itself and in the costs and prices which lie behind it. When, to repeat, the disturbance in the substantive course of trade is moderate, the process of inflationary or deflationary adjustment in the monetary system which alters the demand, in turn, for foreign-trade and home-market goods can be brought about smoothly in a semiautomatic fashion.

Where there is a fixed rate of exchange and the level of costs or prices is seriously altered, however, with resultant undervaluation or overvaluation, the maintenance of the fixed rate of exchange initiates and requires a reversal of the movement of costs and prices. In the case of overvaluation this means deflation. If short-term capital is borrowed from abroad, the pace of the deflation can be slowed down at the expense of exposing the monetary system to sudden withdrawals in the form of gold when foreigners convert their short-term assets into basic metal.

Under- and overvaluation can also be brought about through a movement in the rate of exchange which is itself the result of movements of gold or capital. If the exchange rate is lowered and maintained at a low level, gold will flow into the country unless loans are made abroad through private or official means, with the end result of inflating the monetary system until costs have been raised into equilibrium. If the exchange rate is raised enough above the equilibrium rate to overvalue it seriously, the institutional factors which make downward readjustments in cost and price structures difficult may bring it about that the maintenance of the exchange level is so difficult that as a political and economic measure it has to be abandoned.

[21] The balance of payments is affected somewhat differently in that it is not the total money income which has to change to affect it, but merely its division between foreign-trade and home-market goods.

IX

CYCLICAL MOVEMENTS OF SHORT-TERM FUNDS

The characteristic behavior of the balance of payments during those periodic fluctuations of business activity known as "business cycles" is a subject difficult to analyze systematically. The literature on the subject is largely suggestive in tone, almost necessarily so, so complex and intricate are the variable factors to be dealt with. To pretend to anything approaching exhaustiveness a monograph on the balance of payments in the business cycle[1] would first have to furnish a theory of business-cycle causation (an heroic task!) and superimpose on that as a background a discussion of foreign trade and finance under numberless assumptions regarding the "substantive course of trade," labor and capital movements, the industrial status of the countries involved, and so forth. Thus far articles and volumes on the subject have aspired to throw light on only one or another aspect of the problem. At the most, only hypotheses which inductive studies can disprove but not verify have been advanced to describe typical cyclical behavior. The present chapter, as indeed the entire present work, should be taken in this same tentative spirit.

The fact of an exceedingly rough international concomitance of business cycles, especially in highly developed countries, has been established.[2] The sequence of steps by which alternate waves of prosperity and depression spread between countries must pass through the balance of payments, except insofar as they are transmitted through common psychological causes.

[1] Ohlin has promised such a treatise, which is awaited with great interest. See *op. cit.*, p. 331 n.

[2] See W. C. Mitchell, *Business Cycles: the Problem and Its Setting*, 1927, pp. 424 ff.

Some commentators even find international trade and finance factors at the root of cyclical fluctuations.[3]

Hawtrey's Analysis and Beach's Facts. The standard view of the mechanism of the adjustment of the balance of trade during the business cycle has been presented by Hawtrey in his volume *Currency and Credit.*[4] This treatment has been examined by Beach,[5] who has undertaken an inductive study of the role of gold movements in the cyclical fluctuations of British business from 1881 to 1913. Beach found that the data do not conform to the standard expectations, and he offers alternative hypotheses to explain their actual behavior. The Hawtrey scheme of analysis and the alternatives suggested by Beach may be broadly set forth, without too meticulous regard for the qualifications with which they actually surround their doctrines.

Hawtrey first indicates that the credit mechanism tends to itself to produce wave-like fluctuations in prices, and hence in business activity, because of the characteristic inherent tendency of credit to expand or contract indefinitely. He then points out that the introduction of a standard metallic money tends to check these fluctuations before they attain dangerous proportions. On the one side, the demand of consumers for increased holdings of currency during the periods of rising business activity drains specie from the banking system into internal hand-to-hand circulation. On the external or foreign front, the price-specie-flow mechanism drains gold abroad when credit is expanding to join with the increase in the internal circulation

[3] See below, pp. 145-49, for the views of Hilgerdt and Nurkse on this score. The under-consumptionist, H. G. Moulton, without stating it categorically, suggests that the difference between savings and investment in the 1920's in the United States was partly brought about through foreign lending. See *The Formation of Capital,* 1935, pp. 158 ff.). While lending abroad does not build up capital plant and equipment within the country, from the point of view of money income it is generally identical with domestic investment. When foreign loans are held in the form of balances in the lending country, the income velocity of money as a whole is reduced. If a real transfer of capital in goods and services takes place, however, no purchasing power is "dissipated," even though the loan may afterward turn out to have been uneconomic.

[4] Especially chaps. v and vii.

[5] In *British International Gold Movements and Banking Policy, 1881-1913, op. cit., passim.*

in reducing reserve ratios to the point where credit contraction becomes necessary or at least further expansion impossible.

The external drains may be more thoroughly analyzed. The expansion of credit enables consumers to buy more foreign goods directly and raises the prices of domestic goods until some of them can be more cheaply imported than produced at home. Imports increase and exports decline.[6] The trade balance becomes adverse, and the whole balance of payments becomes unfavorable.[7] Gold flows out of the country, as well as into circulation, until the reserve position of the banking system becomes endangered. At this juncture the discount rate is raised, and this, if effective, sets in motion the forces of deflation. The deflation reduces prices, consumers' incomes and outlays, corrects the unfavorable balance of payments, checks the gold flow, and in time enables a favorable balance of trade to be developed, which brings gold back from abroad. The reduction in consumers' incomes and outlays also brings about a return of specie and currency from circulation. In this way, the standard money, gold, acts as a check upon the inherently unstable factor, credit. The contraction is halted by the reduction of interest rates made possible as gold returns to bank vaults during depression from the pockets of the consuming public and from bullion-dealers' foreign operations.

It is not necessary to point out that Hawtrey's analysis of the adjustment mechanism in the balance of payments is essentially classical.[8] It depends upon a sharp response of prices to changes in interest rates, response operating through the effects of changes in the quantity of money (whether spent or unspent by consumers) on the long and short positions of dealers in

[6] Hawtrey, *op. cit.*, p. 74. He does not explain the causes behind the decline in exports, although he rejects the earlier explanation that this is due to price increases, because of his recognition of the Law of One Price. The clue is to be found, of course, in the shifting of cost curves upward, as the inflation raises the prices of the factors of production.

[7] *Ibid.*, p. 75: "An expansion of credit *causes* an unfavourable balance of payments . . . And of course the balance in question is always the balance of payments, not the balance of trade in the narrower sense of the difference between exports and imports of material commodities [his italics]." Here, evidently, is the crux of his argument.

[8] See Beach, *op. cit.*, pp. 14, 17.

commodities. To this postulated intimate connection between domestic prices and credit conditions he adds the hypothesis of a closely knit world market for international-trade goods, in which the course of trade readily responds to changes in domestic prices in one country or another. On these premises is built the conclusion that gold will flow out of a country during the expansion phase of the business cycle and will return during depression.[9]

Beach has learned from the data that gold movements do not respond in this way. Pursuing a clue furnished by A. A. Young, who discovered from American experience that gold flowed into New York from abroad during prosperity and out again during depression, and going over the ground marked out by Taussig,[10] he examined the facts of English gold movements from 1881 to 1913. His detailed researches reveal that in both England and the United States (which in an Appendix he examines for the period 1896-1913) Young's appraisal of the character of gold movements was correct. "Cyclical fluctuations in the movement of gold to and from England occurred during the pre-war era. There was a tendency for imports to increase during the prosperity stages of business cycles, and for exports to grow during depression."[11] Hawtrey's position on internal coin and currency movements was fully substantiated, however. Cash required for the transaction of domestic business increased during the expansion phase of the cycle and was contracted during depression.

Beach's Alternative Explanations. In accounting for the fact that the data for international gold movements indicate a situation exactly the reverse of what might have been expected on the basis of Hawtrey's theoretical speculations, Beach offers two alternative explanations. He suggests that the classical analysis may be correct (with modifications substituting shifts in demand schedules for sectional price movements), but that in England (and in the United States) the business-cycle pattern

[9] Hawtrey's position has been stated rather succinctly. For a fuller exposition, see Beach, *op. cit.*, pp. 12-19.

[10] See *International Trade*, op. cit., p. 260.

[11] Beach, *op. cit.*, p. 170.

had a smaller amplitude than that in other countries. Thus if all the countries in the world are expanding, for example, the one expanding at the slowest rate may be expected to gain gold on the basis of the classical reasoning, while that inflating at the fastest rate will tend to lose it. Were all countries to expand and contract at approximately the same pace, no gold movements would be expected to occur.

Beach raises two objections to this explanation. In the first place he points out that this thesis requires international trade to react very rapidly to changes in prices and demand. The world market for goods would have to be assumed to be more nearly perfect than it has often been described. Second, he holds that "fluctuations in foreign loans permit relatively higher price levels in borrowing countries during prosperity phases of the cycle, and should bring a greater fall in these levels during depression, as compared with creditor nations, if the classical explanation of the adjustment in the case of foreign loans is correct."[12] While we intend to discuss the cyclical pattern of long-term capital movements below,[13] it may be mentioned here that it is not clear how this constitutes an objection to the classical explanation of gold flows. If prices must lag somewhat behind in creditor countries when capital exports are taking place, it may well be that a further disparity in price levels would enable the country to draw gold during the prosperity phase of the business cycle. The fact that prices were so much lower than in other countries might offset the tendency inherent in capital exports to draw gold. The dispatch with which the trade balance is adjusted to the long-term capital balance under normal circumstances would be increased if prices and expansion lagged behind in the lending country.

Beach's first objection to this explanation is entirely valid, however, when it is applied to the classical analysis stated in terms of prices. The merits of a similar argument, couched in the language of the shifts-in-demand mechanism, will be examined in the following section.

Beach's other explanation runs in terms of short-term capital

[12] *Ibid.*, p. 172. [13] See pp. 141 ff.

movements. In the period studied the banking systems of both England and the United States operated with a small cushion of excess reserves. Moreover, gold coins were largely used in consumer transactions. On this account:

With rising prices in prosperity, the requirements of the public increase, and this drain [of coin into circulation] was more important than the increase of bank credit for the depletion of bank reserves. The pressure on bank reserves led to increased discount rates in the money markets, and the flow of short-term capital, induced as a consequence, may well have been the dominating factor determining gold flows over the cyclical periods.[14]

This conclusion cannot be verified inductively, however, because of the absence of data on short-term capital movements. The close correlation between movements of the rate of interest and business activity nevertheless lends weight to such an interpretation.[15] The gold stock of the Bank of England shows a slight cyclical movement, inasmuch as the ebb of coins into circulation during periods of business expansion was not exactly balanced by the inflow of bullion from abroad.[16] Beach does not attempt to work out lags or leads, and it would probably be meaningless to do so because of the fact that all the data have marked and changing trends. Thus, while Beach's data do not prove the thesis that short-term capital movements, responding to changes in the rate of interest, contravert the classical analysis, yet none of his findings disprove this hypothesis.

Cyclical Behavior of the Balance of Payments. It would have been possible to analyze the cause of the contrary gold movements more rigorously if Beach had not left out a step. In his otherwise competent discussion he fails to measure or discuss the significance of the correlation between British trade cycles and the balance of commodity trade. If the balance of trade is most favorable in depression and least favorable in periods of

[14] *Ibid.*, p. 173; see also p. 180.

[15] Beach gives data on the bank, market, and deposit rates of interest for the 33 years covered. See Table XIV and Chart XVI, pp. 101 ff. No statistical correlation has been worked out, but the eye gives a close correspondence when Chart XVI is compared with Thomas's index of business activity, Table I, p. 41.

[16] See *ibid.*, Chart IX, pp. 71, 91.

expansion, then the Hawtrian analysis is half right. Hawtrey holds that the merchandise balance of trade, which he assumes to vary with business-cycle movements in the manner just described, controls the international cyclical flow of gold.[17] Beach's contrary contention is that the short-term capital balance is the major factor conditioning the direction and extent of gold movements. His position would be stronger if it were demonstrable that in spite of the fact that the merchandise balance of trade reacts in the manner described by Hawtrey, the gold movements take place in the opposite direction.

Beach first doubts that the merchandise trade balance responds rapidly to business-cycle fluctuations because of the weaknesses he finds in the thesis that trade makes rapid adjustments to changes in sectional price levels. If the shifts-in-demand analysis be substituted for the older theory, however, it can be shown readily that imports tend to follow the cyclical pattern described by Hawtrey when the business cycle takes place in one country only or when the country concerned has a wider cyclical swing in its national money income than other countries. The rising national money income during prosperity increases the demand for foreign-trade goods in a degree which is a function of the flexibility of demand for them. Imports increase. In depression, the falling national money income decreases the demand for foreign-trade goods to an extent dependent upon the flexibility of that demand. In depression, imports decrease.[18] The price mechanism can be abandoned altogether; and it is

[17] Hawtrey is not unmindful of capital movements, but he thinks largely in terms of those at long term. These, he asserts, tend to expand with the upswing of the cycle and to contract in depression (*op. cit.*, pp. 115 ff.). Insofar as the normal consequence of a new capital export at long term is an export of gold, he believes implicitly that the cyclical fluctuations in long-term capital assist the merchandise balance of trade in checking expansion and contraction by adding to the amount of gold flows.

[18] That imports tend to move with domestic business activity (and exports with business activity abroad) is suggested by J. M. Clark, *Strategic Factors in Business Cycles*, 1934, pp. 65-66; see also W. C. Mitchell, "The Measurement of Cyclical Fluctuation," in National Bureau of Economic Research, *Bulletin*, No. 57, p. 13, fig. 7. Silverman's use of an index of the value of exports as a description of the business cycle (see "Some International Trade Factors for Great Britain, 1880-1913," *Review of Economic Studies*, XIII (1931), 121, quoted by Beach, *op. cit.*, p. 40 n. apears to have little theoretical justification.

not difficult to see that the adjustment can take place rapidly when it is abandoned.

Insofar as exports are concerned, however, the problem is more complex. On the one hand there is the demand for both types of foreign-trade goods in England, which expands in prosperity and declines during depression. This force would of itself tend to decrease exports in prosperity and increase them in depression had the foreign demand been stable. But the foreign demand was not stable. It was strongly affected by capital exports from England, which, in turn, had a relation to business activity.[19]

Foreign loans enable the borrowing countries to inflate their national money incomes and their demand for foreign-trade goods. If the borrowing countries are young, undeveloped nations they tend to have a relatively flexible demand for foreign-trade goods, which would bring it about that their demand for imports would exceed England's demand for imports in prosperity, even if they were to have business cycles of the same amplitude as England. Conversely, in depression their demand for imports would fall below that of England.[20] In fact, however, borrowing nations are likely to have wider fluctuations in buying power than creditor nations, because the tendency to inflate on the basis of borrowed long-term capital is stronger than the tendency to deflate if capital is loaned abroad.[21] This fact makes exports from lending countries increase in periods of business prosperity and decrease in recession, in wider swings than those of imports, leaving a cyclical fluctuation in the balance of trade which correlates positively with the movement of production and business activity.

[19] See Beach, *op. cit.*, pp. 175 ff., especially Chart XXI, p. 177. Beach uses Hobson's figures, which will receive comment below, pp. 142-44.

[20] See "Flexibility of Demand in International Trade," *op. cit.*, pp. 360-61.

[21] See above, p. 78. Bresciani-Turroni (*op. cit.*, pp. 22-23, 94) suggests that the major weight of the adjustment in the lending country is borne by exports, not by imports, since the capital exports increase the demand in the borrowing country in money amounts more than the demand in the lending country falls off. This is because of the fact that the loan is apt to come out of unused savings (*ibid.*, p. 80). Bresciani-Turroni advances this as a reason why the transfer problem is easier for the remitting nation in the case of a free loan than in the case of a tribute or reparation payment.

This was the case in England. The negative trade balance became less unfavorable in prosperity and more unfavorable in depression.[22] Hawtrey's analysis of the probable character of the merchandise trade balance was in error, even though it was correct as far as imports were concerned. Beach's theory, which denies any connection between the merchandise balance of trade and gold movements, is still left unsubstantiated.

If the merchandise balance of trade was less unfavorable in prosperity and more unfavorable in depression for England,[23] and if the data for gold movements indicate that specie flowed in the exactly opposite direction to the favorable movement in the trade balance, the pre-war cyclical character of English international trade might be declared to be solved. It is also necessary, however, to consider the make-up of the long-term capital balance, which Taussig and Beach declared to vary with the merchandise balance of trade.

Taussig and Beach have used the data prepared by Hobson for their conclusions on pre-war capital movements. Hobson computed estimates of English capital exports for the years 1870-1912,[24] but he did so by the indirect method.[25] His data, as they stand, reveal nothing more than the reverse of the balance of all the income items plus or minus the figure for net movements of gold and silver. If gold movements on balance are small and the service items relatively inelastic, a close inverse correspondence is bound to exist between capital exports, so derived, and the negative balance of trade. Hobson's data make no allowance for the possibility that long- and short-term capital may move in opposite directions.

[22] These results have been estimated roughly. Compare Taussig's chart (*International Trade*, p. 246) with Beach's Chart I (*op. cit.*, p. 1). The former is not corrected for trend, but the comparison, while difficult, is still possible.

[23] This was not the case for the United States, however, which was a debtor nation whose imports during prosperity tended to be increased both by the business cycle itself and by the import of capital. These factors may have been closely related, however.

[24] See Hobson, *The Export of Capital*, pp. 197, 204.

[25] Hobson added estimates of England's invisible credits, (including commissions, freight receipts, immigrant remittances, etc.) and interest and dividends due to England, subtracting from the total the import surplus, which included a provision for the precious metals. This gives the "net export" of capital, including the capital balance on both long- and short-term accounts.

If England attracted short-term capital during expansion, which brought gold in its wake, and lost short-term balances and gold during depression, the long-term capital export from England must have been greater during prosperity by the amount of the short-term capital import and less during the depression by the amount of the short-term capital export. The short-term capital movements may be assumed, for simplicity's sake, to have been of the same order of magnitude as the gold flows. In prosperity and depression, then, the long-term capital outflow would change in roughly equal proportion to the amount of favorable change in the balance of trade,[26] or about the height of Hobson's estimates, with gold added during prosperity and subtracted during depression. It is impossible to relate the movement of merchandise trade to gold movements directly, since that leaves the capital balance altogether out of consideration. More than this cannot be said about the period because of the inadequacy of the data on capital movements.[27]

While one may thus take exception to some of Beach's reasoning and may propose additional steps in his argumentation, yet one must agree that in all probability he has provided the correct explanation of the British pre-war gold flow experience in his second hypothesis. This is the same theory advanced by Laughlin, de Lavaleye, Marshall, and others,[28] freed from all connection with price levels so far as causative influences are concerned. The gold flow in the business cycle would depend upon the rate of exchange and the rate of discount (themselves intimately related), while the balance of trade is largely determined by the flow of long-term capital to the extent that it fluctuates cyclically. This latter, in turn, while it bears a direct relationship to the business cycle as a whole, depends proximately upon the supply of savings in the creditor country and upon the demand for them at home and abroad—in short,

[26] It must be remembered that the merchandise trade balance was continuously unfavorable because of the net balance of credits on invisible current items due to England.

[27] I have not had an opportunity to see A. G. Silverman's *The International Trade of Great Britain, 1880-1913* (a thesis at Harvard), which may throw some light upon the factors involved.

[28] See Beach, *op. cit.*, pp. 21 ff., 35 ff.

upon the difference in rates of interest for long-term obligations between nations.[29] Thus the part played by gold movements and price levels in the cyclical fluctuations of the balance of payments seem in consequence of an examination of the events immediately preceding the world war to have lost a good deal of the significance attached to it in the classical theory. Further examination might reveal this to be the case with the international trade even earlier.[30] It may well be assumed to have been even more true after the war because of the enhanced importance of capital movements in the balance of payments.[31]

Short-Term Capital Movements in the Business Cycle. The short-term capital movements involved in the cyclical flows in England in the pre-war era were of the "income" variety and were brought into play by the desire of international investors to place their funds at interest in the money market where the highest return was available.[32] It will be recalled that equilibrating capital movements and speculative movements do not bring gold movements in their wake. They may, however, hold the rate of exchange near the import or export gold point, so that when income movements do respond to changes in the interest rate or in the current or anticipated rate of profit gold will flow more readily. The cyclical behavior of gold movements indicates, in fact, that long-term capital was transferred from England without the aid of accompanying gold flows.[33] Short-

[29] The many exceptions to this dictum will be discussed in the following chapter.

[30] Iversen (*op. cit.*, p. 116) takes it for granted that the international mobility of capital has increased tremendously during the nineteenth century. Despite the importance of the loans of the Lombards and the Hanseatic towns (See J. H. Williams, "The Theory of International Trade Reconsidered," *Economic Journal*, XXXIX [1929], 205 ff.), the capital items probably played a smaller part in the balance of payments before the Napoleonic Wars.

[31] See, e.g., Viner, *op. cit.*, p. 23, where it is stated that post-war capital movements have been greater, more capricious, and in greater proportion at short term than before the war.

[32] Another important factor was the desire of investors in other countries where the rate of interest was higher to hold sterling assets in order to diversify their investments. See Nurkse's first class of risk above, p. 6 n.

[33] Not on balance, at any rate. Gold movements may have aided in the transfer of specific loans, but with only quarterly data for gold movements and annual (residual) for capital movements, no exact statement can be made about gross capital movements.

term equilibrating capital movements, therefore, appear to have been sufficient to maintain equilibrium in the balance of payments to the extent that the real transfer followed rather than preceded the transfer of purchasing power.

In the post-war period the rate of discount may not have been as important a stimulus to these "income" capital movements as the profits obtainable in the security or forward-exchange markets.[34]

Long-Term Capital as a Cause of Business Cycles. It was mentioned at the outset of this chapter that two other hypotheses have been advanced from other points of view to describe the behavior of the balance of payments in the course of the business cycle. While neither of these relates directly to short-term capital movements and both might hence be considered outside our immediate purview, yet the digression to include them is undertaken because of their indirect importance to the topic at hand.

Hilgerdt's interesting thesis[35] states not only that the export of long-term capital partakes of a typical cyclical pattern but also that it plays an important role in causing the recurrence of wave-like fluctuations in business activity. He shows that in times of prosperity the long-term capital export from creditor nations increases. This is said to render the terms of trade less favorable for such nations, since it raises prices in agricultural and raw-material countries, which are the usual borrowers of international capital.[36] Inasmuch as these countries provide a large portion of the raw materials used by industrial creditor countries, the rise in the prices of basic commodities reacts on the lending nations. Finished-goods prices do not rise com-

[34] See below, chap. xii.

[35] In "Foreign Trade and the Short Business Cycle," *Economic Essays in Honour of Gustav Cassel*, pp. 273-91.

[36] Hilgerdt does not indicate whether his views on the terms of trade rest on a classical view of the transfer problem, or a view akin to that of Nurkse (see pp. 61-64 above). He is content to show statistically that in the period 1922-30 the terms of trade of India, Argentine, and New Zealand have moved approximately inversely to the combined capital exports of Great Britain, France, and the United States.

mensurately, profit margins are reduced, and productive activity falls off. The decline in business activity, coupled in the "short" business cycle with some fortuitous circumstance, cuts off the volume of foreign lending, prices of agricultural commodities fall, profit margins are widened, and business activity in the creditor nations picks up. Thus Hilgerdt ascribes a good measure of causal influence in the business cycle to the international export of capital, which, in its turn, depends for its fluctuations partly upon the state of the business cycle currently undergone.

As Iversen rightly points out, however, it is not clear which is cause and which effect.[37] Were the prices of exportable commodities in agricultural countries to fall for any other reason than the slackening of the rate of capital import, it is clear that the ability of such countries to borrow would be reduced as their credit standing became adversely affected.[38] The export price level depends to some extent upon the rate of capital import, but the latter depends likewise upon the state of export prices. Hilgerdt explains the contraction in lending from the United States, France, and Great Britain combined, in terms of business depression caused by previous lending together with untoward incidents of a political or monetary nature which occasioned losses of confidence. In 1923 the Ruhr incident, in 1926 the British gold resumption and the subsequent general strike, and in 1928 the French stabilization slowed down the rate of foreign lending from the three countries combined and resulted in the business recessions of 1924, 1927, and 1929. Many authorities, on the other hand, have explained a large part of the business depression initiated in 1929 by the collapse of agricultural prices, the foundations of which were laid in

[37] *Op. cit.*, p. 75. Hilgerdt mentions this possibility, *op. cit.*, p. 276. See also the Macmillan report, *op. cit.*, p. 81.

[38] Perhaps the tendency of raw-material prices to rise first in the recovery phase of the business cycle can be explained in terms of the flexibility of demand in industrial countries. The demand for tin, copper, cotton, rubber, wool, and so forth, tends to expand very sharply from depression lows as recovery takes hold, because of the necessity placed upon manufacturers of such products to build up inventory. Compare, for example, the recent rise in the prices of English import goods (1935-36) with her relatively stable domestic price level, at a time when the business of foreign lending has not been resumed.

the war and post-war agricultural boom in non-European nations.[39]

Nurkse inclines in part to the view of Hilgerdt, setting up his analysis of capital exports in the business cycle in terms of Austrian monetary theory.[40] When the market rate of interest falls below the natural rate, an inflationary expansion takes place in the creditor country. This induces an inflationary expansion in capital exports and monetary expansion, with a business boom, in borrowing countries.[41] When, however, the market rate falls below the natural rate, not because of a fall in the former, but due to a rise in the latter, the situation is considerably different. Capital movements take place toward the country where the interest movements occur, not away from it. This brings about a depression in the countries from which capital is attracted, since the market rate there is driven above the natural rate. Nurkse concludes that when the market rate of interest moves, long-term capital exports will correlate positively with business-cycle activity. When the natural rate of interest moves, however, the symmetry is broken; capital exports tend to move inversely.[42] The same general rule applies to deflationary discrepancies between the market and natural rates of interest.[43]

Nurkse illustrates this analysis by reference to the post-war American capital export. He regards the period of 1925 to 1929 as one of substantial inflation in the United States, in which price levels did not rise because of the large increase in productivity, occasioned by a high rate of invention and a rise in labor efficiency brought about by scientific management.[44] The inflation, which was the basis for the huge capital export prior to 1928, was tempered by the fact that much of the foreign borrowing went into New York balances of debtor nations

[39] For a description of the manner in which agricultural crises may generate general business depressions see A. C. Pigou, *Industrial Fluctuations*, 1927, pp. 36-41.

[40] To which he does not unreservedly subscribe. See *op. cit.*, pp. 164 n., 200 n.

[41] *Ibid.*, pp. 200-201. [42] *Ibid.*, p. 202. [43] *Ibid.*, p. 203. [44] *Ibid.*, p. 207.

operating on the gold-exchange standard.[45] The high-tariff policy of the same period and the sterilization of gold reserves also tended to mitigate the effects of the inflationary divergence between the market and natural rates of interest on prices and incomes.[46] Nurkse claims that the market rate of interest was below the natural rate up to 1928, presumably because the former had been artificially lowered by Federal Reserve action.

In 1928, however, Nurkse detects a change taking place in the natural rate of interest, which rose as a result of overoptimistic anticipations of future capital values and profits. This led to a cessation and reversal of the capital outflow, caused a fall in raw-material prices of a world-wide character, stranded "abortive capital" abroad, and so forth.[47] In Hilgerdt's view the fall in raw-material prices should have restored profit margins to finished-goods manufacturers and have led to an increase in production in creditor countries. Nurkse holds, however, that the capital drawn by the United States from the other creditor countries caused depressions in them, as well as incidental depressions in the raw-material countries, brought about by their inability to import capital. He does not make clear his opinion concerning the cause of the spread of the crisis to the United States, but probably he believes that the inflation in America was leading to its own inevitable collapse.

Nurkse's emphasis on the distinctive patterns taken by the capital flow, when attention is paid to the question whether the market or the natural rate of interest moves first, may perhaps be more readily comprehended in the terms of our analysis above.[48] The facts of the case show that the actual (or market) rate of interest did rise in the period beginning early in 1928, as even the lagging discount rate of the New York Federal Reserve Bank reveals.[49] The anticipated rate of profit having increased, borrowers were more eager to acquire the use of funds, and, on the assumption of an unchanged willingness of banks and others to lend, loans expanded as the rate of

[45] *Ibid.*, p. 207; see also Iversen, *op. cit.*, p. 407 n.

[46] *Ibid.*, p. 208. [47] *Ibid.*, pp. 209-10. [48] See above, p. 36 n. [49] See above, p. 131 n.

interest increased. The amount of capital export fell off in response to the rise of the anticipated rate of profit and the actual rate of interest. An import of capital at short term took place in the form of loans to the New York money market and in direct purchases of equity securities.[50] If the capital import into the United States from 1928 to 1930 be thus regarded, it will be seen that the phenomenon was similar to that discovered by Beach in pre-war England. Two differences stand out: (1) The discount rate of the Federal Reserve Bank of New York did not serve as the magnet drawing liquid funds from abroad. It was below that of the Bank of England until August, 1929. The rate of interest in the call-loan market, and the anticipated rate of profit derived from holding equity securities served as the going rates in the money market; (2) the short-term capital, being conditioned by unstable, psychological factors did not enter in a steady, continuous flow calculated to produce a one-way movement of gold. Gold movements were highly irregular, and the account showed import surpluses for 1926 and 1929, with export balances for 1927 and 1928. In 1929 the gold import perhaps had its origin in the fact that all rates of interest were above those of France and England for a short time after August.

Short-Term Funds and the International Timing of Cycles. To conclude this chapter, which has dealt with the relations of short-term capital movements to the business cycle in a necessarily somewhat haphazard way, it may be worth while to con-

[50] See Iversen's criticism of Angell's position (*op. cit.*, pp. 72-73). The rise in the rate of interest, although it affects the prices of fixed securities, will not be likely to lead to an import of capital in that form to a creditor nation as long as business is still in the expansion phase of the business cycle. When the crisis is reached, at which time the rate of interest is highest and bonds of equal risk are lowest in price, some repurchase of bonds will occur. This will apply only to those debtor nations least affected by the depression, since those affected will be in no position at such a time to take advantage of the opportunity to repurchase their bonds cheaply. One may agree with Angell (*op. cit.*, pp. 527-28) that equity and fixed-yield obligations will tend to move in opposite directions during the business cycle, but it is improbable that the movements will follow the lines he suggests. It will be remembered that we include ordinary purchases of stocks among short-term capital movements, since the presumption is that foreign investors are interested in intermediate short-term appreciation rather than long-term income prospects (see above, p. 4).

sider the positions taken by Nielsen and Nurkse on short-term capital as an international regulator of business and credit expansion. The former believes that such short-term movements "serve to maintain equilibrium in the pace at which credit is expanded in different countries."[51] The latter makes the suggestion, which he does not pursue analytically, that short-term capital movements synchronize business cycles among creditor nations, while long-term capital movements spread these fluctuations to the raw-material countries.[52] These statements evidently apply to gold-standard conditions. A country which tries to expand credit alone will tend to lose short-term capital to markets with higher rates of interest until rates of interest either fall abroad or are raised at home or both. When one nation attempts to restrict credit, while other nations abroad are expanding, short-term capital will be attracted and gold imported until either foreign countries are compelled to initiate a deflationary policy or contraction in the single country is abandoned.

This thesis is the same as that of Hawtrey, except that the influence of the merchandise trade balance is left out of account, and short-term capital movements, which Hawtrey considered an auxiliary factor working in the direction of the international synchronization of credit policy[53] are made to operate alone so far as concerns relations between countries with highly developed money markets.

There is a contradiction in this position, however, which is especially marked in the case of Nurkse. He maintains that: (1) short-term capital movements tend to synchronize the business cycle internationally; and (2) the rise in the anticipated

[51] See Iversen, *op. cit.*, p. 238 (Iversen's italics omitted). The present writer is unfortunately unable to consider Axel Nielsen's contributions in the original because of the fact that his volume *Bankpolitik*, Vols. I-II, 1923 and 1930, is available only in Danish. He is therefore compelled to rely upon Iversen's summary of Nielsen's work in the former's treatise, *op. cit.*, pp. 238-42.

[52] *Op. cit.*, p. 228: "Diese konjunktursynchronisierende Wirkung der Kurzkredite gilt normalerweise wohl vornehmlich für die Gruppe der Glaübigerländer unter sich, während die Konjunkturausbreitung auf die kapitalarmen Rohstoffländer in der Regel hauptsächlich mittels langfristiger Kapitalexporte vor sich geht."

[53] See *Currency and Credit*, p. 139.

rate of profit in the United States, as inflation proceeded to a peak, caused a depression abroad by diverting capital from raw-material countries. Expansion, as Beach also found, instead of driving short-term capital out, attracted it from abroad. This was especially true in the pre-war era, when narrow gold reserves, the circulation of gold coins, and so forth operated to make short-term rates of interest more sensitive to credit fluctuations. But it was also true in the case of the post-war United States.

The paradox can probably be resolved in terms of lags and leads in the timing of international business cycles or by frictions in the mechanism.[54] When in an international expansion in the prosperity phase of the business cycle one country gets ahead of the others, and when the rate of interest there rises above that abroad, these facts themselves will tend to hold back credit expansion in the country out of step. Such capital as it draws from abroad will not be enough in the usual case to halt materially the rate of credit expansion by tightening interest rates there. The American experience in 1928 must be set down as an exception to the general rule prevailing in the past, since on that occasion it was not so much the rate of interest or the current rate of profit which attracted funds, but the anticipated rate of gain from stock-market speculation. This was necessarily an illusion, since the paper profits from stock-market speculation could not be realized *en masse*.

Beach's results fit into this general picture of a rough international concurrence of business cycles maintained through movements of short-term capital. It must be remembered with respect to his findings that the greater part of the imports of gold took place just before the crisis at the peak of prosperity, while the greatest drain took place, as a general rule, immediately afterward. These shifts of international short-term funds are essentially of a cyclical nature and are determined by the

[54] See Nielsen's statement (Iversen, *op. cit.*, p. 239) that "in general it is only interest differentials that are expected to last for some time which will release international capital flows." This contradicts Nielsen's fundamental position that short-term capital is sufficiently fluid to maintain all countries in line with respect to credit policy.

shape of the whole cycle. Those referred to by Nielsen and Nurkse presumably take place intermittently back and forth throughout the cycle. Beach's findings apply to net gold movements for the expansion and contraction phases of the cycle; Nielsen's and Nurkse's remarks are intended rather to relate to gross movements within these phases.

Summary. The present chapter has attempted to review several of the strands of theory fashioned by other writers to explain the role of short-term capital movements in the course of the business cycle. There has been no comprehensive treatment of the subject elsewhere in economic literature, and none was offered here.

First, Hawtrey's thesis that the balance of payments turns unfavorable in prosperity and favorable during depression was examined. It was found that Hawtrey's dependence upon the price-specie-flow mechanism in this connection did not affect the basic validity of his theory within his assumptions, since the conclusions of the shifts-in-demand analysis would have been the same. It was noticed, however, that Hawtrey did not take into consideration the effects of the movement of long-term capital. This item in the balance of payments, which increases during prosperity and declines during depression, brings it about that the merchandise balance of trade is more favorable in industrial creditor countries during prosperity and less favorable during depression. It does this by causing wider fluctuations in purchasing power in the young borrowing countries, since the effect of the transfer mechanism is to tend to make the borrower inflate to a greater extent than the lender deflates. In addition, the fact that the demand for foreign-trade goods is likely to be more flexible in young countries than in highly developed nations may be an accentuating factor, increasing the foreign demand for the lender's products in prosperity when capital exports are high more than the lender's demand for the borrower's products increases by virtue of the business-cycle expansion.

If the merchandise balance of trade or the whole income trade balance may thus be paired with the long-term capital balance—although strictly, of course, no two items in the balance of payments may be linked together—the course of gold movements is still to be explained. In an inductive study of English gold movements in the thirty-two years before the war Beach found that gold moved in an opposite fashion in the business cycle to that expected by Hawtrey. In prosperity gold flowed into England; in depression it flowed out. This may now be attributed to the movement of short-term capital which was attracted to England as the opportunities for profits, and the rate of interest, increased during prosperity and fell during depression. This thesis cannot be verified by an appeal to statistics, since the data for capital movements of the period are not broken down into long- and short-term items. But it is nevertheless a far more satisfying hypothesis than that of Hawtrey, which, as we have seen, contains a demonstrable error.

Further attention was directed to Hilgerdt's original theory that long-term capital movements caused short business cycles, by affecting the terms of trade and thus profit margins in industrial lending countries. It was pointed out that this sequence of events was unlikely: (1) because foreign trade raw-material prices are probably a relatively small factor in the total costs of manufactured goods in industrial countries; (2) because the interrelation between the terms of trade and capital movements is not clearly established—raw-material prices tending to rise early in the recovery stage of the business cycle even without capital movements; and (3) because changes in the terms of trade may cause the capital movements, not vice versa.

Then Nurkse's analysis of business-cycle movements of long-term capital was investigated, and it was found that his distinction between the natural and market rates of interest was somewhat artificial. His theory can be subsumed under the type of analysis presented in this monograph by paying separate attention to the demand and supply factors involved in the rate of interest.

Finally Nielsen's and Nurkse's contention that short-term capital regulates the international timing of business cycles was reviewed. It was decided that within any one phase of the business cycle international liquid funds might act in this fashion to synchronize the pace of expansion and contraction to some extent in industrially developed countries. Over the full course of a given cycle, however, the other analysis, as modified in the light of Beach's findings, was believed to be valid.

X

"ABNORMAL" CAPITAL MOVEMENTS

The preceding chapters have been concerned with an analysis which was based on the assumption that autonomous capital movements, that is, those which arise in response to fears for the safety of money principal, were not present. Before leaving the discussion of the mechanics of capital movements and proceeding to a treatment of the general problem of stabilization presented by them, some attention must be given to "abnormal" as distinguished from "normal" capital flow.

The subject of "abnormal" capital movements has received little direct theoretical attention in economic literature until recently.[1] In part this has been due to the fact that the practical importance of the problem has been fully recognized only of late;[2] and in part it is because the causes and effects of such movements have generally been considered so evident as to re-

[1] Keynes and Ohlin evidently touched on the subject in their reparations controversy but did not carefully distinguish between the "normal" and the "abnormal" case. Directly on the subject are F. Machlup's original "Theorie des Kapitalflucht," *Weltwirtschaftliches Archiv*, XXXVI (1932), and M. Fanno's *I transferimenti anormali dei capitali e le crisi*, 1935. We shall rely on these treatments to a considerable extent in the following discussion. Iversen and Nurkse, it will be remembered, attempt to deal with "abnormal" capital in the general theory of capital movements. The former (*op. cit.*, pp. 107-8) denies the necessity for any revision of the general theory for "abnormal" movements; the latter admits the necessity for a distinct treatment but does not offer a full one. Among the other writers contributing to the discussion directly, perhaps Einzig stands out. From his prolific pen have come a score of volumes and innumerable articles in the last decade, many of which deal specifically, if journalistically, with the problem. The French "psychological" school of foreign exchange should also be mentioned. It regards the so-called "abnormal" capital flight as normal and builds its theory of foreign exchange around them (see above, p. 106 n.).

[2] The problem of abnormal capital movements, with consequent default, frozen credits, currency depreciation, and the like, is of course not new. A reading of Jenks's *The Migration of British Capital to 1875* reveals that in this respect, as in so many other respects, the aftermath of the Napoleonic wars anticipated many of the problems the twentieth century has had to face as a result of the world war.

quire no particularized treatment. Yet the exigencies of practical policy evidently give point to attempts to penetrate more closely into their theoretical orientation.

Definitions. The problem of definition arises first. What distinguishes a "normal" from an "abnormal" capital movement?[3] The latter term, when used at all, is generally applied to capital flight; but other types of capital movements have been considered abnormal by different writers. Does the abnormality of a particular movement of capital arise in connection with its causes, the mechanism of its transfer, or both? These and corollary questions will be examined in the present chapter, with the aid of the authors just mentioned.

It may broadly be stated that an abnormal capital movement is one that takes place from a country where the rate of interest is higher than that in the country to which the capital is brought. This definition should be related to gross, not net, rates of interest. Fanno is in error when he states that the net rate of interest (the market rate minus a premium for the risk) should be considered.[4] Heuser, in his review of Fanno's monograph, points out this error, but suggests a clumsy alternative concept: that "capital flight is the result of a divergence between the actual difference between the market-risk premium paid in the two countries involved and the individual estimates of the difference in risk involved."[5] Inasmuch as the divergences are all in one direction, it may more simply be said that capital flight takes place from a country with a high rate of interest to one with a lower rate.

Machlup maintains that the broad basis for all capital flight can be summed up in the expression "uneconomic considerations."[6] The use of the rate-of-interest criterion evidently gives

[3] The words "normal" and "abnormal" are probably unfortunate because of their connotations for equilibrium economics and their possible confusion with short- and long-run tendencies. Moreover, "abnormal" capital movements imply a derogatory value-judgment. It is to be hoped, however, that the reader will be willing to accept the use of the terms without attributing to them any meaning other than that contributed by the discussion. On this assumption the quotation marks, which are irksome to the "normal" reader, will be abandoned.

[4] See *op. cit.*, pp. 9, 11, 23.

[5] See *Economica*, II (1935), 491-93.

[6] *Op. cit.*, p. 514.

precision to this somewhat vague statement. Iversen holds that capital flight is as fully economic as so-called normal capital movements, since minimizing losses and maximizing gains are part of the same motivation. He does indicate, however, that reparations and intergovernmental war-debt payments should be placed in a separate category, since they are "arbitrary" and "out of proportion to other elements in the situation."[7]

If these vague descriptions be left aside as saying little or nothing, it can be shown that the interest-rate criterion can subsume all abnormal capital movements. We may use Fanno's survey of the causes and types of these movements for purposes of demonstration. He lists six causes or conditions under which abnormal capital movements arise: (1) payment of reparations or war debts; (2) high taxes; (3) fear of high taxes; (4) various political or social motives; (5) distrust of the national banking system; and (6) fear of monetary devaluation.[8] He further remarks that abnormal capital movements may take the form, in addition to war debt and reparation payments, of: (1) a flight of national capital; (2) a withdrawal of funds temporarily deposited in a country for safe keeping; and (3) a sudden recall of funds invested in a country in the normal course of international financial relations.

It is readily seen that capital flight of all sorts takes place from countries with higher rates of interest to those with lower. The same forces that induce people to attempt to expatriate their capital make them unwilling to lend freely at home. It has likewise been true that in cases in which the prospect of monetary devaluation is faced, the country concerned attempts to tighten interest rates, to some extent at least, as a measure of keeping capital at home.

With respect to war debts and reparations, the likelihood is that such payments are owed by nations with high rates of interest to those with lower. This is not because "otherwise they [the capital movements] would have taken place voluntarily."[9]

[7] *Op. cit.*, p. 59.

[8] *Op. cit.*, p. 23.

[9] See Iversen, *op. cit.*, p. 59 n., and Nurkse, "Ursache und Wirkungen der Kapitalbewegungen," *Zeitschrift fur Nationalökonomie*, V (1934), 79.

This statement begs the question. The *a priori* probability is that the capital of modern nations engaged in war, especially that of the vanquished country, will be relatively exhausted at the conclusion of hostilities.

Another type of abnormal capital flight may be added to the list suggested by Fanno. When a country which has borrowed heavily abroad is unable to borrow further and is required to pay interest and sinking-fund charges or to repay matured loans, the situation is in many respects similar to that involved in the reparations question. That the transfer problem is similar will be indicated in the following section. At present, however, it can be shown that the capital moves from a country with a higher to a country with a lower rate of interest. If the country concerned cannot borrow abroad at the rates of interest quoted there, it means that its effective rate of interest is higher, even though a lower rate of interest may be nominally quoted. The abnormality may be emphasized again if it is remembered that normal capital movements can take place or not at the discretion of the proprietors of the capital. Sinking-fund payments or the redemption of matured loans involve contractual obligations which from an economic point of view are as binding as those implied in war debt or reparations settlements.

In terms of the market phenomena, then, an abnormal capital movement is one that takes place from a country with a higher to a country with a lower rate of interest. It may be mentioned further that from the point of view of proximate cause the normal movement of capital is attracted *to* a country; while the abnormal movement is that which is propelled *from* a country—in the case of capital flight by reason of any one or more of a complex list of fears and suspicions, and in the case of war debts, reparations, and old-loan payments, by reason of contractual obligations.[10] The line of differentiation is not precise.

[10] An exception may be noted here for loan repayment which takes the form of repurchase of securities formerly issued abroad in advance of their maturity. Here the capital movement is evidently attracted by the low price of the obligation, not drawn abroad by the compulsion of a legal contract. If the bonds have fallen in price in the creditor country because of high rates of interest there, the movement may be considered normal. More subtle is the case

It does, however, suffice to furnish a broad basis for distinguishing normal from abnormal capital movements in terms of motives, on a level of discourse where precision is impossible.

Capital Flight and Credit Policy. Before proceeding to discuss the transfer process as related to abnormal capital movements, a word may be devoted to Machlup's contention that the problem of capital flight is unimportant if proper credit policy be followed. He argues that if the money capital to be expatriated is raised in the same fashion in which it would be raised if the supply of means of payment were unchanged, that is, from hoards, from savings, or from amortization quotas of industry, it will not be harmful. He notes a minor exception that will occur when the original currency, gold or foreign exchange in which the transfer takes place, is hoarded abroad.[11] If there is no increase in credit the process of acquiring the money capital will be deflationary and will initiate the transfer process through which goods will be exported. If the banks or the central bank grant loans, however, whether at penalty rates or not, this deflation will not be effective, the transfer process will not get under way, and the monetary system will collapse.[12] Machlup leaves the inference that the dangers of capital flight can be avoided by a refusal of the authorities to extend credit when capital is

in which the bond repurchase occurs after the bonds have fallen in price because of fears of default by the debtor or even actual default. It is widely believed that Germany devoted a considerable portion of the foreign exchange acquired by foreign-exchange control from 1931 to 1935 to buy in her outstanding bonds at bargain prices. Similarly, in 1932, Japan bought in Japanese dollar and sterling bonds held abroad to some extent in order further to depress the yen. This export of capital was similar in its effects to a private capital flight but was actually a part of monetary policy.

[11] *Op. cit.*, p. 518 nn. For the importance of this exception see below, the present chapter.

[12] *Ibid.*, pp. 527-29. Machlup recognizes that when the money capital is raised by the repayment of loans (as depositors demand currency for their credit balances at banks, and banks in turn attempt to liquidate), serious consequences are involved for the community (pp. 524-25). In company with the Austrian monetary school, however, Machlup regards deflation as a wholesome process. Those that suffer losses from it have only themselves to blame for their misuse of credit (p. 525). See also his article, "Why Bother with Methodology?" *Economica*, III (1936), *passim*, especially p. 41, where he refers to Von Mises's view that in the face of bank failures credit expansion offers greater evils than those resulting from such failures.

taking refuge abroad. Iversen explicitly follows Machlup on this point.[13]

Machlup's fundamental position, which Iversen adopts, can be summed up in the assertion that a limit is imposed upon the duration of capital flight by the possibility that the banking system will collapse. This is not wrong; it is, however, out of place in Machlup's 1932 article. The paper professes to make the point that politicians overemphasize the dangers of capital flight. The statement, however valid, does not lead to any such optimistic conclusion. It is all very well as a straightforward, though not very profound, scientific remark to say that death in the human body places a limit on the duration of heart disease.

Transfer through Opposite Normal Capital Flow. When a man in one country wishes to exchange his assets in that country for foreign assets denominated in another currency, he can do so, as long as a fixed rate of exchange is maintained, by trading assets with someone. The other party to the exchange may be a foreigner or a countryman with foreign assets. As a last resort he can demand foreign assets of the central bank. In the present section we shall assume that he is able to export his capital because a similar inflow of capital occurs. In the following section we shall assume that he is unable to find a person willing to give up foreign for domestic assets at a rate higher than that at which the central bank is compelled to sell him gold or foreign exchange. Thus the outflow of capital may be transferred in a monetary sense (1) by opposite inflows and (2) by the loss of the country's gold or foreign exchange reserves.[14]

Machlup and Iversen point out that when a local capitalist buys a foreign bond formerly held within the country and sends it to a foreign market for sale abroad, no net flow of capital has

[13] *Op. cit.*, pp. 59-62.

[14] For the general purposes of this chapter the foreign exchange reserves of a central bank will be considered equivalent to the central bank's gold holdings, and changes in it will not be regarded as a capital movement. This conforms to the logic of the situation. To say that when capital flight is financed by foreign exchange of a central bank no net capital movement has taken place (see Iversen, *op. cit.*, p. 61) is a curious side-stepping of an important problem.

taken place.[15] Similarly, when local securities quoted on foreign security markets are bought at home and sold abroad, no net capital movement occurs. Viewed in terms of double-entry bookkeeping the first operation involves a shift in the form of foreign assets, bonds being exchanged for foreign deposits; the second means that a foreign asset has been acquired in exchange for a foreign liability—domestic securities held by foreigners. Machlup does point out, following the lead of E. Welter, that when local securities are sold in foreign markets no actual demand for money capital arises in the domestic sphere, but that a "potential" demand from abroad is created.[16]

The question is one of considerable importance. A capital outflow may be balanced and offset by any one or more of a number of types of capital inflow. Various grades of foreign assets may be replaced by other grades. In some cases the shift is potentially more dangerous than in others, that is, a long-term foreign asset may be acquired in exchange for a short-term foreign liability, or a foreign asset which is not likely to be available immediately may be exchanged for a foreign liability which may soon have to be repaid. In his discussion of reparations Fanno notes that the type of capital import which enabled the Germans to maintain their schedule of payments to the Allied governments was the key factor in the determination of the length of time during which these payments might be continued. Long-term commercial loans first supplied the necessary funds. When these dried up, German bank balances were sold to foreigners. These deposits, being callable on demand, were the proximate cause of Germany's default.[17] Presumably the sale of three-month acceptance and finance paper, which was engaged in during that period, was less dangerous than the sale of demand deposits but more so than that of long-term bonds.

It may be possible to range the various methods by which capital flight can be financed by normal opposite capital movements, in the order in which they hold forth the promise of danger in the future. Any such list is arbitrary and subject to

[15] See Machlup, *op. cit.*, p. 520; Iversen, *op. cit.*, p. 60.

[16] See Machlup, *op. cit.*, p. 523.

[17] See Fanno, *op. cit.*, p. 43.

differences of opinion. But certainly the task of compiling such a list affords a more fruitful approach to the problem than that of Machlup or Iversen, who imply that when no net movement of capital takes place, there is little that can be said of interest.

The case of a matured commercial debt may be cited. An Australian public utility company meets with the necessity of repaying a bond issue floated in the London capital market. Various possibilities exist as to the means by which repayment may be made. It may be assumed, however, that the company is not in a position to retire the issue from built-up reserves and in the second place that, should its credit standing or the state of the capital market in London prevent it from borrowing there, it enjoys a preferred position among borrowers in Melbourne and could float an issue there so long as the rate of interest is adjusted to the narrow market for savings. The possibilities, ranged in the order of their actually or potentially pernicious influence on the Australian international position, are, going from the harmless to the most harmful:

(1) That the company is able to refund its issue at good rates in New York and London.

(2) That the company has lost its good name in foreign capital centers, but that it can borrow in Melbourne and buy foreign exchange on London in the necessary amounts because of the flow of loans to other Australian borrowers, both private and governmental.

(3) That by borrowing in Melbourne the company can buy sufficient amounts of foreign bonds in Melbourne, sell them in New York and London, and retire the matured issue with the proceeds.

(4) That by borrowing in Melbourne it can buy local (for example) governmental two-currency bonds, sell them in London, and retire its foreign bond issue with the proceeds.

(5) That, the amount of long-term capital flowing to Australia being reduced, it is forced to borrow in Melbourne at a high rate, but that the short-term rate of interest is high at the same time and attracts funds from abroad, which supply the foreign exchange necessary to enable it to retire its debt.

(6) That, other methods failing, it turns to the Australian central bank for the necessary foreign exchange and that the cen-

tral bank in turn raises foreign funds by a short-term guaranteed loan floated in the London market.

(7) That, if this fails, the Australian central bank draws upon its reserves of London exchange to enable the issue to be retired.

In the case of the repayment of the matured long-term capital loans it is likely that methods 1 and 2 will suffice to enable the transfer to take place except in periods of acute depression. Under such circumstances the international balance sheet of the country will not be adversely affected. But the transfer of German reparations sped down the list of less desirable alternatives, until the fifth and sixth methods had to be utilized if the gold reserve of the country was to be retained even in part. In cases of severe capital flight, likewise, the first four alternatives are quickly exhausted, and methods 5, 6, and 7 are employed to save the currency *in extremis.*

In each of these methods no net outflow of capital has taken place. Yet it is clear that the borrowing of the central bank abroad, whether from the money market or in dire necessity from foreign governments and central banks, only occurs when the abnormal capital flight has already been transferred partly in gold. Gold would probably start to leave a country which possessed it in its banking system in the transition period between alternatives 4 and 5, and it would not cease, unless the gold standard was abandoned, as each of the last three methods was employed in turn.

It is impossible to measure the degree of danger each method progressively contains for the currency of the country employing or submitting to it. It may be said, however, that the appearance of method 3 is a symptom of difficulties to come and that each subsequent method, as it comes into use, reveals the ebbing hope that the currency will be successfully maintained. Capital flight, or in general, abnormal capital movements, which are transferred by normal capital movements in the opposite direction and hence involve no net flow of funds, are not lightly to be dismissed.

Transfer through Loss of Gold or Foreign Exchange Reserves. In case no capital movements in the opposite direction are available or forthcoming Machlup in effect distinguishes three possibilities: (1) that the money capital will be raised by deflation in the country, in which case the transfer, with a minor exception in case (2) the funds so transferred are hoarded abroad; and (3) that the money capital is raised by credit expansion and thus involves no net deflation, in which instance the capital can only be transferred through the reduction of the central bank's reserves of gold and foreign exchange.

Nurkse does not deal thoroughly with the transfer problem in relation to abnormal capital movements, but suggests in connection with "autonomous" short-term flows that they will be likely to be transferred in gold because of the fact that their sudden and capricious appearance will not be likely to stimulate the normal movement of private short-term funds in the opposite direction.[18] Similarly, after giving reasons why short-term capital movements will not take place in the opposite direction at a time of monetary instability,[19] Fanno maintains that goods cannot respond quickly enough to equalize abnormal capital movements. His reasoning is that there are not sufficient stocks of exportable goods on hand at such times and that therefore the transfer must take place in gold.[20] The implication in both Nurkse's and Fanno's argument is that after a time goods will flow to complete the transfer in normal fashion.

In his discussion of reparations, another form of abnormal capital movement, Fanno points out that normal capital movements have as their motivation the desire of the borrower to spend funds. Hence they assure that demand will be increased in the debtor country before, during, or after the purchasing-power transfer. Reparations, on the other hand, do not increase demand;[21] and this fact adds to the difficulties of transferring

[18] *Op. cit.*, p. 229. [19] *Ibid.*, p. 66. [20] *Ibid.*, p. 67.

[21] *Ibid.*, p. 38. This statement is not quite precise. The receipt of net new imports of normal capital involve an increase in the national money income and an increase in the demand for foreign-trade goods at one or more of the three stages of the transfer mentioned above, p. 56. The receipt of reparations does not increase demand at the first stage. It may increase demand at the second stage, if the funds received are used to add to the recipient government's outlay, rather than to retire debt. It is likely, after the elapse of time to increase demand at the third stage, if less than full employment exists, by clearing the

reparations. Later he points out the problem and the dangers of expanding credit on the basis of gold imported from a country which is undergoing capital flight. The funds may suddenly be repatriated and involve deflationary consequences in the debtor country as it returns the gold in the first instance.[22] On the basis of these passages Heuser credits Fanno with the position that "the reason why funds exported under conditions of a flight of capital have to be transferred almost entirely in the form of gold or foreign exchange is . . . the probable failure of buying activity to increase previously to, simultaneously with, or after the money transfer.[23]

This statement strikes closer to the heart of the problem than its alternative—that capital will be easily and naturally transferred in goods. The exception which Machlup considers minor, that is, that hoarding abroad may take place after the purchasing-power transfer has been made in gold or foreign exchange, may be said to represent the general case.

The important point regarding the transfer of capital between countries in the form of goods and services is not so much whether deflation takes place in the capital-exporting country as whether inflation of money incomes takes place abroad in the receiving country.[24] With normal capital movements, the major share of the adjustment falls on the borrowing country. With abnormal capital movements, the gold received merely increases excess reserves of the banking system in the country of refuge if the reduction in the country's foreign short-term assets does not lead to an increase in the national money income. The capital flight will then continue to be financed solely through the expropriation of basic banking reserves of the capital-losing country. This will continue until either the capital flight is halted or the battle to maintain the currency is given up and the ex-

market of a portion of the government borrowing, thus making possible a reduction in the long-term rate of interest. It can safely be asserted, however, that reparations do not increase the national money income with anything like the speed or sureness that private capital movements would. To this extent, Fanno's statement is correct.

[22] *Ibid.*, pp. 76-77.

[23] *Economica*, p. 492.

[24] See above, pp. 78, 141 n.

changes are allowed to depreciate or foreign-exchange control is initiated.

It may be mentioned as a relatively unimportant exception to the foregoing statements that flight capital will be transferred in goods when the money capital is raised by purchasing goods salable on foreign markets, shipping them abroad, and retaining the proceeds in foreign assets. This, however, cannot be done on a large scale. Exporters may build up their foreign balances disproportionately in this fashion, but the general public is ill equipped by temperament and experience to use this method of capital export.

The Long- and Short-Term Rates of Interest. Abnormal capital transfers, with the above exception, may be affected in three ways, which may on occasion be consecutive alternatives. In the first, the transfer is made possible by long-term capital movements in the opposite direction; in the second, by similar short-term capital movements; in the final method, the transfer is carried out by reductions in the country's gold and foreign exchange reserves. At a given time all three of these methods of transfer may be current, but one or another of them is likely to predominate. The abnormal capital movement may be halted at any time before the final method has been fully used by the reversal of the flight or by default. If the flight proceeds until the third method alone is effective and continues undiminished or in increased measure, the prospect of devaluation or official moratoria to avert national bankruptcy looms for the country concerned.[25]

[25] Fanno devotes an entire chapter (*op. cit.*, chap. v) to distinguishing the necessity for "freezing" credits in cases where a simple devaluation would not meet the problem. Where no assets are available to pay off foreign debts and to leave over enough gold and foreign exchange to enable the banking system to obtain a fresh start, devaluation, he maintains, provides no remedy. The foreign debts are apt to be written in other currencies, and no amount of depreciation would be able to raise the necessary funds to repay them unless capital can be attracted from abroad. It is necessary to examine Fanno's contention that there will be cases in which foreign assets will not be available and in which other capital from abroad cannot be attracted by a devaluation program. If domestic capital has already been transferred abroad in large amounts a decisive devaluation, if the necessary steps to restore confidence were taken, would be likely to induce a repatriation of capital, which would enable the foreign credits to be repaid. There are, of course, cases in which domestic capital is slow to return. But such a situation is within the power of the country concerned to correct.

Sufficient attention has already been devoted in this chapter to the stage in which the abnormal capital is transferred by inward normal long-term movements (Stage 1), and to that in which the movement is made possible by reductions in the country's gold and foreign exchange reserves. It is therefore in order to occupy ourselves briefly with the second stage, in which liquid funds flow into the country and make possible the movement of abnormal capital outward.

It has been reaffirmed recently on the basis of empirical evidence that the short-term rate of interest tends to have a different cyclical pattern from the long-term rate (for example, the yield on high-grade corporate bonds).[26] So long as the transfer of the abnormal capital movement is being carried out without strain by the borrowing of other funds on long-term account or the sale of foreign long-term assets, it is probable that the short- and long-term rates of interest within the country from which the capital is moving are in the same relationship that exists in the prosperity phase of the business cycle. This implies that the long-term rate is higher than the short-term rate, but that the latter is closing up the gap. The relationship between the two rates can be maintained by short-term capital movements in the form of security arbitrage.[27] When the abnormal capital outflow continues until strain appears—and by strain is meant that there are no further foreign assets to sell or that foreign loans available to satisfy the local demand for loans are being exhausted—the long-term rate of interest rises unduly in relation to the short-term.[28] Whether this is the pattern followed by the two rates of interest in the business cycle is not clear; but the generalization may be made that in the business cycle, too, the short-term rate of interest passes the long-term rate after the latter has risen. In the case of international capital movements, moreover, the fact that long-term capital becomes more expen-

[26] See W. C. Mitchell, "The Measurement of Cyclical Fluctuations," *op. cit.*, p. 9.

[27] See Iversen, *op. cit.*, p. 175.

[28] Bresciani-Turroni (*op. cit.*, p. 18) attributes the rise in the long-term rate of interest, which changed the form of German borrowing from long term to short term, to current world credit conditions. The German demand for capital might have affected this. See, however, Nurkse, *op. cit.*, p. 209.

sive leads to a subsequent increase in the volume of funds being borrowed at short term, so that the short-term rate rises above the long-term rate. At this point one might expect the long-term interest rate to become a going rate again; but such does not appear to be the case. Despite the fact that the short-term rate is higher than the long-term, all current borrowing in the international capital market takes place in the form of short-term loans. This continues until either confidence reappears in the ability of the banking system to withstand the strain or the system collapses and resorts to devaluation or moratoria.

This type of action in rates of interest when abnormal capital movements are taking place is at first sight puzzling. One might expect that the shift from long- to short-term loans would continue only so long as the rate of interest was favorable to borrowing at short term. Thereafter, it might be believed, the borrowers would be able to obtain funds at long term until the position of the two rates was again reversed.

Yet what actually happened in the case of Germany was that the flow of long-term capital to that country, when reversed in favor of short-term loans in 1928, was not resumed.[29] Thereafter the long-term rate of interest for foreign capital was largely nominal, since foreign estimates of the risk premium necessary to induce them to make long-term loans was so great that an attempt to move the long-term rate to a point at which transactions would take place would have been extremely oppressive to German industry. At short term, with a definite maturity of three months or less, more exact calculations could be made of the risk of lending to Germany. The going rate for short-term funds was higher than the rate for long-term, because the latter was nominal and Germany did not expect to be able to borrow from abroad at that rate.

This analysis can be carried through to the point at which further short-term loans from abroad are not available to a country as it tries to transfer abnormal capital movements. If short-term loans are not sufficient to meet the strain, and (for example) either the rate goes higher or gold flows abroad or

[29] *Ibid.*, p. 18.

both, the subjective estimates of the risk on short-term loans increase, and short-term lenders withdraw their offers. Up to a certain point raising the rate of interest for short maturities will bring replacement funds from abroad. If, however, the situation goes from bad to worse, a point will be reached at which the short-term rates for foreign loans becomes nominal. To raise the rate to the point at which the subjective risk estimates of foreigners would be overcome would be to involve the country in ruinous deflation. In such circumstances the country pays out gold and foreign exchange until it decides to capitulate and devalue or declare a moratorium.[30]

[30] The foregoing discussion relies upon the implicit assumption of a gold standard. Where an unregulated paper standard prevails, the analysis follows similar lines, except that a "fall in the rate of exchange" must be substituted for movements of gold and foreign exchange reserves. That is, abnormal capital movements on the unregulated paper standard alter the rate of exchange, except in cases in which they are offset by movements of funds in the opposite direction. The likelihood of such opposing capital movements is greatly reduced by the fact that the exchange rate is free to vary. On this account cumulative depreciation may set in which can only be halted by a very low rate of exchange (at which rate no gain can be expected from transferring funds abroad) or by foreign-exchange control.

The present writer has been unable to follow the analysis of P. B. Whale in "The Theory of International Trade in the Absence of an International Standard," *Economica,* III (1936), 24-38.

Whale defines "equilibrium" in terms of some unexplained norm of trade, with "undervaluation" representing a relative "undue" expansion of exports to imports, and "overvaluation" the opposite (p. 33). He insists on this definition, even though he admits that undervaluation (some other kind?) may cause deflation abroad and thus not be reflected in the trade figures (p. 37). His discussion of the term "undue" leads him to consider "abnormal capital movements" on which they depend, but although he indicates that his analysis requires their definition (p. 34) he fails to provide it.

In his discussion of abnormal capital movements on the paper standard, he assumes that the rate of exchange will not move, since he holds that the abnormal capital movement is automatically transferred, being equal to the difference between exports and imports (p. 34). This assumption is implicit in his treatment, despite the fact that he has set out to describe what happens when the rate of exchange is free to move. Where stabilization fund authorities peg the rate, evidently an international standard does exist. Moreover, Whale fails to indicate whether he means by equilibrium that exports exactly balance imports or more generally, the balance of payments on income account equals zero, and if so, over what period of time.

The rare confusions of concepts in this article reach their high point with the simple assertion offered on page 32 without any theoretical substantiation: "Variations in the quantity of money required by international capital movements would be compatible with a policy of internal price or income stabilization." The variations in money he deems required (but see above, pp. 64-67,

Summary. "Abnormal" capital movements are those that are propelled from a country by reason of contractual obligations or the fear on the part of the owners of the capital, whether foreigners or natives, of losses in the future. In this they contrast with "normal" capital movements which are attracted to a country. The distinction is not theoretically precise and does not go very deep. On any more fundamental level of analysis, however, nothing can be said about the motivation behind a movement of capital except that the proprietor of it thought thereby to maximize his utilities.

If more tangible criteria be needed, it may be said that abnormal capital movements are those that take place from countries with high to countries with low rates of interest. In this instance it is the gross, not the net, rate of interest which must be considered, since the net rate of interest for the person moving the capital is always higher in the country to which he is moving the capital than in the country left.

Certain major types of abnormal capital movements may be recognized: capital flight, behind which any one of a number of proximate causes may lie; reparations; war debts and the repayment of matured commercial long-term loans. In all cases their transfer may be facilitated by (1) long-term loans; (2) short-term loans; and (3) the depletion of the country's gold and foreign exchange reserves. The abnormal capital transferred by an inward flow of funds involves on balance no net movement of capital, but the balance-sheet position of the country may be weakened if short-term liabilities are acquired in exchange for assets not readily available. In the same manner a bank may be able to meet a run by discounting its government bonds and paying out cash to the head of the line of depositors demanding repayment; and the fact that its assets still balance its liabilities when its cash and government bonds are nearly

and pp. 89-95, where it is pointed out that transfer is possible without money changes), quite obviously upset a policy of price or income stabilization. Either money incomes are raised sufficiently to expand the demand for foreign-trade goods, or foreign-trade goods are lowered in price in the capital-importing country or both if the transfer is to be accomplished. But see below, chap. xi.

exhausted is no earnest of its ability to maintain its capital unimpaired.

Abnormal capital is unlikely to be transferred in goods, largely because of the fact that its movement does not increase demand for foreign-trade goods in the recipient country. In the case of capital flight the foreign deposits acquired by persons expatriating their funds are likely to be hoarded, pending the restoration of confidence at home and a return to employment there. In the case of reparations and war debts the receipt of funds by creditor governments is not likely to lead to an equal increase in the government's spending. While in the long run the withdrawal of the government receiving reparations from the capital market may lead to an expansion of loans to other borrowers and a resultant increase in the national money income, yet this expansion may again take the form of foreign loans and thus move further into the distance the possibility that the abnormal capital movement will be transferred in goods. In addition, the problem of raising the capital in the paying country for abnormal transfer involves deflation, except in the extreme case in which large hoards have already been accumulated. If the abnormal movement is large, the deflation necessary to raise the money capital will be correspondingly great and will lead to a cumulative capital flight as capitalists seek to avoid the country of business depression and avoid the possibility of national bankruptcy. Normal capital movements, on the other hand, are transferred in goods and services by the fact that demand increases in the capital-importing country. They rarely involve a serious deflation in the lending country, since the money capital to be transferred is likely to come out of idle balances.

When capital, on the gold standard, can be transferred neither by an export of goods nor through the import of foreign capital on private account (because the rise in the risk premium individually demanded by foreign prospective lenders keeps ahead of actual increases in rates of interest) gold must flow out or foreign exchange reserves must be paid out. To be sure, recourse will have been made to the method of giving claims on foreign money to the inhabitants of the country in exchange for their domestic claims while the bulk of the demand was still being satisfied by foreign lenders. When the supply of long-term loans falls off, however, followed by a refusal of foreign potential lenders at short term to respond to increases in the rate of interest offered, gold and foreign exchange reserves must bear the brunt of the remaining capital transfer. And this abnormal movement, if it were originally capital flight, has now added to it the repayment of the foreign loans at short term, which were borrowed to finance the first part of the capital flight and which have now matured. Unless the tide can be turned by a dramatic gesture, such as heroic budget balancing, overnight devaluation, or the accession of a "strong man" to power, the banking system must collapse because of the undermining of its reserves or the foreign debts must be frozen by debt moratoria and foreign-exchange control.

Part IV

INTERNATIONAL MONETARY INTERDEPENDENCE

XI

CREDIT POLICY AND THE BALANCE OF PAYMENTS

If the analysis of the foregoing chapters is to be related to current international monetary problems, certain questions remain to be resolved. In the first place, the relations of domestic credit policy to the balance of payments must be clarified. Secondly, some analysis should be undertaken of the various mechanisms which have been devised to curb the influence of those short-term capital movements which make for disequilibrium in the balance. The latter capital movements are, on the one hand, the autonomous movements discussed in the previous chapter; and, on the other, the ever-growing volume of funds which move internationally in response to anticipated profits from security speculation rather than in response to exact calculations of the monetary returns currently obtainable. The mechanisms devised to curb these capital movements in their effects may be discussed under the headings of forward exchanges and of stabilization funds. The gold standard and the opposite extreme, the freely fluctuating paper standard, will receive such additional treatment as they require in the present chapter.

Internal and External Monetary Stability. Any discussion of the mechanisms of adjustment in the balance of payments, to achieve a semblance of reality, must be presented in terms of some type of credit policy, explicitly or implicitly assumed. The point has been made frequently,[1] but it bears repetition. The association between the balance of payments and credit policy is also of interest for a more significant reason. Many economists have seen a fundamental conflict between the types of credit policy appropriate to the maintenance of equilibrium in the

[1] See, e.g., Ohlin, *op. cit.*, pp. 395, 441; Iversen, *op. cit.*, pp. 320-21, 470; Nurkse, *op. cit.*, pp. 140-41.

balance of payments at a fixed level of exchange and that desirable on other grounds for the attainment of specific objectives of internal policy. A study of international capital movements at short term must deal with this problem, since such movements may either work for adjustment in the balance of payments, extend a given credit policy beyond the national borders,[2] or even require a modification of domestic or external monetary policy.

The discussion of the problems of internal and external monetary equilibrium and their alleged conflict is at the present time in a state of vast confusion. If internal stability be broadly defined to relate to the elimination or moderation of the internal business cycle and external stability be limited to stability of exchange rates, the controversialists may be divided into a number of camps. The following list is complete neither in the number of points of view represented nor in the adherents assigned to any one of them. At best it is intended merely to be suggestive of the wide number of views currently held.

The groups are principally composed of:

(1) Those who maintain that internal and external stability are incompatible:

a. Those who hold that internal stability is attainable if external stability be abandoned[3]

b. Those who believe that internal stability is approachable only if external stability be abandoned[4]

c. Those who hold that internal stability requires, or at least is aided by, a definite type and degree of external instability[5]

[2] See above, pp. 149-52.

[3] See Shone, *op. cit.*, *passim*: Henderson, *op. cit.*, *passim*, Durbin, *op. cit.*, pp. 206-13, among others.

[4] See J. W. Angell, "Monetary Control and General Business Stabilization," in *Economic Essays in Honour of Gustav Cassel*, p. 26; and "The 100 Per Cent Reserve Plan," *Quarterly Journal of Economics*, XLIX (1935).

[5] There are several subgroups which might be ranged under this classification. The principal one consists in those who advocate some form of Fisher's compensated dollar plan: the Committee for the Nation in the United States, and Sir Morgan-Webb, in England. Of particular interest, however, is the position of Myrdal, in Sweden, who is credited by Brinley Thomas with the view that an independent credit policy (which is desirable) presupposes an "international margin" supplied by a favorable balance of payments. See B. Thomas, *Monetary Policy and Crises—a Study of Swedish Experience* (1936), pp. 119-21.

(2) Those who believe that internal stability is impossible so long as certain institutions prevail in external relations[6]

(3) Those who hold that internal stability is a will-o'-the-wisp, especially if pursued by means now in favor among economists, and that some form of external stability is all that can be hoped for in the present state of knowledge[7]

(4) Those who hold that external and internal stability may be compatible or incompatible depending upon the definitions used and the methods pursued to attain one or the other, and who believe especially that the implications of neither have been sufficiently explored to permit broad generalizations[8]

(5) Those who believe that credit policies in one country must have repercussions abroad and that what is desirable as an objective is external stabilization for each given country, with the elimination of the business cycle so far as possible for the sum total of all countries[9]

(6) Those who feel that given the proper credit policy internal and external stability are compatible,[10] and that they are even concomitantly inherent in the particular type of credit policy[11]

As mentioned above, this confused assortment of grades of opinion, being intended only to be representative, is by no means complete. Doubtless, too, many of those assigned by footnotes to a particular opinion would object to being associated with the doctrines in question, and would insist, if consulted, upon being granted a separate and unique category, whose description would in each case require a separate chapter. Many names are omitted from the footnotes, those of Keynes, Ohlin,

[6] See C. R. Noyes, "Stable Prices vs. Stable Exchanges," *Econometrica*, III (1935); and L. Currie, "Domestic Stability and the Mechanism of Trade Adjustment to International Capital Movements" in *Exploration in Economics*, 1936, pp. 46-56.

[7] This, I take it, is the average of opinion of the gold-standard group of economists, represented in the United States by men such as the late H. P. Willis, W. P. Spahr, E. W. Kemmerer, and in France by Charles Rist, Frederic Jenny, and others.

[8] See J. H. Williams, "The World's Monetary Dilemma—Internal Stability versus External Monetary Stability," Academy of Political Science, *Proceedings*, XVI (1934), 62-68.

[9] See F. A. Hayek, "A Regulated Gold Standard," *The Economist*, CXX (May 11, 1935), 1077-78.

[10] See P. B. Whale, "The Theory of International Trade in the Absence of an International Standard," p. 32.

[11] See J. Robinson, "Banking Policy and the Foreign Exchanges," *Review of Economic Studies*, III (1936), 226 ff.

and Harrod being outstanding. Keynes and Ohlin have frequently presented their views on both internal and external stability without achieving satisfactory positions relating the two problems.[12] Harrod has written at length[13] on the subject of the proper exchange policy to combine with an internal credit policy designed to stabilize employment; but his treatment is largely negative and riddled with gaps and qualifications.

Internal Stability in a Closed System. The concept of external stability, if defined with reference to exchange rates free to move only within narrow limits, is precise and clear-cut. The concept of internal stability, on the other hand, whether defined with reference to employment, prices, income, or production, cannot be as satisfactorily related to a concrete formula of policy. It is necessary, therefore, to devote some attention to the question of whether the criteria of internal stability currently put forward offer a satisfactory basis for discussing the alleged conflict between it and external stability.

For the purposes of the present treatment only three types of monetary policy need be examined: (1) that of maintaining constant money per capita; (2) that of maintaining prices constant; (3) that of maintaining incomes per capita constant. Stabilization of employment is implied by both of the two latter

[12] Ohlin (*op. cit.*, p. 375) expresses his advocacy of a credit policy of maintaining money incomes constant per capita in the same chapter that goes on to discuss adjustments to disequilibria in the balance of payments arising out of capital movements. The impression is given that he feels with Whale (*op. cit.*, p. 32) that a capital transfer is compatible with a policy of constant incomes. To read this error into his chapter, however, would be unfair in the absence of a statement as explicit as that of Whale. As for the omission of Keynes, a history of his views on the subject as they have been modified from 1912 to the present would be very interesting but would present a task so imposing as to lie outside the scope of the present work. In his *Treatise on Money* Keynes belongs fairly clearly to group (1), as he surely does in *Essays in Persuasion*, although in the former work he does qualify his position (Vol. II, chaps. xxxvi and xxxviii) by discussing the merits of a world currency and credit-control scheme. In his article "The Future of the Foreign Exchanges," he implicitly advocates a high degree of foreign-exchange stability—within wide gold points—but does not discuss its relation to domestic stability. In the *General Theory of Employment, Interest and Money* he is very little concerned with the problems of an "open" economy.

[13] See *International Economics*, chaps. vii and viii.

and therefore does not require separate discussion.[14] The implications of these policies will be examined for a closed system in order to ascertain their inherent consistency. Thereafter, on the assumption that they are capable of being attained in a closed system they will be examined in terms of an open system on the basis both of fixed and of fluctuating exchange rates.

A policy of constant money, advocated in the United States by Angell (among others) and in England by J. C. Gilbert,[15] is evidently self-consistent. Its adherents, however, do not claim that it provides a solution of the problem of stabilizing economic activity within a country.[16] Their only claim is that constant money would eliminate the cumulative inflationary and deflationary effects of the credit system on employment and productive activity.[17] Provided that money can be adequately defined, a policy of sterilizing gold movements by offsetting open-market operations and undertaking further open-market operations to change the amount of bank deposits in accordance with the secular change in the population will carry it out.[18]

A policy of maintaining prices constant is evidently conceptually difficult. The problem presented by the complexities of the index numbers to be used need not be dwelt upon here.[19] If it be assumed that there is available an index number of wholesale prices which accorded to each price its relative im-

[14] Both those who advocate constancy of prices and those who advocate constancy of incomes per capita are really interested in stabilizing employment and differ merely on the method of accomplishing this end. The merits of their respective positions need not be discussed here. It will be noticed that Hayek's objective of monetary policy, the stabilization of the product term, money times exchange velocity, under certain qualifications (see *Prices and Production*, p. 106), has been omitted from consideration. This is because of the fact that sufficiently weighty objections have been leveled against this type of credit policy on *a priori* grounds (see Durbin, *op. cit.*, pp. 120-28), and, on the basis of its practical aspects (see J. W. Angell, *The Behavior of Money*, p. 127) to discredit it (but see L. Currie's review of Angell's *Behavior of Money*, in the *American Economic Review*, XXVI [1936], 791).

[15] See "Banking Policy and the Income Velocity of Circulation of Money," *Economica*, Vol. I (1934), pp. 242-45.

[16] See Angell, "Monetary Control and General Business Stabilization," *op. cit.*, p. 58.

[17] *Ibid.*, pp. 57-58.

[18] Further adjustments through open-market operations would have to be undertaken if the member-bank reserve ratios were subject to short-run change.

[19] See Gottfried Haberler, *Der Sinn der Index Zahlen*, 1931, *passim*.

portance in the community, the stabilization of such an index still presents a bewildering problem. Suppose that an industry of considerable importance experiences a decline in the demand for its products because of a change in the real income of the community or even because of a change in tastes. Constant prices would require another industry of increasing importance to exhibit a rising trend of prices to counteract the fall of the former. This might be difficult to bring about by monetary means. In addition, the point noted by such critics as Durbin may be cited. If prices do fall in an economy having full employment as a result of an increase in productivity uncompensated for by a proportionate increase in the rewards to factors of production, the injection into the system of new money sufficient to raise prices to their former level is dangerous. If dislocations among the resources available to different industries are to be avoided so far as possible, the additions to the money supply will have to take the form of consumers' credits.[20] Even then the price index chosen for stabilization is not apt to remain stabilized unless the weighting be changed, since the consumers' choices among the range of commodities open for their selection will alter as a function of income in accordance with the complex of income elasticities for various goods. As a final objection to constant prices as a basis for monetary policy capable of precise formulation it may be mentioned that if prices fall at a time of deflation brought about by hoarding (that is, at a time when the national money income falls as a result of a decline in the income velocity of money), it is not clear that monetary action can restore the former level of prices. In the present state of economic science it might be years before additions and subtractions from the monetary supply finally would bring the price level to the position from which it started, within the permitted degree of fluctuation. This objection may be more broadly stated. In the absence of complete knowledge concerning the reactions of entrepreneurs, factors of production, and consumers to given changes in the monetary supply, the change in money called for by a given change in price must be unknow-

[20] See Durbin, *op. cit.*, pp. 128-38.

able unless the limits of permitted fluctuation be wide. If these limits are wide, the "constancy" of prices under a constant price policy of this sort is open to question.

There may be much the same range of exceptions to a policy of maintaining incomes constant in a closed economy. If one industry gains at the expense of others, those others will not be likely to decrease income payments in the same absolute amounts that the expanding industry is increasing them. They may continue to pay out incomes to factors at a loss to themselves, or they may shut down the plant entirely. In the first instance the gross money income will be increased; in the second, decreased. Not only will different rates of growth among individual industries result in complications under a policy of constant incomes but also different rates of growth among factors of production will cause dislocations. Should capital accumulate faster than the labor supply expands, for example, a constant income-per-capita policy might require the reduction of rates of return to labor if a larger absolute amount of the total national income is to be paid to owners of capital.

It is, perhaps, unnecessary to labor the point. Suffice it to say that the proponents of a policy of maintaining money constant admit that they do not solve the major problems involved in the attainment of monetary equilibrium; while the adherents of constant prices and constant incomes as objectives of monetary policy have not carefully formulated the many exceptions to their respective proposals that are necessary for equilibrium maintenance nor provided precise rules for monetary management to use in the pursuit of their respective ends. These weaknesses apply to the remedies advocated even when they are considered in a closed economy.

Internal Stability in an Open System. When an open economy is envisaged, the policies of constant money, constant prices, or constant incomes become even more difficult to formulate. The problems added by applying these policies to one country in a world where many countries exist and where international trade is being carried on can be discussed separately for each proposal.

Constant money may be maintained in the face of gold movements by having the central bank or treasury offset such movements through open-market operations or by merely holding the gold out of reserves through the operation of a stabilization fund of the credit type.[21] There is no guaranty, however, that the effective money, that is, the industrial circulation, will remain unchanged by events having their origin within the national borders. When world changes are considered, it seems likely that the industrial circulation will not remain unchanged. A rise in national money incomes abroad may be expected, under certain conditions, to increase the foreign demand for the country's exports and to lead to an inflow of gold or an outflow of short-term funds. The increase in the money supply would occur in the industrial circulation in the absence of central-bank or stabilization-fund intervention as exporters expanded their profits and their operations. Any decrease that occurred through steps taken by the monetary authorities would be likely to affect the financial circulation, at least in the first instance. Even without changes in the total money supply, including foreign balances, a shift in the ownership of deposits between foreigners and inhabitants of the country would be likely to involve a shift in the national money income, inasmuch as the income velocity of domestic and foreign deposits differs widely.[22] Thus, keeping the money supply stable will not succeed in isolating the country concerned from the influence of foreign disturbances.

An objection more serious than this can be raised, however. Cases will arise in which the amount of money (in the industrial circulation) ought to be changed in order to minimize disturbances which have their origin abroad. The example most commonly cited in present-day economic discussion is that of international capital movements. If the country is an importer of capital because of the scarcity of domestic savings, that importation of capital should be accompanied by an expansion of money in order to facilitate the mechanism of the capital transfer. Less compulsion exists for the reduction of the indus-

[21] See below, pp. 213-16.

[22] See above, p. 23 n.

trial circulation when the country exports capital anew on a large scale.

If it be objected to this example, however, that it is a relatively easy matter to rule out international capital transfers or to permit them only when they are linked to specific merchandise transactions (many of those who advocate national monetary policies have seen the dangers arising on the international front under any standard) [23] the classical example may be substituted for capital movements. If a country which has been accustomed to import a large portion of its food supply from overseas suddenly finds that the prices it is required to pay for such products have risen drastically because of foreign crop failures, its policy of maintaining money constant might well be modified to minimize the resultant disturbances. The classical gold-standard remedy of deflating until other imports are reduced and/or exports sufficiently increased in value to make up the deficiency in the trade balance has real merit in such a situation. If the national monetary policy were not trimmed and if an inelastic and inflexible demand for food from abroad be assumed, serious disruptions might ensue. The high prices for foodstuffs would increase the costs of imports. Unless gold were paid out in the short run, the currency would depreciate. This depreciation ultimately would act in the same fashion as deflation to reduce other imports and to increase exports. Its immediate effects, however, would be to stimulate other imports and postpone exports, as in the case of depreciating countries. And, further, it would have different effects with respect to the distribution of income among the various sections of the community. The foreign crop failure must have an effect upon the national real income. Deflation of a noncumulative sort (which is only likely to arise if the currency had been originally maintained at an artificial level by dint of a previous inflow of capital) spreads this decrease widely over the entire population by seeing to it that food prices are the only ones that change as a

[23] See Currie, *op. cit.*; Keynes, "The Future of the Foreign Exchanges," *op. cit.*; Noyes, *op. cit.*

result of the crop failure. Depreciation, on the other hand, would raise the costs of all imports at the expense of the entire population and would tend immediately to increase the money incomes of exporters in relation to the factors of production engaged in producing goods and services for home-market consumption.

Another aspect of the same point may be more clearly set forth if we consider food-producing countries. In New Zealand and Australia, for example, the real national income in a given year depends in large part upon the amount of foreign borrowing and on the state of the demand and supply for important raw-material exports. A policy of maintaining a stable amount of money in Australia would appear somewhat arbitrary. When the foreign demands for wheat and wool are strong and the harvests abundant, the national money supply and the national money income are expanded as a result of maintaining the rate of exchange; and this has the effect of permitting everyone except wheat farmers and sheep ranchers to share immediately in the increase in the national real income. When the sale of these products brings a lower-than-average return, the fall in the national money income accompanied by a reduction in the money supply penalizes the entire community rather than merely the producers for export.

If the quantity of money were kept constant, real income would not be constant and, of course, money income would not be constant either. The inability of a country to maintain constant money and a fixed rate of exchange at the same time would mean that the relative prices of home-market and of foreign-trade goods would fluctuate erratically, and perhaps factors of production would shift continuously between the two types of goods. It has been seen that a policy of constant money is clearly beside the point in a country where the real national income depends largely on one or two export products. In a more balanced economy, such as that of the United States, a policy of constant money is equally misguided analytically, even though perhaps it might prove satisfactory statistically, because of the mutual cancellation of the effects of random disruptive influences arising beyond the national borders.[24]

A policy of constant prices is open to the same objection—that it fails to aid in the adjustment of the national economy to disturbances arising beyond the national borders. These disturbances necessarily have an effect on the national real income. If the country is an importer of capital, the smooth accomplishment of the inward transfer of capital in goods and services may require some upward movement in prices. Conversely, although with a lower degree of certainty, a capital export may require a relative decline of the prices. If the adherent of constant prices as a monetary policy rules out international capital movements by hypothesis, however, price stability would still be impossible in an open economy. This is true whether fixed or fluctuating exchanges be in effect.[25] Changes in international demand, in costs of transfer, including tariff duties, and in real costs of pro-

[24] The problem of eliminating cumulative inflation and deflation arising from gold flows is a real one. If the rate of exchange be kept in equilibrium, however, the danger from this source is minimized. Thus movements in gold plus or minus short-term foreign assets or liabilities only should be permitted to affect the money supply, and all gold movements which are accompanied by opposing changes in short-term foreign net assets should not be allowed to affect the credit base.

[25] Currie's demonstration (*op. cit., passim,* especially pp. 55-56) that capital imports have an inflationary effect on the gold standard and a deflationary effect on an unmanaged paper standard and that capital exports have an inflationary effect on an unmanaged paper standard but a deflationary effect on the gold standard is not convincing. The thesis contains a good many assumptions, both explicit and implicit, and a number of these have little pertinence to the facts of the real world: e.g., that the adjustment involved in the transfer mechanism is left to one country only; that short-term capital movements will not take place on the paper standard to limit the amplitude of exchange-rate fluctuations, or on the gold standard to limit the flow of specie; that changes in the gold supply inevitably occur on the gold standard (because the loan is expended entirely at home in the first stage of the transfer process), etc. In addition, Currie cites briefly V. F. Coe's article, "The Gains of Trade" (*Canadian Journal of Economics and Political Science,* I, 1935) to suggest that Coe denies the existence of gains from international trade, whereas the latter merely quarrels with Harrod's attempt to measure them arithmetically. Currie's essay represents an interesting awakening of American monetary theorists to the idea that international complications may disturb the application of certain monetary nostrums to a national economy, even when the rate of exchange is free to vary. But his demonstration of the manner in which specific disturbances operate is not conclusive; and his proposal to regulate (and eliminate) international capital movements fails to meet the difficulties he cites. Evidently he should entirely close the economy.

duction at home and abroad may also disturb monetary stability. A crop failure again provides a case which would be difficult to rule out by hypothesis. If the exchanges be fixed, a crop failure at home may require an export of gold, deflation, and a downward readjustment of prices. If the exchanges be free to fluctuate, the crop failure may well result in exchange depreciation, which would tend to raise the prices of internationally traded commodities. Constant price policy, then, appears to suffer as a theoretically satisfactory doctrine if it is thought of in terms of a world economy.

Much the same reasoning may be applied to constant money incomes per capita as a solution for the problem of monetary equilibrium in an open economy. If disturbances beyond the national borders or in the production of goods which are to be shipped abroad can affect the real national income, there seems to be little virtue in arbitrarily requiring that the whole effect shall be felt in prices and that the national money income shall be left unchanged. No assurance can be provided that if a domestic crop failure reduces the monetary incomes of a given group a monetary attempt to maintain the total national money income unchanged will affect the distribution of real income in appropriate fashion. Thus far economic science has only been able to affect the distribution of real income, with any precision, through taxation and subsidy.

A constant-money income per capita is an answer to a hypothetical (and important) question raised in a hypothetical state where a given rate of advance in techniques of production applies to all types of commodities produced and consumed by the community. As such it serves the purpose of pointing out the weaknesses in other hypothetical answers for similar and dissimilar hypothetical states and may even prove satisfactory as an objective of monetary policy in given countries under ideal conditions. To refuse to modify it to meet the requirements of internal and external changes in the data, that is, to random and erratic changes in real income, appears to be slighting realities for theoretical symmetry. Certainly, constant money, income, or prices as objectives of monetary policy can be made to appear inadequate if discussed in terms of the requirements of Argentina, Australia, or Brazil. When applied to the United States or to Great Britain they are theoretically as ill fitted to cope with realities, even though at first sight they apprently have more semblance of appropriateness in terms of the data.

Internal Stability in an Open System, continued. We may conclude the present chapter by drawing more tightly lines of the present discussion and by relating the above section to the other types of position mentioned at the outset of the chapter.[26] Those who have preconceived ideas about internal stability, couched in terms of constant money, prices, or incomes and who believe that internal and external stability are incompatible belong largely to the first two subgroups of the first group or to the second group, which feels that internal stability could be achieved if it were not for external interferences of specific sorts.[27] Those in the third subgroup of the first main group, who advocate a particular type of external instability to achieve internal stability, evidently desire currency undervaluation. This is the case whether they be members of the Committee for the Nation, anxious to correct any fall in dollar wholesale raw-material prices by a change in the price of gold, or Swedish economists desirous of facilitating a reflationary program by cultivating an "international margin." Such undervaluation may, of course, benefit one country in given circumstances, but it can hardly be applied broadly by many countries, since undervaluation for one vis-à-vis another involves a reciprocal overvaluation. While undervaluation may be used freely by small countries whose products do not play important roles in international markets (although often at a cost to them through adverse changes in their terms of trade), yet it cannot suffice as a weapon in the economic armory of large nations. It invariably results in

[26] See above, pp. 176-77.

[27] It is perhaps unfair to group Noyes and Currie together. Whereas Currie is primarily interested in indicating that the presence of international capital movements makes internal stability impossible, no matter what be done about external stability, Noyes is at pains to demonstrate—in a somewhat involved fashion—that the antithesis between external and internal stability existing in the minds of many economists is an oversimplification of the real situation.

repercussions abroad of a deflationary sort. If these are understood, undervaluation is likely to invite reprisals.

The gold-standard position in the writings of its orthodox proponents is equally untenable as a permanent solution to monetary ills. It is unnecessary here to dilate on the merits and the demerits of the gold standard in its many variations. It is perhaps sufficient to point out that, while an international standard may be needed, the gold standard, as it has operated and as it is understood, fails to live up to the obvious requirement of such an international standard, that is, that it foster as much internal stability as is compatible with an international standard. Two objections are paramount: (1) that the secular trend in the supply of new gold has borne no definite relationship to the requirements for new money, at times having been excessive and having induced inflation beyond full employment, but at other times having failed to keep pace with the advances in productive technique in the world and having thereby exerted a deflationary influence; and (2) that the gold standard as it has been operated has failed readily to disclose over- and undervaluations of currencies, since gold movements have not been interpreted in the light of movements of short-term international capital.[28] If the gold standard be put forward seriously today as a proposal for international agreement, these glaring defects would first need correction.[29]

The fourth and fifth shades of opinion distilled out of the mass of literature on the subject are evidently both theoretically correct as far as they go. Professor Williams doubtless has today

[28] Actually, no sufficiently broad attempt to measure the movement of international short-term capital was made until the Macmillan report of 1931. It is only lately that the crude methods employed in that study have been superseded by the frequent concise reports made to banking authorities, at least in the United States, Great Britain, France, and Belgium, and these data, except in the United States, are confidential. See appendix, below.

[29] The first defect may be overcome possibly by some such remedy as proposed by Professor Hayek in the article already alluded to. The second evidently requires that adequate information concerning short-term capital movements be gathered, and that the net balance of gold and net short-term foreign liabilities be allowed to affect national monetary policy. Any movement in gold compensated for by a movement in short-term funds, on the other hand, should be prevented from having any effect.

more concrete ideas on the implications of external and internal stability, based on the additions to the literature that have appeared since 1934. Professor Hayek's desideratum of a world economy functioning as one economic unit and maintaining world stability is essentially romantic. In a world of rigid costs, international trade barriers, stabilization funds, and so forth, it fails to take note of two considerations. The first is economic nationalism. The second is that nowhere in the world are economic choices made and their consequences faced. If the city of Detroit, for example, expands credit at a rate more rapid than the rest of the country and is later threatened with a more serious deflation, R.F.C. loans and W.P.A. grants of relief money are used to save the situation. In a world where deflation is politically and economically difficult, the adage that good money should not be sent after bad does not apply. Good money is sent after bad within a national economy through the operations of governmental agencies. So long as it cannot be done in the international world and so long as nationalistic reflationary programs are therefore necessary upon occasion, the prospect of stable exchange rates for the whole world is remote indeed.

Mrs. Robinson and Barrett Whale occupy the position of theoretical heretics, presenting the opinion that there may be no conflict between internal and external stability under given conditions. The former suggests that owing to the fluidity of international capital an increased investment within a country (on certain simplified assumptions) cannot affect the rate of exchange because of the automatic increase in savings from abroad. This equalizes savings and investment and offsets the negative balance of payments on income account arising from the increased national money income. This position evidently assumes that the rate of exchange will stay stable and that no gold will flow out, for only on those assumptions will borrowing from abroad make up the differences. If the rate of exchange were not pegged or were otherwise free to vary, foreigners might not purchase domestic securities in sufficient volume to bring about the automatic equation of savings and investment, and the rate of exchange would depreciate. The equation of savings and investment (in the 1936 Keynsian terminology) would result from the depreciation of the foreign buying power of the inhabitants of the country. In case purchases of capital goods from abroad should be increased (investment) and no foreigners should appear to buy domestic securities in sufficient volume to furnish the exchange necessary for these purchases at a stable price, it is evident that those importers and others whose domestic currency will buy them less foreign exchange abroad will have made up the necessary savings. Mrs. Robinson's adherence to the new Keynsian tautological equality between savings and investment, at a time when she retains the gold standard "fundamental equation," $I' - S = I'_1 - S_1$[30] has resulted in a begging of the question and considerable confusion.[31] Her "formal proof" that the exchanges cannot depreciate if liquidity preference and increases in the active circulation required by higher money incomes be taken care of fails to accord with the factual evidence and turns out to be no proof whatsoever.

Whale's assertion of the compatibility of internal and external stability during the period of an international capital transfer has been commented upon above.[32] It is perhaps unnecessary to repeat, after the demonstration of the previous section, that constant prices and constant incomes are not maintainable in all countries during a period of international capital transfer or, in fact, during any period when disturbances in the substantive course of trade require adjustments in the balance of payments.

Summary. The process of tracing out the interrelationships of the factors involved in adjustments in the balance of payments is only possible in terms of some course of action (or inaction) which is pursued by the country's banking system. This course of action must be assumed for analytical purposes,

[30] See Keynes, *Treatise on Money*, I, 162.

[31] That the "General Theory" equality of savings and investment has on occasion confused even Keynes himself can be gathered from one or two passages in the later volume where he talks about bringing savings up to investment in the "*Treatise*" sense, when actually savings and investment are equal in the beginning by definition. See *The General Theory of Employment, Interest and Money*, p. 261.

[32] See p. 169 n.

whether explicitly or implicitly. Whether it is one step in a series of planned moves toward a particular objective or merely the opportunistic and haphazard result of quixotic decisions on the part of Treasury officials or central bankers, its general character may be described by the inclusive term "credit policy."

As a result of relating the balance of payments to credit policy the larger questions of idealized types of credit policy are opened up. Should a theoretically perfect credit policy for a country be geared to domestic or to external needs for stability? How should internal and external stability be defined? After it has been defined, is internal stability possible of attainment in an economy where external disturbances are in evidence?

We have seen that the answers given to these questions are varied and diffuse. Those, on the one hand, who answer that economic science knows too little about either internal or external stability and those who, on the other, maintain that what is necessary is world stability are all on safe ground. But the question has been pursued to a point further than these positions. There are those who argue that internal stability is attainable if all thought of maintaining exchange rates stable between nations is abandoned. There are those, again, who insist that a specific type of external instability (that is, currency undervaluation) is needed to make internal stability possible or at least to assist in its attainment. Others maintain that the quest of internal stability is handicapped by the persistence of external disturbances, no matter whether exchange rates be fixed or flexible. Still others hold the position that the gold standard provides external stability, which should be sought and clung to in the absence of a formula for the achievement of domestic monetary equilibrium. Finally, there are those who take the view that stability of exchange rates and internal stability are inherently compatible.

To this assortment of conflicting views we have attempted to make answers. Constant money, constant prices, and constant incomes per capita suffer as objectives of internal credit policy in that the first is inadequate to achieve the elimination of the business cycle and the latter two are incapable of being maintained precisely when a change in the substantive course of trade occurs. Such a change may be an international transfer of capital or it may be a change that cannot be controlled through legislative action, such as an alteration of foreign tariffs, in foreign demand, or a crop failure at home or abroad.

Those who would foster undervaluation of a national currency in order to further the maintenance of domestic stability are advocates of a policy of only limited application. Under certain conditions, too elaborate to be specified here, undervaluation may prove a useful national device. Inasmuch as the undervaluation of one currency involves the overvaluation of others relative to it, however, the device has no general merit.

One may raise numerous objections to the solution put forward by gold-standard adherents insofar as they advocate the gold standard as it was known previous to the World War and during the period between 1925 and 1931. Foremost among these objections, perhaps, are two: (1) the supply of gold in the long run bears no necessary relation to the world's monetary needs; and (2) the failure of the gold standard to bring about necessary readjustments in costs and prices leaves open the possibility of serious undervaluation and overvaluation. This may be detected only if gold plus net short-term capital assets and liabilities abroad be watched and if increases in the aggregate of gold plus net foreign short-term assets result in expansion of the monetary supply while decreases bring about contraction.

Finally, it may be asserted that those who feel that external and internal stability are mutually compatible under given credit policy are wrong. Under any economic or monetary system, crop failures, shifts in demand, and changes in methods of production will result in disturbances in the smooth production and distribution of goods and services. Insofar as part of the goods and services consumed by a given country are obtained in exchange for other goods and services sold abroad, where different currency systems, distribution methods, types of economic protection, and degrees of paternalism exist, the frictions are multiplied. This is partly because of the problem of transfer through space and partly by reason of the diverse and varying regulations, customs, and habits which apply to such interchanges of goods.

It is possible to emphasize the production and exchange of goods within the national borders at the expense of the exchange of goods and services across such borders. Neither type of production and exchange can be frictionless. It is the task of the monetary theorist interested in international trade problems to see how far internal frictions may be eliminated without adding to the external frictions, and vice versa. Doubtless an optimum point is attainable, beyond which to smooth external frictions would be to add to internal disturbances more than was gained and beyond which to add to internal stability would be to multiply in an undesired fashion the disturbances to external trade.

XII

THE THEORY OF THE FORWARD EXCHANGES

One of the suggestions put forward for the preservation of external stability by keeping exchange rates stable within narrow limits (in the short run at least) at the same time that the domestic requirements of credit policy are being served is to permit the central banks to buy and sell forward exchange. Keynes has perhaps been the most ardent advocate of this device.[1] Through it he hopes to enable the central bank to ensure that there will be one rate of interest for external transactions, while another prevails in the domestic money market. The Bank of England, for example, could attract short-term funds, if they were needed to preserve the day-to-day stability of the foreign-exchange market, by selling forward dollars. The increase in the discount on forward dollars or the decrease in the premium would induce short-term funds to move to London, these movements being covered by forward purchases of the dollars sold by the Bank. American banks, for example, would be encouraged by the artificially induced premium on forward sterling to buy spot and sell forward.

In order to be able to weigh the merits of this plan more precisely it is necessary that the subject of the forward exchanges be examined with some care. The previous sections of this monograph have referred only occasionally to the subject. This has been due to the fact that only a limited number of variables can be conveniently handled in the argument at one time. To render the statements made about the foreign-exchange market more in accord with actual practice the forward-exchange market should have been taken into consideration frequently. Especially is this true in Chapter I, where the various types of short-term capital movements were discussed. The deficiencies of that

[1] See, e.g., "The Future of the Foreign Exchanges," *op. cit.*, pp. 530-31.

analysis, as well as the merits of the Keynsian proposal for separating the domestic from the external money market, may now be jointly considered in terms of the theory of the forward exchanges.

The Interest-Rate Differential. The literature on the subject of forward exchange is still sparse, but it is growing. In 1924 Keynes's *Tract on Monetary Reform*[2] appeared, furnishing the first widely read discussion of the topic. Later, in an article entitled "The Arithmetic of the Sterling Exchange,"[3] he again furnished a lucid and compact analysis of the topic. More recently other writers[4] have been giving passing attention to the matter, without casting any new light upon the theory. Lately, however, a series of articles by various writers have appeared,[5] developing the theory to a point where the complexities of the interrelationships among spot rates, forward rates, and short-term interest rates can be set forth in greater clarity than was possible ten years ago.

We have mentioned above[6] that the forward exchange premium or discount, expressed as a per-annum percentage of the spot rate in the absence of speculative movements of capital, tends to equal the difference between money-market rates of interest. This theory was first developed in terms of the activity of banks and foreign-exchange dealers in offering persons with commercial requirements opportunities for hedging. So long as the bank could sell (let us say) as much three-month forward

[2] *Op. cit.*, pp. 125-51. It is interesting to note that the writers of textbooks on foreign exchange are finally beginning to take cognizance of the growing forward market. See, e.g., S. Evelyn Thomas, *The Principles and Arithmetic of Foreign Exchange*, rev. ed., 1934. It is only in the last two years, however, that the New York newspapers have begun to publish forward-exchange quotations. Even since then it has been done in a haphazard fashion. Until October, 1936, indeed, the *New York Times* gave forward rates on Paris, Zurich, and Amsterdam, but omitted London.

[3] *The Nation and the Athenæum*, June 13, 1925, p. 338.

[4] See Harrod, *International Economics*, pp. 93-96; N. F. Hall, *The Exchange Equilization Account*, 1935, pp. 38 ff.; L. L. B. Angas, *op. cit.*, pp. 84 ff.

[5] See "Bank Rate and Forward Exchange," by a Correspondent, *The Banker* (London), February, 1936, pp. 130-38; J. H. Huizinga, "Central Banks and Forward Exchange," idem, May, 1936; W. W. Syrett, "A Revision of the Theory of Forward Exchanges," idem, June, 1936; P. Einzig, "The Theory of Forward Exchange," *Economic Journal*, XLVI (1936), pp. 462-70.

[6] See p. 9.

exchange to prospective importers as it bought from prospective exporters, it would not be interested in the rates at which these transactions would be undertaken. Such a balancing, however, would be brought about only fortuitously. If importers want to buy more foreign exchange than exporters have to sell, the bank can provide the forward exchange without running a speculative risk only by building up covering spot balances abroad. The bank will be unwilling to do this if it is costly. On the other hand, the bank will be willing to pay for the privilege of covering the exchange risk of moving its funds abroad if it can earn more money in the foreign money market than it can earn at home. On this account, if the rate of interest is lower abroad than at home, it will charge a premium for foreign forward currencies; while if the rate of interest is higher abroad, it will be willing to sell forward exchange at a discount. Thus, in the absence of speculation the forward premium or discount on forward exchange tends to equal the difference between the two rates of interest in the countries concerned. The forward rate for the currency of the country with the higher rate of interest will tend to be at a discount compared with the other.

So long as the forward-exchange market is thought of in these relatively simple terms, it is evident that the premium or discount on forward exchange cannot differ from the spot rate by an amount more than the difference between the spot rate and the gold points. Were it otherwise, bidding or selling of forward exchange at a discount below or a premium above the gold points would quickly bring the forward rate to the gold point, since the fact that no speculation is taking place shows that spot transactions will take place at or within the gold points when the forward contracts mature. Given gold points of $4.89 and $4.83 for sterling in New York, then, with the spot rate at $4.86, the three-month forward rate on sterling will not rise beyond a three-cent premium nor fall below a similar discount so long as the ability of both the United States and Great Britain to maintain the gold standard (for at least three months) is not called into question. This would be the equivalent of a 2.44 percent[7] per annum rate of discount or premium. On the assumption that the safety of the gold standard is assured and so long as the short-term rates of interest do not differ between New York and London by more than 2.44 percent, the forward rate would tend to be set by the difference between the two rates of interest, with the spot rate at $4.86. This would be true, however, only if there were no assurance in the market that the interest-rate differential would continue beyond three months. If the money market could confidently expect the rate of interest to remain for a year higher (for example) in London than in New York, a lower degree of interest difference would drive the three-month forward sterling discount to the gold import point. This would be the case because New York dealers could count on getting a favorable interest differential during four three-month periods and would hence be willing to pay a premium on forward dollars equal to four times the interest-rate difference in order to cover their exchange risk. The usual belief in the money market, however, and hence the usual analytical assumption, is that three months constitute the longest period of time for which confidence can be maintained in the spread between interest rates. The banker can be sure of getting a given rate of interest for three months if he can invest in three-month obligations.

The above exposition, however, oversimplifies the relations between the gold points and the forward-exchange rates. It neglects to indicate that changes in interest rates and also changes in the forward premium or discount on a currency will reciprocally affect the spot rate. If the rates of interest are identical in New York and London and if the spot rate is $4.86, with forward exchange selling flat (at the spot rate), then an increase in the London rate of interest will not only drive forward sterling to a discount (forward dollars to a premium) but also raise the price of spot sterling. If the interest-rate differential is expected to be permanent, the spot rate will be sent to the gold export point in New York, while the forward rate is moved to the gold import point. Since, however, the going

[7] $\$0.03 \times 4 \div \$4.86$.

differential rate of interest on three-month investments will determine the forward discount alone, under those conditions the spot rate will rise by an indeterminate amount and the discount on forward sterling will take a position determined by the interest-rate differential. It is evident, however, that the possible difference between the rates of interest is enlarged by the fact that the spot rate has moved. With gold points at $4.89 and $4.83, a difference of 4.88 percent[8] between money rates in New York and London could be sustained with the spot rate at the gold export point in New York.

One further point may be mentioned before the assumption of no speculation is removed. If only banks hold foreign balances and form the entire foreign-exchange market, a completely nonspeculative position would require that they cover their foreign balances by sales of forward currency against them. If, however, the banks' customers want to sell more forward exchange than they buy, the banks can, up to a point, maintain a covered position by drawing down their foreign balances. Presumably these foreign balances could be drawn down to zero and then overdrawn, the banks keeping their foreign debts covered by the forward exchange purchased from their customers. In practice, however, domestic banks buy and sell forward exchange to foreign banks. If banks in New York were offered large amounts of forward sterling, they might in turn sell it to British banks and maintain their balances at a working level. The English banks would then have a short position in dollars unless it were covered. The cover, however, is readily secured if the English banks acquire spot balances in New York and bring up foreign balances here. It may thus be seen that the forward market need not function only passively as a reflector of spot exchange transactions but may well take an active role. It may induce changes both in the spot-exchange rates and in the current foreign assets and liabilities of exchange dealers.

Forward Exchange and Speculation. If the assumption of no speculation be removed and along with it the further assump-

[8] $\$0.06 \times 4 \div \$4.89$.

tion that the gold standard is believed to be impregnable, the analysis becomes more complex. Two points require discussion: (1) the fact that the discount or premium on forward exchange can assume commanding importance in affecting the spot-exchange rate and the interest-rate differential;[9] and (2) the relationship between foreign-exchange equilibrium and the forward-exchange rate.[10]

With the removal of the assumption of the gold standard or merely of confidence in it, it is clear that the forward rate of exchange can move beyond the limits otherwise imposed by the gold points. For purposes of exposition we may first discuss the case of the gold standard when confidence in it has been lost. Under this circumstance a higher rate of interest in the country whose ability to maintain the standard is suspect will not necessarily be effective in attracting spot funds. The rate of interest may be considerably higher in such a country than it is elsewhere, with the rate of exchange at the gold-export point. At the same time, the forward rate will be at a discount considerably below the gold-export point. The spot rate and forward rate, instead of tending to move toward opposite gold points as they do when the gold standard is not threatened and a difference in interest rates prevails, will move in the same direction from the mint parity.

When this condition occurs, it is evident that banks with balances in such a country can earn higher returns than are likely to exist in any one money market by selling spot exchange and covering the sale with a purchase of forward. In addition to receiving whatever rate of interest is attainable outside the country, the banks also earn the difference between the forward and spot rate of exchange. In other words, it becomes profitable to withdraw funds from the market with the higher rate of interest. Few foreign banks will be able to do this, since as a rule and *a fortiori* under the stated assumptions, they would not hold uncovered balances in the country under suspicion. If the facilities are available, however, it will pay them to borrow

[9] This is developed by Einzig, *op. cit.*, especially pp. 463-65.
[10] Cf. Syrett, *op. cit.*, *passim.*

spot exchange and sell it against forward cover so long as the rate of interest paid for the spot funds does not exceed the "swap margin" (the difference between the spot and forward rates) profit from the exchange operation. This will tend to drive the rate of interest up to a point where it equals the swap margin. Domestic banks, likewise, could buy spot exchange and sell forward cover against it at handsome profits, and their ability to do this, if unhampered, will bring it about that a high discount on the exchange will make domestic banks willing to lend to their domestic customers only at high rates of interest. In reality, however, the quoted rate of interest rarely responds to the forward-exchange discount in any perfect sense. Monetary authorities discourage domestic banks both from lending to their foreign correspondents for speculative purposes of this sort and from conducting such operations on their own behalf. In addition, banks in a deflated country may not have the available resources to invest in this way; and all banks may have practical limits as to the proportion of their funds they are willing to lend abroad through the forward market. The moral suasion exerted, however, does not prevent some dealings in the foreign-exchange market by the domestic banks, reducing their willingness to lend to their domestic customers at lower rates of interest than they can earn in the other manner.[11]

When the gold standard is on the defensive the limit on the discount to which the forward-exchange rate can fall is determined partly by the limits to which the speculators think that the currency would depreciate or be devalued if the gold standard were abandoned and partly by the extent to which foreign and domestic banks sell spot exchange and buy forward cover against it. This is limited in turn by the moral suasion of the authorities mentioned above and by the amount of liquid resources which the banks have, or consider to be, available. If the banking system is free to discount with the central bank, however, these liquid resources are determined, not by the

[11] See Einzig, *op. cit.*, pp. 464-65: "It is of the utmost importance . . . to realize that the Forward Exchange market provides a loan market which is a rival of internal loan markets, and which escapes, to a large extent, the influences of the traditional discount policy pursued by the authorities."

banks' reserve requirements, but by the discount rate of the central bank. If the authorities in charge of the central bank feel that a rate of discount sufficiently high to make it unprofitable for domestic banks to lend abroad through covered purchases of foreign currency would be detrimental to business and governmental fiscal interests, their only recourse is moral suasion.

The effect of the forward-exchange market when a gold currency is threatened is thus to render the bank rate of discount inoperative.[12] In Western countries the bank rate is not traditionally raised beyond 20 percent, and since the war the deflationary effects of high rates of interest have become so widely recognized that the highest rate of interest charged by central banks in France, England, and the United States has been 6 percent. Contrasted with this is the fact that from May, 1935, to September, 1936, French banks could earn "seldom less than 15 percent per annum, and . . . at times, as much as 50 to 60 percent"[13] by employing their funds in loans abroad covered by forward franc purchases. The rate of discount, then, is effective in the presence of an active market for forward exchange only so long as the stability of the gold standard is not called into question. Thereafter, the heavy discounts to which forward rates fall on those countries whose exchange is under attack make it possible for them to halt the weakness in spot exchange only by using extra-banking means to see that no spot exchange is available or by raising the discount rate to the point where the swap margin will be offset. This, of course, applies only so long as the monetary authorities do not enter the forward-exchange market themselves.

Forward Exchange and the Paper Standard. When the gold standard has not only been attacked but also abandoned, the relation between interest rates and spot and forward exchanges is somewhat different. In this circumstance both spot and for-

[12] For a clear account of the manner in which the heavy discounts on the French and Swiss francs and the Dutch guilder rendered the bank rate manipulation of those countries ineffectual during 1935 see "Bank Rate and Forward Exchange," *op. cit., passim.*

[13] See Einzig, *op. cit.*, p. 464.

ward rates are free to move without limit unless stabilization controls affect either or both. If the monetary authorities have pegged the spot rate of exchange, the forward rate will depend upon interest-rate differentials so long as no one-sided speculative movement takes place. If the market abroad and at home believes that the currency is going to appreciate or depreciate, however, the forward rate of exchange will affect the going rate of interest as well as be affected by it. In addition, of course, heavy speculative buying or selling of the forward exchanges will require the stabilization fund, if it is determined to maintain the spot rate of exchange, to buy or sell spot foreign currencies (or gold). If the customers of New York banks wish to buy forward sterling in large amounts, for example, the New York banks will have to buy spot sterling as cover. Unless the British stabilization authorities are willing under such circumstances to witness a rise in the price of spot sterling, they will have to be prepared to buy dollars or gold in New York.

When no stabilization control intervenes in either the spot or forward market, the spot and forward rate will act together in the same manner that spot and future prices act in commodities. A movement in the forward rate will affect the spot rate, and similarly a movement in the spot rate will affect the forward rate. In the absence of heavy one-sided speculation in either, their relationship will be determined largely by the interest-rate differential between the money markets concerned. So long, too, as banks are free to deal in the foreign exchanges and to lend without limit for foreign-exchange speculation, this relationship will prevail in spite of the speculation. If excessive short sales of their own country's spot exchange by banks earn the disapproval of monetary authorities, however, the relationship between spot and forward exchange will affect the differential between going rates of interest, as well as be affected by it.

Forward Exchange and the Equilibrium Rate. W. W. Syrett and Paul Einzig have recently pioneered in exploring the relationships between the equilibrium rate of exchange and the forward rate. Syrett, although he was the originator of the theory later elaborated by Einzig, oversimplifies the discussion in his effort to make his point.[14] The present treatment, therefore, will deal entirely with Einzig's presentation.[15]

The "interest-parity" level of the forward exchanges may be defined as that rate which would exist in the absence of speculation by reason of the interest-rate differential between two money markets and with commercial requirements in balance. When speculation takes place, however, Einzig expresses the relation between the equilibrium rate of exchange,[16] the spot rate prevailing in the market, and the market forward rate as follows:

> . . . it is probable that if the spot exchange is over-valued or under-valued the Interest Parities will be between the spot exchange and its equilibrium level; and the actual forward rates will be between their Interest Parities and the equilibrium level of the spot exchange. It is nevertheless important to emphasize that in the case of wide discrepancies (between the actual spot rate and the equilibrium rate) the adjustment of either Interest Parities or even actual forward rates to the equilibrium level of the spot exchanges is never likely to be complete.[17]

Six reasons are given for arriving at this conclusion. If an exchange is overvalued, the forward rate tends to move to a discount because:

> (1) Interest rates in the country with an over-valued currency tend to rise, especially if it is defended by more or less orthodox methods . . . or if . . . over-valuation leads to an outflow of gold. In countries not on a gold standard the effect of over-valuation upon interest rates is not so pronounced, but in case of prolonged . . . pressure . . . it is likely to manifest itself to some extent.
>
> (2) The trade balance of a country with over-valued currency tends to become adverse, and consequently, other things equal, forward selling of the national currency for commercial account.

[14] For example, Syrett assumes that his explanation of the theory of the forward exchanges is a complete revision of that theory, which should supersede the older analysis. It can readily be shown, however, that his findings constitute an "emendation" in the other theory rather than a "revision" of it.

[15] Einzig urges the necessity for economists to develop the theory of the forward exchanges further along the lines indicated by Syrett. Within the limits of the present monograph, however, such development is hardly possible. We shall have to be content to state the substance of the theory as presented by Einzig, with a few generalizations concerning its validity and usefulness.

[16] See above, chap. vii.

[17] Einzig, *op. cit.*, p. 467.

It is possible, however, to avoid this effect by import restrictions, export subsidies, etc.

(3) Even if the over-valuation of the currency does not produce a trade deficit, commercial forward selling will exceed commercial forward buying, owing to the pessimistic view taken by merchants. . . . Those who expect payments in that currency are likely to cover their exchange risks, while those who have to make payment at a future date will leave the exchange uncovered in the hope of benefiting by its future depreciation. Should the discount become prohibitive, however, this factor may be reversed.

(4) The same considerations as under (3) hold good regarding hedging against assets in an over-valued currency.

(5) Speculation, anticipation of devaluation, or depreciation of an over-valued currency are an important cause for the widening of the forward discount. Here again the tendency may become reversed as soon as the discount has, in the opinion of the market, become excessive.

(6) The over-valuation of a currency tends to tighten credit resources, as a result of the defense of the currency, or through flight of capital. This is important, because, owing to lack of liquid resources, interest arbitrage is unable to take advantage of the discrepancy between forward rates and their Interest Parities, and is thus unable to counteract the widening influence of the forward discount.[18]

The same set of factors operate in the opposite direction if the currency is undervalued.

Einzig admits at least two limitations to the theory as thus set forth. In the case of gold-standard countries where confidence in the stability of the exchanges is not impaired, the gold points will set limits to the forward premium or discount; and in the case of an undervalued but depreciating currency, the prospect of a lower level in the future will be apt to drive the forward rate to a discount.

Purchasing Power Parity and Forward Rates. The previous section has attempted to summarize the views of Dr. Einzig and in part those of Syrett, without comment. Before leaving them, a word of evaluation may not be amiss.

The "revised" theory of the forward exchange in effect merely restates what may be inferred from forward-exchange discussion

[18] *Ibid.*, pp. 466-67.

based upon the interest differential and speculation theory. Einzig's six points, for example, are reducible to aspects of these two factors, with the exception of point two, which deals with the actual trade balance. The first and sixth points, which really belong together, relate to the effect of the forward exchanges on the interest-rate differential. The other three are all aspects of speculation, involving (*a*) exporters and importers; (*b*) those owning foreign assets; (*c*) pure foreign exchange speculators. If these three groups in the economic community take a short position in a currency, they will send the forward rate to a discount. Their opinion of when and how much to go short may well be related to currency overvaluation, but it bears no necessary, and certainly no determinate, relationship to it.[19]

Despite this protest that Syrett and Einzig have said nothing new, their work is helpful insofar as it adopts a somewhat different view of the subject. It is, however, to be deplored that their implicit understanding of undervaluation and overvaluation and of foreign-exchange equilibrium is in terms of simple purchasing-power parity. It may be granted that equilibrium must be conceived of for this purpose in terms of prices and costs. If the short-term-capital-movement criterion of equilibrium is used, the theorist is able only to say that if a currency is already weak, as the movement of funds necessary to support it indicates, it may be made still weaker if speculation against it sets in. But the reservations which must be imposed upon any theory of foreign-exchange equilibrium based on prices appear to be absent from Einzig's and from Syrett's analysis.

Monetary Authorities and Forward Exchange. After this considerable digression into the theory of the forward exchanges it should be relatively easy to examine the pros and cons of forward-exchange operations as a means whereby central banks can insulate their domestic money markets from foreign disturbances. We may begin with a relatively simple case.

Let us assume that the English balance of merchandise trade is weak for three months in the fall and that the exchange au-

[19] Both Syrett (*op. cit.*, p. 206) and Einzig (*op. cit.*, p. 468) grant that a mathematical approach to the subject is impossible.

thorities want to peg the rate without tightening the short-term rate of interest. It would be possible for them, of course, to let the rate of exchange fall to the gold export point and then to sell gold. If the gold came out of the equalization account, the account would then buy bills from the market and thus replenish the market's supply of sterling. Or the Bank of England, if the gold came from it, could buy bills from the market and replenish bank reserves. In either event credit conditions in England will not necessarily be affected.

But suppose that the monetary authorities have been impressed with Mr. Keynes's exhortation to operate in the forward market. They therefore sell forward dollars and drive forward sterling to a premium (on the assumption that the rate of interest had previously been the same both in New York and London, with forward dollars selling flat). It now becomes profitable for banks and dealers in New York to buy spot sterling and sell it forward. They thus build up London balances to an amount necessary to eliminate the profit. The level of spot sterling is maintained, the rate of interest in London is unaltered, and the Bank of England is left with a short position in dollars. At the end of the three months, assuming that the balance of payments will then tend to make sterling strong, the Bank of England can purchase spot dollars and fulfill its contracts. What it has accomplished is to postpone for three months the necessity for buying dollars by borrowing them from the market.

In the case cited the Bank of England pays what amounts to an interest charge for the dollars it has borrowed by the discount to which it drives the forward dollar. If it had merely let the exchange depreciate to the gold export point and then paid out gold, it would be required to buy back gold when the exchanges turned favorable. It might earn money if there were a difference between its buying and selling prices for gold. It would certainly earn interest if it bought bills from the market to replenish the banking system's reserves.

The only real difference between operating in the forward market and letting the gold mechanism operate, carefully offset in its effects on bank reserves, is this minor one associated with the Bank's earnings. In either case, under the assumptions stated, the rate of exchange moves only within limits, the rate of interest not at all, and the situation is restored to the *status quo* after the seasonal weakness.

When the authorities are managing a paper standard, buying or selling forward exchange requires them to take an open position even though the range of possible rate movement is not limited by gold points. To be sure, they can always cover an open short position with spot exchange bought with gold, so long as they have gold with which to operate. But in this instance they might better have paid out gold originally.

The only circumstance suggesting itself under which the authorities might well operate in the forward rather than the spot market is that occurring when a weakness or strength in the currency develops which the authorities know will be reversed in a given period of time. In this case they can lend or borrow through the forward market and thus induce an outward or inward movement of spot funds in exactly the manner recounted in the previous paragraph. The advantage of the forward operation lies only in the possibility that by protecting the spot rate of exchange from movement, without the aid of flows of gold, the authorities may forestall a cumulative pressure on either side and thus limit the necessity of managing the exchanges in the long run.

Under other circumstances, however, particularly when the managing authority has settled upon no level of the spot exchange which it is determined and able to hold, taking a forward position in the currency may be dangerous. Thus, suppose that a country devalues its currency, but that the market retains a short position in the currency, and suppose that a moderate forward discount, which is still greater than the interest parity, opens up. To attempt to reduce the forward discount by selling foreign currencies forward will be a risky business indeed. In the first place, it encourages foreign speculation against the given currency by making it cheaper, and by providing a counter-party for those going short of the exchange, with the possible result that such speculation will become cumulative and will force the authorities to buy ever-increasing amounts of forward exchange. In the second place, this step will not induce strength in the spot exchange sufficient to bring about an inflow of gold—if the authorities want to make a show of strength—unless the forward discount is forced below the interest parity. The ability of the authorities to do this, with additional speculation to be reckoned with and forward purchases of foreign currencies accompanying each purchase of spot exchange, is open to doubt. Finally, if the policy does not bring about a change in the speculators' estimate of the situation, which it will not be likely to do if the exchange market is aware of what is taking place, the authorities will be left, when their forward contracts mature, with the obligation to deliver foreign currencies or gold. It seems evident, therefore, that the simplest way to protect such a currency would be to defend the spot rate. The forward discount cannot long continue if the spot rate can be successfully defended. As those who have sold spot exchange at an excessive discount have their contracts mature, they must pay a penalty.

It may thus be seen that it makes little difference whether central banks operate in the forward or spot exchanges on most occasions. In the case of deep-seated disequilibria, Mr. Keynes admits, dealing forward has little to recommend it[20] and much against it. For day-to-day fluctuations, on the other hand, there is as little to be said for the forward exchanges as for the spot market or even for gold flows. The "great technical advantage" of forward operations is not very great if central banks are willing to offset changes in the banking system's holdings with open-market policy under given circumstances. A possible disadvantage might result from central-bank and stabilization-fund operations in the forward markets if they became widespread. The authorities might not be content to borrow merely short-term funds from foreign money markets for definite and ephemeral purposes; they might also borrow gold in this fashion. If a currency were weak at the same time that the monetary system

[20] See Keynes, *op. cit.*, p. 531.

was expanding rapidly, the authorities might upon occasion refrain from bringing about a needed contraction in the monetary base and might sell forward currencies in great abundance and thus induce an inflow of gold. Such a point should carry little weight, but it may be suggested that if allowed to go unchecked Mr. Keynes's contagious enthusiasm for the forward exchanges may lead authorities to regard the device as a solution for all types of difficulties.

Summary. The theory of the forward exchanges requires the analysis of a number of related factors, including the spot-exchange rate, the gold points, the rates of interest in the money markets between which the foreign-exchange rate is quoted, the presence or absence of speculation, and (if desired) the equilibrium rate of foreign exchange. In the absence of speculation the forward rate on a market with the higher rate of interest will tend to a discount, since it will pay dealers to buy spot exchange on that center and to cover the exchange risk with a sale of forward exchange. This process will stop at the point at which the discount on forward exchange absorbs the advantage to be gained from being able to lend funds at a higher rate of interest. This statement holds true so long as full confidence is maintained in the prevailing gold standard, in which case the limit to the forward discount is the gold export point of the foreign market. If the interest-rate differential were considered permanent, an infinitely small difference in interest rates would suffice to move the spot rate of exchange to the gold import point and the forward discount to the gold export point. In practice, however, the interest-rate difference is only assured for the length of time of the credit instruments in which funds can be readily invested, usually three-month bills. The gold points set limits upon the amount of the interest-rate differential that can be sustained between two markets, with all exchange contracts covered, but this difference is wide normally, since the forward rate will tend to move in the opposite direction from the spot rate.

When allowance is made for speculation under conditions in which the safety of the gold standard is not assured, the forward discount or premium on currencies will be likely to move outside of the range of the gold points. The forward premium or discount will then exert an influence on the interest-rate differential, as well as be affected by it. The fact of credit stringency in the money market of the currency under attack or the fact that banking authorities may exert moral pressure to prevent banks taking advantage of the favorable returns to be made from lending abroad may prevent the interest-rate differential and the forward discount from reaching equality. On the paper standard, movements of the forward rate may affect the spot rate without limit, unless the spot rate be pegged. So long as no credit stringency is evident in a given market and so long as the banking authorities forebear from interference with exchange operations, the interest-rate differential and the forward discount or premium will be equal.

A currency under attack is liable to be one that is overvalued in terms of cost-price relationships. From this fact may be deduced the general and only broadly acceptable doctrine, that the forward rate will tend to lie between the spot rate and the equilibrium rate of exchange and to exceed the interest-rate differential.

So far as operations in the forward exchanges by central banks are concerned, there appear to be no weighty reasons for or against them in ordinary times. When it is known that a periodic weakness or strength in the spot position of a currency will take place, there may be some merit in having the central bank finance this by borrowing or lending in the forward markets, rather than by paying out or buying gold. Especially would this be the case if the gold movement were to give the economic community encouragement in speculative operations. On the other hand, it is equally clear that the central bank's forward operations, when its ability to maintain the spot rate over the period of the forward transaction is in doubt, may result in serious losses, which would accrue to the speculators it had financed. By and large, however, it may be said that the forward market for central-bank operations offers no royal road to salvation.

XIII

THE STABILIZATION-FUND TECHNIQUE

One prominent ailment of the gold standard as it was operated in the post-war period, according to the verdict of experts who have conducted money autopsies since 1931, has been that gold movements did not in all cases result in accompanying changes in the credit structure and therefore in prices and income. The Gold Delegation of the League of Nations particularly stressed the pernicious character of the practice of "offsetting" gold movements, as had been done in the United States through open-market operations.[1] By selling government bonds when gold flowed into the country the Federal Reserve system in the United States had interfered with the automatic balancing mechanism in the gold standard brought about a maldistribution of gold[2] and contributed to the breakdown of the gold standard.[3] In any reinstitution of the gold standard, it was emphasized by the Gold Delegation and by other economists as well,[4] it was imperative that movements of gold be permitted to have the fullest possible effects upon the monetary economies concerned.

The Rationale of Offsetting Gold Movements. Curiously enough, however, at the same time that these verdicts and admonitions were being delivered the practice of offsetting gold movements was developed to a fine point in 1932 with the establishment of the Exchange Equalization Account in England. Subsequently, too, the United States Treasury took steps to sterilize imports of gold into the United States. The anomaly afforded by this disparity between orthodox economic doctrine and actual practice may be in part explained by the

[1] See Gold Delegation of the League of Nations, *Report,* 1932, paragraph 81.

[2] See Gayer, *Monetary Policy and Economic Stabilization,* pp. 98-105. See also, Bowen, H., "The Mal-distribution of Gold," *American Economic Review,* XXVI (1936), 666.

[3] See Gayer, *op. cit.,* p. 19.

[4] *Ibid.,* p. 168.

failure of certain economists to recognize that gold movements which accompany changes in short-term foreign assets or in short-term liabilities to foreigners do not call for changes in the credit base; whereas changes in net short-term foreign assets unaccompanied by gold movements should be met by a change in the conditions of credit within the country if the long-run equilibrium of the foreign exchanges is to be maintained.

As we have seen in the earlier portions of this monograph, the types of capital movements most likely to produce accompanying gold movements are (1) the abnormal sort, in particular capital flight, and (2) the income variety. It is the purpose of the present chapter to examine the way in which the stabilization-fund technique, under certain conditions, lends itself to the task of offsetting gold movements accompanying such capital flows. Incidentally we shall show that some types of stabilization funds do not serve this purpose.

It should be noticed, first of all, however, that the stabilization fund, although in certain cases it achieves the result of offsetting the effects of capital movements on the credit base, was originally a device intended to enable countries with paper currencies to maintain any desired degree of exchange-rate stability or flexibility. Originally these funds were devices to enable the financial authorities of a country to enter the foreign-exchange market without their operations being known to the public through the medium of a central bank weekly statement and to indulge in or to refrain from operations calculated to peg or to change the rate of foreign exchange. Thus the powers granted the Bank of France by the law of August 6, 1926, under which it was permitted to buy and sell foreign exchange at any price it desired, would have been sufficient to serve the original purpose of the stabilization funds created since 1932, had it not been for the fact that secrecy was sought by the authorities in order to combat speculators.[5] It was only later that it was realized that the stabilization-fund technique as developed in England

[5] This secrecy was obtained in the case of the Bank of France to a considerable extent by the simple expedient of carrying gold and foreign exchange bought pursuant to the law of August, 1926, under Miscellaneous Assets, until the revision of the Bank's statutes in June, 1928.

permitted the authorities not only to take full command over the course of the movement of the exchange rate but also to insulate the money market, at least to a considerable degree, from the effects of international capital movements.

Credit Stabilization Funds. Two types of stabilization fund have been developed since 1932: (1) the credit type; and (2) the gold type. The only pure credit stabilization fund is the Exchange Equalization Account in England, the Dutch fund of 1936 being apparently quickly filled with gold. Gold funds have been set up by the United States, Belgium, France, Switzerland and Czechoslovakia.

The credit type of stabilization fund is very simple in operation. If the authorities want to decrease the value of their currency on the foreign exchanges or to prevent a rise which would otherwise take place, they borrow in the domestic money market and with the proceeds buy foreign currencies or gold. If the authorities desire to increase the value of their currency on the foreign exchanges or to prevent a fall, they merely sell foreign currencies or gold abroad in exchange for their own currency and with the proceeds buy securities (treasury bills) in the domestic money market. In effect, if they keep the exchange rate stable, they provide investments for foreigners wanting to lend in their own market and take the place of former lenders who have decided to withdraw loans. In this fashion the domestic money market can be insulated from the effects of those international capital movements which are considered undesirable.

The Exchange Equalization Account as it has operated in England has been peculiarly successful because of the predilection of foreign exporters of capital to England, or more usually the banks that hold their funds on deposit, for the English treasury bills which the fund is equipped to sell to them or buy from them. Were a similar technique applied to the United States, with a fund operating entirely in short-term obligations of the Government, the results would not be as happy. If, for example, a rise in the long-term rate of interest were to coincide with rising profits and rising stock-market prices, an inflow of funds into the New York stock market, offset by a sale of Treasury bills, would raise stock prices and at the same time tighten interest rates. To insulate the economy against foreign capital movements under these conditions would require that the Stabilization Fund be able to sell the foreigners the assets they wanted to buy, that is, equity stocks. If the Fund sells Treasury bills, it takes funds out of a section of the money market different from that into which foreigners are putting their funds. The illustration serves to show, however, that the Exchange Equalization Account has been peculiarly fortunate in and exceedingly well adapted to the institutional framework within which it operated.

The present section is not intended as a history of the operations of the Exchange Equalization Account. That history has been treated by other authors.[6] A brief résumé of other views of the purpose and functions of the Account, however, may clarify the present discussion.

Paish has said, ". . . the main purpose of the Account . . . was to offset speculative movements in sterling exchange rates, while allowing 'real' movements to have their normal effects."[7] This statement, however, is ambiguous and gives no adequate definition and explanation of the criteria by which "real" and "speculative" movements may be differentiated. N. F. Hall has attempted to be more explicit:

> The objective of the authorities was to prevent changes in foreign balances (short-term capital movements) moving the exchange away from the equilibrium rate at which it was tending to settle under the influence of normal long-term industrial factors . . . this . . . is much less complicated than it appears to be at first sight. The authority simply has to watch the quantities of foreign currency which are being purchased at any particular rate of exchange. It has then to examine whether these quantities of foreign currency are greater or less than the volume of sterling deposits that have been acquired on foreign account during the period. If the volume of foreign currency is greater than the increase in

[6] See F. W. Paish, "The British Exchange Equalization Fund," *Economica* II (1935), 61-69, and III (1936), 78-83; N. F. Hall, *The Exchange Equalization Account, passim.*

[7] *Op. cit.* (1935), p. 61.

foreign deposits, then the rate is too high . . . if it is less, then the rate is too low. . . . This will be true, of course, only if the balance of payments is neutral. So long as those responsible for the management of an exchange equalization account adhere to the principle of not attempting to influence the basic rate of exchange and content themselves with acquiring foreign currencies in proportion to the increase in foreign balances, the industrial factors will come slowly into equilibrium during the period in which it is operating.[8]

If in this paragraph, "foreign gold" be substituted wherever "foreign currencies" are mentioned, since the Account actually operates largely in gold, and if the expression "sterling deposits" be expanded to "sterling short-term assets," since foreigners buy treasury bills (directly or indirectly), Hall's prescription can be reduced to the simple injunction to exchange authorities to keep short-term capital and gold movements combined equal to zero, so long as the balance of payments is neutral. But, it may be pointed out, if the balance of payments is neutral, there will be no net movement of gold and short-term capital, at least in the static economy which Hall envisages. There would, therefore, be no need for a stabilization fund to operate. If the balance of payments were not neutral and Hall's injunction to prevent net short-term capital and gold movements were obeyed, the rate of exchange would be varied from day to day and the stabilization fund would find that it was not stabilizing.

That Hall's own formulation of the problem is not as simple as this passage would indicate may be gathered from his discussion through the volume of the relation of such problems as the government bond market,[9] the character of short-term liabilities,[10] price movements,[11] forward exchanges,[12] seasonal fluctuations,[13] and gold reserves.[14] His discussion, however, suffers here, as it suffers in the passage already cited, by reason of his lack of a clear conception of foreign-exchange equilibrium in a temporal sense.[15]

[8] See Hall, *op. cit.*, pp. 4-5.

[9] *Ibid.*, pp. 21, 35 ff.

[10] *Ibid.*, pp. 16 ff.

[11] *Ibid.*, chap. vi.

[12] *Ibid.*, p. 32.

[13] *Ibid.*, pp. 52 ff.

[14] *Ibid.*, pp. 63 ff.

[15] See above, pp. 102-3

It may be granted that Hall's injunction, above, that short-term capital movements plus gold movements should equal zero for the maintenance of equilibrium holds good in the long run. On a daily, monthly, quarterly, or even, for some purposes, an annual basis, however, it is not adequate. Some short-term capital movements in the short run may be necessary to the maintenance of equilibrium over a longer period of time.[16] And evidence may be pointed out from Hall's own argument to sustain this point.[17]

It can thus be seen that the equalization fund of the credit type cannot keep short-term capital movements and gold equal to zero on a daily or monthly basis and still equalize or stabilize. It may either decide on a rate of exchange and simply peg that, or it may undertake to offset only certain types of short-term capital or gold movements. What these types are should be clear from the foregoing chapters of the present monograph. They will, however, be dealt with again in summary fashion in a later section of this chapter. Before proceeding, a word may be inserted about gold stabilization funds.

Gold Stabilization Funds. The stabilization fund in a gold-standard country has a less complicated function to perform.

[16] See above, pp. 155 ff.

[17] The case of the pound sterling in the fall of 1932, with which Hall deals extensively, may be cited. Hall maintains:

(1) that the danger of a seriously overvalued pound in the early summer of 1932 was by no means an imaginary one (*op. cit.*, pp. 37-38);

(2) that the price indices suggest (although [p. 61] "in very short periods movements of prices do not give much help in determining what the appropriate rate of exchange should be") that by the time the account was actually started—the end of June—there was no actual overvaluation (p. 39); and

(3) that after the event, it appears that it would have been wise for the Account to have aimed at a lower sterling rate in July, August and September of 1932, in order that the fall weakness of the pound might have been combated by the sale of foreign currencies thus acquired (p. 52). When October arrived, the fund had few or no foreign assets available to support sterling (see also Paish, *op. cit.*, 1935, p. 66).

The basis for this confusion lies in Hall's difficulty with equilibrium over a period of time. Evidently a sterling rate of exchange to be in equilibrium for the entire year must be undervalued in the spring, when exports are seasonally high, since it will be overvalued in the fall, when imports are at a peak. Equilibrium, conceived of in terms of short-term capital and gold movements, must be sought on at least an annual basis, as opposed to a monthly or quarterly one, when seasonal fluctuations are important in the balance of payments.

Unless it is implemented with powers to borrow directly from the market, all its purchases and sales of foreign exchange affect the reserves of the banking system unless otherwise offset. Inasmuch as normal gold movements function in the same way without the intervention of a gold stabilization fund, such a fund, so far as the foreign-exchange market is concerned,[18] is useful only if it shrouds the foreign-exchange market in secrecy, which may or may not frighten foreign-exchange speculators (insofar as it holds gold, generally from revaluation "profits") out of the banking system. For the preservation of stability in the foreign-exchange market the normal policy of the central bank in buying and selling gold for international transactions is sufficient.[19]

A stabilization fund of the gold type operating in conjunction with the gold standard may forestall gold shipments, which it later expects to be reversed by earmarking gold and releasing it from earmark at home and abroad. It is fulfilling a useful function in so doing, however, only when it operates within the gold points; since if it operates at the gold points, it is merely making profits which would otherwise accrue to commercial banks, bullion dealers, and steamship companies and which contribute no distinct service.[20]

The gold stabilization fund then performs no useful function

[18] The fund may also be called upon to stabilize the government bond market without being given the power to issue new securities. Its purchases here evidently affect reserves in the same manner as purchases of foreign exchange. Its sales likewise affect reserves, but must await an accumulation of a portfolio from purchases.

[19] See Bank for International Settlements, *Annual Report,* April 1, 1935, to March 31, 1936, p. 15: "As, however, the United States dollar was re-linked to gold at the same time that the Fund was instituted, there has been no need for the Fund to intervene to prevent the gold value of the dollar from fluctuating."

[20] An exception may be noted when shipping facilities for gold are exhausted and the gold points widen in consequence. Under such circumstances, the stabilization fund, by holding gold under earmark when the old gold point has been reached, will check the downward swing of the currency concerned and may allay panic, which would otherwise result. Such appears to have been the nature of the operation of the Stabilization Fund in June, 1935, when gold shipments from France were halted by the exhaustion of shipping and insurance facilities, and Jean Tannery, governor of the Bank of France, stated that the American Stabilization Fund had been used to aid France. See *The New York Times,* June 17, 1935: p. 1, col. 1.

so far as the stabilizing of exchange rates is concerned unless a stability of narrower range than that provided by the normal gold points is desired. Moreover, with regard to preventing international movements of capital from affecting the banking system, it performs no function similar to that of a credit stabilization fund unless it is implemented with open-market powers granted to Treasury, fund, or central bank, which are used to offset gold movements by taking funds out of the market when gold enters the country and put them back when it leaves.[21] If these open-market powers exist so that they may be used for this purpose, however, there is no need for a gold stabilization fund.

It may be mentioned that a credit stabilization fund may be operated so that it functions like a gold standard.[22] Thus, the Bank of England has bought gold from the Equalization Account on frequent occasions since 1932 to expand the reserves behind the increased note circulation. By so doing it has allowed part of the inflow of foreign funds to affect the credit base; and it has followed a tenet of the gold-standard psychology (in its expansion phase) which it had previously rejoiced to reject. A gold stabilization fund, however, automatically affects reserves when it buys foreign currency or gold, unless offsetting action is elsewhere taken. Inasmuch as the gold standard itself is capable of preserving the stability of the exchange within limits generally deemed desirable, a gold fund is useful only in that it may hold reserves out of the banking system, which may be desirable under certain circumstances and only if it awes the exchange market sufficiently to reduce the volume of speculative dealings.

Offsetting Gold Movements and the Reserve Ratio. One further point may be mentioned before leaving the subject of the technical operation of stabilization funds. It has been

[21] Such a policy of offsetting gold flows was announced for the Treasury by Secretary Morgenthau on December 21, 1936. See *The New York Times*, December 22, 1936; p. 1, col. 6.

[22] See P. B. Whale, "The Theory of International Trade in the Absence of an International Standard," *op. cit.*, p. 32 n.

claimed by the editor of *The Economist*[23] that whereas a capital inflow in the form of a gold import into a gold-standard country tends to reduce interest rates and hence to exert an inflationary influence upon the money structure, a similar inflow of funds into England, when offset by the Equalization Account, may have a deflationary effect upon the banking system unless the Bank of England takes steps to correct it. The example cited may be used by way of illustration. If British foreign balances increase, the Account sells bills, presumably to the joint-stock banks gaining the deposits, and with the sterling proceeds it buys the foreign exchange offered (which it converts into gold). The joint-stock banks have acquired deposits and Treasury bills in equal amounts; but inasmuch as their reserves remain unchanged, their cash proportion is reduced and any attempts on their part to restore this ratio will make credit less easy. It should be noted, however, that this assumes that the original increase in foreign deposits is hoarded by foreigners, not spent on goods or investments. If the latter assumption holds true and if the joint-stock banks do not allow any reduction to take place in their cash ratios, the inflow of funds would be deflationary unless the Bank of England takes offsetting steps by buying either securities in the open market or gold from the Equalization Account.

In the United States, however, an inflow of capital, even if offset by Treasury borrowing in the amount of the gold, would not of itself be deflationary. In the first place, the foreign funds which have flowed to this country between January 2, 1935, and September 30, 1936, and brought gold with them have gone in large part into the stock market, that is, they have been used not entirely to create foreign balances but rather in goodly proportion to increase domestic deposits. These domestic deposits are first of all placed in the hands of sellers of securities, going thereafter into general circulation. In the second place, the banking system in the United States has been possessed of excess reserves since early 1933, so that no effort has been made to keep reserve ratios constant. So long as excess reserves exist,

[23] *Money and Banking Leader*, CXXV, No. 4859 (October 10, 1936), 68.

therefore, and so long as funds coming into New York are used in good part for security transactions, the Treasury policy of offsetting gold imports by sales of bills in the amount of the gold bought by it, prevents any increase in the banking system's excess reserves[24] but does not prevent a one-to-one expansion in deposits in the hands of the public. To the extent to which the gold import increases demand deposits at the disposal of Americans, it is, therefore, inflationary, despite the fact that it is offset.

Selective Offsetting of Gold Flows. While the objective of stabilization funds at the time of their origin was to enable the monetary authorities to keep a desired degree of exchange stability without being involved in any long-run commitment as to the gold value of the currency, yet the credit type of stabilization fund, or its equivalent in the United States of Treasury or Federal Reserve open-market operations associated with gold movements, has come to be thought of primarily in connection with the problem of the foreign influences which should be allowed to affect the credit base. The problem of stabilizing the currency for short periods is not essentially a new one, since even on the old gold standard the various sovereign powers continually enjoyed the right to alter the value of their currencies. They were likewise free to offset gold movements or so to alter their banking statutes that they might do so. The development of the stabilization-fund technique has worked principally to give countries an opportunity to regularize the basis on which decisions may be taken concerning the question of whether gold movements shall be offset in their effects on the national credit structures.[25] The 1924-27 gold-offsetting

[24] Actually the policy decreases excess reserves, although it leaves the level of total reserves unchanged, since the legal reserves of the banking system will increase when deposits are increased and leave a smaller amount of free or excess reserves.

[25] This applies primarily to stabilization funds of the credit type. The gold stabilization funds set up by France and Switzerland in September, 1936, at the time of the gold-bloc devaluation, had as their principal objective the preservation of secrecy in case the repatriation of capital was not as enthusiastic as was hoped for. In Switzerland, when gold was offered in profusion to the Swiss National Bank the Bank refused to buy all the gold available (see *The New York Times*, December 29, 1936, p. 29, col. 4). This is essentially a negation of

policy of the Federal Reserve system was part of no integrated long-run policy of credit control, but was rather a response to what were then considered special circumstances.

If the practice of offsetting gold movements under certain circumstances is to be regularized, certain canons of practice will have to be established. It has been the purpose of this monograph to indicate that when gold moves as a result of a change in the ownership of short-term balances, the credit structure should not be altered, or, in other words, the gold movement should be offset. Perhaps this cardinal point may be made clearer by an analysis of possible types of gold movements.

Whitaker has presented a classification of various types of gold movements, which Beach considers "admirable in many respects."[26] He distinguishes: (1) producers, (2) commercial, and (3) financial or money-market shipments. Financial shipments differ from commercial shipments in that "A commercial shipment of gold always serves to discharge a previous international debt, but an initial financial shipment creates a debt and looks to a future and early return shipment of gold."[27]

This set of distinctions does not go far enough for the present purposes. While it is unscientific to link together various items in the balance of payments in causal relations, yet on a rough basis, it may be permissible to suggest another system of classification. Excluding producers' gold shipments, which belong in the commodity balance of trade of the country of export, we may distinguish the following types of gold movements on the gold standard among financially developed communities:

1. Those movements resulting from a capital export at long term and occasioned by the fact that foreign demand for the coun-

the gold standard and would tend, under different circumstances than those which prevailed, to drive the Swiss franc to a premium unless the Bank of Switzerland were willing to acquire foreign balances. A policy of sterilization, while expensive in that the Swiss government would have to pay interest on the debt outstanding to cover gold purchases, would seem to be more in keeping with what has been termed, since September 26, 1936, the "new gold standard."

[26] See Beach, *op. cit.*, p. 24.

[27] See A. C. Whitaker, "The Ricardian Theory of Gold Movements and Professor Laughlin's Views of Money," *Quarterly Journal of Economics*, XVIII (1904), 224.

try's goods at the first stage of income change in the transfer mechanism is not sufficiently flexible to permit the transfer in goods without delay and because sufficient short-term capital is not imported to allow that part of the loan not immediately transferred in goods to be transferred through a balancing of short-term against long-term capital items.[28]

2. Those flows that occurred regularly in the business cycle in pre-war England as a result of cyclical fluctuations of short-term capital, toward England in prosperity, and away from England in depression, occasioned by cyclical fluctuations in the short-term rate of interest.[29]

3. Net gold movements over fairly long periods of time which are due to deep-seated disequilibrium occasioned by the resistance of money costs to deflation at a time when the rate of exchange is being held constant. These occur most clearly when the movement of long-term capital is unchanged (from that which it had been before) and when short-term capital is not moving, on balance, or is moving to the country losing gold.[30]

4. Gold movements resulting from changes in international demand, in costs of transfer, or in real costs of production for foreign trade goods, and occurring in the transition from one equilibrium position to another in relation to the long-run adjustment of costs internationally.[31]

5. Movements due to seasonal factors in the income balance of payments which are not offset by opposite seasonal movements in capital items.[32]

6. Gold movements due to shifts in liquid of speculative short-term funds from country to country where the rate of interest fails to guide capital movements because of high estimates of the desired premium for risk, or because of higher anticipated profits from capital appreciation in countries with lower prevailing rates of interest.[33]

These types of gold flow, classified analytically on the basis of the present monograph may be more concisely described as

[28] See above, pp. 81-86. [29] See above, pp. 135-37.
[30] See above, pp. 114-16. [31] See above, pp. 104-8.
[32] See J. M. Keynes, *Monetary Reform*, p. 116. See also M. A. Rifaat, *The Monetary System of Egypt*, 1935, pp. 50-52, especially table xi, p. 51, where the seasonal flow of gold in and out of pre-war Egypt (before the establishment of the sterling-exchange standard) is recorded. The one-crop system of exports brought gold into the country when cotton was being marketed abroad in the fall, and this gold was paid out again from January to August.
[33] See above, pp. 163-66.

follows: (1) long-term capital export flows; (2) short-term capital cyclical flows; (3) fundamental disequilibrium flows; (4) flows resulting from changes in the substantive course of trade (other than capital movements at long-term); (5) seasonal gold flows; and (6) abnormal capital gold flows.

It is exceedingly difficult at times to assign a particular gold movement to one or the other category. The tremendous import of gold to the United States from 1934 to date (January, 1937) may be taken as an example. When data on the capital movements between the United States and foreign countries for the period January, 1935, to September, 1936, inclusive,[34] were published, and when the large volume of purchases of foreign and American securities in the United States was revealed, it might have been said that a substantial part of the gold flow was the direct result of the long-term capital movement. This would make it fall in the first category. According to another view, the American devaluation of the dollar to an undervalued level might be held responsible, bringing the gold movement into the third type. Finally, those who believe that the accelerated rate of purchase of securities in this market was due to speculative buying in anticipation of capital gains and to capital flight from Europe in the form of short-term balances and security purchases, might prefer to classify the gold movement under the sixth type—that is, to view it as caused by an abnormal movement of capital to the United States. The answer to this perplexing question is of real importance, since upon it should be based the decision as to whether or not to permit the gold movement to have its full effect upon the credit structure.[35]

[34] See U. S. Treasury Department, *Statistics of Capital Movements between the United States and Foreign Countries and of Purchases and Sales of Foreign Exchange in the United States*, summary Table A, p. 12.

[35] Without going too deeply into this question, it is my own view that the gold movement to the United States since 1933 was largely of Type 3 prior to 1935, but thereafter predominately of Type 6. That the long-term capital movement to the United States is not a normal one (Type 1) is easily seen from the low rates of interest here and the higher rates prevailing in every other country in the world, with England no exception. Whether in 1936 an upward revaluation of the dollar would have stopped much of the security purchase is a question that cannot be answered. If the dollar was then seriously undervalued, however, it did not manifest itself in a disproportionate increase in

The first and fourth types of gold movement, those resulting from long-term capital export or from minor changes[36] in the substantive course of trade, should be permitted to have their full effect upon the credit supply and the banking system, since the gold movement is here a symptom of the necessity of changing from one level of equilibrium to another. In the one case the deflation or the inflation attendant upon the gold flow resulting from the movement of long-term capital aids the real transfer of the capital in goods. In the other, the necessity for a readjustment in the items in the income balance is met by the response of the credit system to the gold shift.

With respect to deep-seated disequilibria, arising either from a violent disturbance in the substantive course of trade or from a monetary inflation or deflation within one country, which is not matched abroad, no *a priori* judgments may be laid down. In some cases, perhaps, it will be well to allow the gold flow to have its effect in changing the income balance or in readjusting the credit situation by imposing deflation on an inflating system or fostering inflation in a deflating economy. Under other circumstances, however, it may prove more feasible to readjust the rate of exchange. In some cases the choice does not make a great deal of difference to the country as a whole so far as real income is concerned, though it may affect the distribution of that income. Such an example is that afforded by the "young country" in a world depression, when the demand for the few products on which its real income depends decreases. If this demand is inelastic with respect to price, currency depreciation will not increase real income, since foreigners will not buy sufficiently greater amounts at the reduced prices to enable the country

exports relative to imports. Perhaps the most important cause of the import of capital through security transactions was the fact that England and the sterling bloc were ahead of the United States on the road to recovery, so that higher profits were anticipated here than in those countries; whereas during the period up to gold-bloc devaluation at least, the other European countries not subject to exchange controls had not yet given sure indications that they were to experience recovery.

[36] A major change in the conditions of trade, of course, would entail a fundamental disequilibrium in the international system and would have to be treated as such.

concerned to purchase increased amounts of imports in terms of foreign currencies. It will, however, sustain the incomes of the producers of the export goods in terms of the local currency. On the other hand, it may make interest on debt more difficult to raise when the debts are denominated in foreign currencies. Deflation spreads the loss of income more slowly, unless the deflation takes place by means of direct measures. Both methods combined may be preferable to the use of either alone. But no hard and fast rules may be laid down concerning which response should be undertaken. In the case of large trading countries gold seldom moves first in disequilibrium condition of this sort, despite the Thornton-Mill price-specie-flow theory, since short-term capital is much more sensitive than gold. It is only for the smaller countries that the gold supply is a useful indication of the state of equilibrium existing between the balance of payments, the monetary situation, and the exchange rate. For them, moreover, the question of whether to let the gold flow have its effect upon the monetary system cannot be decided without a full examination of the other pertinent factors.

The remaining types of gold flow, the cyclical, the seasonal, and that caused by abnormal capital movements, should probably be uniformly offset. The complete argument to sustain this contention is long and complex and will not be attempted here. The first type comes under our general rule that when a gold movement results from a short-term capital movement the effects of the gold movement should be offset. Likewise the third type clearly falls within this rule, since funds moving to a country for purposes of short-term speculation or for temporary safekeeping are liable to be withdrawn without notice; and any credit expansion based on them or on the gold brought into a country as a result of them is precariously founded. The seasonal movements of gold are happily no great problem today, as a result of the development of more highly integrated banking practice. When they take place, however, they should be permitted to have little effect, if the changing season tends to reverse them completely.

As a corollary of these remarks about practice with relation to gold movements, it follows that short-term capital movements may be somewhat similarly analyzed with respect to their origin in the balance of payments. When short-term capital movements are accompanied by gold flows, neither the shift in the ownership of deposits nor the increase or decrease in gold should be permitted to affect the banking system. When a change in short-term balances occurs without a gold movement, however, it becomes necessary to decide whether it requires a response in the banking system. An increase in gold without a change in net short-term foreign assets or liabilities may be due either to a long-term capital movement, a deep-seated equilibrium change, or a change in the substantive course of trade. Similarly, a change in net short-term foreign assets or liabilities without a change in gold movements may arise from one of the same causes. An increase in net short-term foreign assets (decrease in net liabilities) should be regarded as an increase in gold. In effect it is an addition to claims on gold abroad or a subtraction to claims of foreigners on the domestic gold supply. An increase in short-term liabilities to foreigners (an increase in foreign short-term assets) should be regarded as a decrease in gold.

Recognition of Types of Gold Flow. There remains the problem of distinguishing among the various types of gold flow when they take place, in order that the appropriate response can be made to them. This is not a problem of theory, but one requiring experience and judgment. The most that the theorist is able to do is to mark the outlines of the problem and to leave to the combined efforts of the foreign-exchange trader and the central banker, both acting after consultation with the international-trade theorist and the monetary theorist, the task of directing the operations of the system.

Happily, in most countries today a signal advance has been made toward the implementation of this approach to the problem by the collection of detailed data on international capital movements. The various types of series available for study will be found in the Appendix.

Both the data which are published and other confidential

figures being gathered in other countries give the central banker a much greater opportunity to conceive the problem in terms of the realities of the given situation. To take but one example, the data on short-term assets and liabilities now possessed by the Bank of England, if available in 1925, would probably have lessened considerably any desire upon the part of the authorities to return to the gold standard at the pre-war sterling rate.

Summary. The development of the stabilization-fund technique, originally devised to give flexibility to the monetary authorities' power to regulate the foreign exchanges from the point of view of rate fluctuation, called attention to the problem of what foreign influences should be allowed to play a part in the domestic banking situation and what influences should be conteracted. Whereas under the gold standard as it had existed before 1931 movements of gold were offset in their effects on bank reserves through open-market operations, no clear expression of opinion had been given as to the wisdom of such steps as a part of considered policy, except by orthodox critics who universally condemned it. With the development of the credit stabilization fund, however, it was found that all movements of capital in and out of the money market could be readily offset in their effects. Thus, for example, if the stabilization-fund technique is applied to all movements of capital in and out of a country, none of those movements affect the money market except as they alter the reserve ratios of the banks. As funds come into the market, the stabilization fund absorbs them by issuing securities with which to buy the foreign exchange offered; as funds leave the market, the stabilization fund sells the foreign exchange (or gold) demanded and with the proceeds in the local currency, retires securities formerly issued to the market, thus restoring funds to it. The money market may be influenced if central bank policy requires it; and these changes may coincide with operations of the stabilization fund. The central bank may buy gold from or sell gold to the stabilization fund. But so far as the operations of the fund itself are concerned, the money market is effectively insulated against outside influences except as the monetary authorities desire to let them have their effects.

The use of stabilization funds equipped with gold does not operate in this way. If the gold fund sells gold to the central bank at the outset of its operations, thereafter using the currency, and proceeds to supply foreigners with exchange on that country, using gold to supply foreign exchange to the market when the exchange is weak, the domestic currency proceeds of the gold sales being deposited with the central bank, all operations of the fund affect directly the banking system's reserves. When it is desired to prevent this effect, open-market policy conducted by the central bank, fund, or treasury authorities must be coördinated with the operations of the stabilization fund.

Thus while the open-market powers of central banks, as they existed prior to 1931, provided the power to offset movements of funds between countries, these powers have now been regularized by the development of the stabilization-fund technique. Clearly, however, not all movements of funds should be offset. If this were done, the entire international regulatory credit mechanism would break down, leaving no indications of the development of maladjustments between economic systems. The simplest rule for the operation of a policy of offsetting gold movements is that of offsetting those which are brought about by equivalent movements of short-term capital, that is, to consider gold and short-term capital together, and to take no monetary steps in response to a movement in either one when the sum total of both is zero. It follows from this that when one moves without the other, the monetary response should follow. Whether this response should take place in the credit system or in the rate of exchange (since sometimes the response of the monetary system demanded by a movement in gold or short-term funds would be of too far-reaching a character to be accomplished easily through the credit mechanism) is impossible to tell except in the particular circumstances surrounding the case in question.

Authorities on central banking and stabilization funds are

in a much better position today than they were formerly to determine their short-run policies with respect to the requirements of the international monetary situation, because of the fact that data on short-term capital movements and international security transactions are now being gathered in most of the important financial centers of the world. International credit control has made considerable progress since the days of the Macmillan report, thanks to the systematized collection and study of data dealing with the ebb and flow of capital in and out of the world's chief financial centers.

XIV

INTERNATIONAL MONETARY INTERDEPENDENCE

The present discussion of the role of short-term capital movements in the balance of payments, on the one hand and in the domestic monetary system, on the other, has been essentially an attempt to throw light both on several of the theoretical problems and several of the purely mechanical ones involved in international monetary relations. The entire discussion has presupposed that international monetary relations will continue to exist. Should international trade be abandoned in favor of autarchy, the problem would largely disappear. On the other hand, should the capitalistic system be superseded by the planned state, whether corporative in higher degree than those of the present day or communistic, the planned barter in international trade which would take the place of the open-market system would render much of the present discussion irrelevant.

With international trade playing an important part in the welfare of nations and with an open-market system prevailing in internal and external economic relationships (in an important part of the world at least) it is vital that the question of international monetary organization be discussed. The assumptions on which this monograph is based do not necessarily imply an acceptance of these institutions by the author. They are needed, however, to give point to the problem.

It is perhaps unnecessary to labor the conclusion reached in Chapter XI, that it is impossible, on the assumptions just noted, to disregard the problem of international monetary relations. So long as the economy depends in some way on external trade, events which have their origin abroad will affect it. A monetary policy based entirely upon the requirements of the internal economy will be based at one remove on external factors. Under these circumstances it is impossible to say that the external problem can be avoided by some expedient such as allowing the exchange rate to take care of itself. Such a decision would constitute a disposition of the problem that would in no way insulate the economy from the outside world. The response of external events would merely be felt through a different sequence of economic stimuli and repercussions.

Types of Monetary Organization. Of the various types of organization which have been suggested on the international monetary front, leaving foreign-exchange control out of consideration, perhaps the extremes are a completely free and uncontrolled rate of foreign exchange, on the one hand, and on the other, a rigid gold standard, unrelieved by the intermediation of central banking.[1] In either case, it is unnecessary to add, the economy will be affected by changes in international demand, changes in tariffs, changes in the costs of production of international trade goods, capital movements, and changes in the money incomes of foreign nations. When the foreign-exchange rate is uncontrolled, the economy will be affected through changes in this rate; when a rigid gold standard is in operation, the economy will be affected through movements of gold which result in changes in the domestic money supply.

When these two extremes are presented in the foregoing bald form, it is evident that they are both distasteful. What is desired is a compromise between them that will achieve the greatest possible stability of exchange relationships and at the same time permit each country the utmost freedom to pursue its own monetary policy. Such a compromise, however, is impossible to achieve unless the monetary ends sought in the domestic sphere by all the countries concerned coincide, at least roughly. It is quite out of the question, for example, to expect that the

[1] These extremes are mentioned by, among others, Dr. Williams in a paper given before the American Economic Association on December 29, 1936 (see J. H. Williams, "The Adequacy of Existing Currency Mechanisms under Varying Circumstances," *American Economic Review*, XXVII (1937), Supplement, 158-59). Between these extremes he lists eight compromises and suggests that the real debate in the international monetary sphere is over the merits of the two or three central alternatives.

sterling-dollar relationship prevailing at the present time can be preserved if the United States undergoes a rapid monetary expansion, increasing its national money income by fifty per-cent, while at the same time the English national money in-come is maintained stable. This will occur only if the classical expectation of an increase in American imports from England, along with reduced exports to England, coincides with a flow of capital from England to the United States in search of profits to be made as a result of the expansion. When the national money income has expanded the full amount desired in the United States, however, and if England has been able to avoid at the same time an inflation arising from the increased demand for its exports and a deflation arising from its loss of capital, the original capital flow from England will cease or even will return to some extent. This will have the result that England will be called upon either to allow its national money income to expand or to allow its currency to appreciate. When the choice is between internal deflation and foreign-exchange de-preciation, economists and those charged with authority in monetary matters are generally prone to let the exchange rate fend for itself. Where the choice lies between exchange appre-ciation and internal inflation, however, it does not follow that exchange appreciation will be as readily singled out for the burden of the adjustment.

What is being sought in the maze of currency and banking experiments which have been undertaken since the war is con-trol over the monetary mechanism: control, on the one hand, over the national money income and, on the other, over the value of the currency unit in dealings with foreign countries. Control of the latter sort is understood. The gold standard (despite the inability of man to regulate the rate at which the world's monetary stock of gold is increased annually) can be made to control the external value of a currency, although in times when the world supply of gold is not expanding at the pace of the advance in the production of goods, this can be done only by exposing the economy to inflationary or defla-tionary pressure or by devising new controls to economize or sterilize the use of gold. Control over the national money income is being achieved more slowly, although, with the advances in monetary theory and practice since 1930 and the development of the devices of open-market policy, government spending, government subsidies, and discriminatory taxation, signal progress has been made in the direction of such control. What will be needed when these two controls have been perfected is a theory integrating them. Some progress has already been made along this line by the development of the stabilization fund, of open-market operations designed to offset certain types of gold flows, of artificially-widened gold points, and so forth. But there remains much of the problems of controlling the national money income and of relating that control to movements in the substantive course of trade and to changes in the national money income in other countries.

The Role of Short-Term Capital Movements. Most writers interested in the latter phase of this problem have dwelt upon the subject of gold and the gold standard. It has been the object of this study, however, to indicate that short-term capital movements also should always be considered, especially when financially developed communities are under discussion. Whereas the fundamental link between money systems has been gold and whereas it may still remain so for the purpose of fixing mint parities and limits of permissible foreign exchange rate fluctuation, yet short-term capital is a much more active item in the balance of payments from day to day. Short-term capital and gold should be taken as the principal guides to monetary policy so far as the latter is concerned with the preservation of foreign-exchange equilibrium.

This foreign-exchange rate equilibrium is not solely a function of the demand and supply of exchange at a given time. Back of demand and supply stand the price and cost factors which, together with the various demands for internationally traded goods, govern merchandise trade and the service items. Back of them, too, stand the demand and supply of savings at home and abroad which determine the movement of long-term capital and a complex of psychological factors which underlie the autonomous movement of long- and short-term capital. A disequilibrium in the balance of payments, therefore, requires an adjustment of the national price and cost structure, or more briefly, an adjustment of the national money income to the balance of payments and the rate of exchange; or an adjustment of the rate of exchange to the national money income. Despite the fact that it is thus far impossible to arrive at accurate statistical estimates of disequilibrium through costs or prices, because of the difficulties of choosing a basic period of equilibrium and because it is well-nigh impossible to allow for changes in the substantive course of trade, yet some more accurate idea of equilibrium can be obtained from examination of gold plus or minus net short-term foreign assets or liabilities.

A recent attempt has been made to suggest that equilibrium in the balance of payments should be defined in terms only of short-term capital movements.[2] The emphasis on short-term capital movements, following their long neglect in this connection should be welcomed. It may be pointed out, however, that if equilibrium in the balance of payments be related to the broader problem of the proper relationships among the national money income, the balance of payments, and the rate of exchange, the omission of gold from the definition is a serious one. To take a simple case, if a central bank of a country on an exchange standard decides to shift its foreign exchange reserves from one country to another, the sale of the exchange on the country where the reserves were originally held and the purchase of the exchange on the country to which they are to be moved may well cause a gold flow from the former to the latter. If gold be the evidence of disequilibrium in the balance of payments, requiring a response either in the monetary system or in the rate of exchange, then the first country should deflate and the second country should expand its means of payment. If

[2] Past and current; i.e., "a country's international payments are 'out of equilibrium' whenever short-term funds are moving to or from it, net . . . or whenever the short-term or demand balances on either side of the country's international accounts currently exceed or fall below the normal working requirements." See J. W. Angell, "Equilibrium in International Payments: the United States, 1919-1935," in *Explorations in Economics*, 1936, p. 14.

short-term capital movements be the sole criterion, then the first country having experienced a reduction in its net short-term liabilities—an outflow of short-term capital—should inflate and the second country, with increased net short-term foreign liabilities, should deflate. But if the gold outflow and inflow be set off against the short-term capital outflow and inflow, respectively, then it is seen that no change in the means of payment should be permitted to take place, which requires that the gold movements should be offset in both countries. This is evidently what should take place from the point of view of the relations of the national money income, the rate of exchange, and the balance of payments, since the equilibrium existing among these factors has not been disturbed fundamentally by the outside central bank's desire to change the form of its liquid reserves.

If net gold plus or minus net short-term foreign assets or liabilities be the criterion of equilibrium in the balance of payments and in the factors lying back of the various items in the balance, it follows that if either gold or short-term capital move of itself without an offsetting response in the other or if gold flows out at the same time that net short-term liabilities to foreigners are increasing or flows in when net short-term foreign assets are mounting, a disturbance in equilibrium has occurred. If this disturbance is due to seasonal factors in the balance of payments, it should be disregarded. If it is slight, it may be advisable to maintain the exchange rate and permit the called-for adjustment in the national monetary income to take place at its own pace. When the disturbance is an important one, however, and when it indicates a fundamental change in the conditions under which international trade is being carried on or a significant variation of the national money income at home or abroad, a choice must be made between changing the national money income in the required direction or shifting the rate of exchange into the equilibrium position indicated by the changed circumstances.

International Repercussions of the Business Cycle. The most pressing domestic problem is that of eliminating the business cycle. The present writer adheres to the opinion that this is essentially a monetary problem and one that will cease to exist when monetary authorities obtain greater control over the national money income. Meanwhile the problem exists both as a monetary problem, with violent fluctuations in the national money income, and as a real problem, with similar fluctuations in employment and output. And so long as the business cycle exists as a real problem in one country or more, it will continue to exist in some degree for all countries; it will continue while men produce and exchange goods internationally in the open market.

For the small country dependent upon external trade for the maintenance of what it considers its optimum standard of living, the business cycle cannot be avoided if its foreign markets suffer from cycles. When the foreign money demand for its product falls off, it cannot depreciate its exchange rate, or deflate its national money income and continue to import and export in as large quantities as before, except in case foreign costs of production had fallen to the same extent as foreign national incomes. In this case there would be no business cycle abroad, if the business cycle is defined as a fluctuation in economic activity. Moreover, the small country is usually faced with the necessity to transfer interest and amortization charges on foreign debt previously contracted, which means in the face of the falling (generally inelastic) foreign demand, that it must sell a greater money volume of goods, when long-term capital imports dry up in depression, if it is to maintain its ability to import.

For the important trading country the advent of a business depression in a foreign country imposes an equally unpleasant dilemma. As money income falls in the latter country (that is, on the assumption that there are only two countries), the first can maintain equilibrium in the foreign exchanges either by deflating at an equal pace or by lowering its exchange rate in step with the deflation abroad. The first possibility will not be favorably regarded in the country trying to ward off depression; the second will not be approved by the foreign country trying to stem the tide of deflation. If the demand of the latter for the products of the former is flexible, that is, if it decreases faster than the national money income as a whole, then there is no means, neither deflation nor depreciation, by which the spread of deflation can be avoided. It is only if the demand of the depressed country for the other's goods and services is perfectly inflexible, that is, if no matter how low its income sinks it will continue to purchase the same quantity of imports at the same prices, that the export industries of the nondepressed country can rest unaffected by the depression.

The international problems involved in the appearance of deflation in one country are complex and important. The foregoing paragraph, which can only hastily suggest some of them, at least points the general conclusion that the primary responsibility of monetary authorities in all countries should be to eliminate or to modify the business cycle as much as they themselves can and by so doing to avoid a whole range of problems of perplexing difficulty.[3] Until this is accomplished, it is difficult to see economically, and probably impossible to see politically, how one country can avoid suffering important repercussions from the economic difficulties encountered by others.

International Trade Theory and the National Money Income. In conclusion, the opinion may be hazarded that perhaps the time has come to rewrite the theory of international trade in terms of the national money income. Toward the accomplishment of this task the present monograph has indicated only a few of the important monetary problems involved. It is hoped, however, that it has concentrated attention on a key variable in the balance of international payments, the movement of gold plus or minus changes in net short-term foreign assets.

Such a rewriting of the theory of international trade would not constitute a revision of the body of analysis that has been developing continuously from generation to generation from the days of Smith and Ricardo down to Taussig, Viner, Angell, Williams, and the other outstanding contributors to the field. It would be more in the way of a translation of that body of analysis from "real" terms to money terms. Such a translation

[3] See J. H. Williams, "The World's Monetary Dilemma," p. 67.

is, however, of vital importance if the subject of international trade is to be related to the principal topic of interest in the field of economics today—the business cycle. The need for it can be seen clearly in the case of the tariff. Thus far, the only orthodox argument in favor of tariffs has been the infant-industry argument. Were it possible to prove, however, that under given circumstances the imposition of a tariff relieves a country of deflationary pressure from abroad which is likely to become cumulative, the immediate loss in the real terms of trade would be small compared with the loss in domestic employment arising from the reduction in the national money income which the imposition of the tariff had spared the country.

Perhaps a tentative start can be made on this task of "translation" by emphasizing the suggestion made above that international equilibrium can be defined in terms of the effects of the balance of payments on the national money income.[4] A country's rate of exchange may be said to be in equilibrium when the balance of payments exerted no pressure on the country's banking system tending to increase or decrease the national money income. If the balance of payments tended to make the national money income rise, that is, if the country had a "favorable international margin" in the words of the Swedish economists, the currency could be said to be undervalued. If the balance of payments tended to make the national money income decline, the currency would be said to be overvalued.

Stated in these terms, the range of international trade and monetary problems can be seen to have an exceedingly important relevance to the domestic monetary problem—a relevance which economists absorbed with the problem of eliminating the business cycle in a theoretically "closed" economy have been apt to neglect. First, the periphery of the economy requires constant examination and close attention when the national money income is being controlled, in order to insure that the rate of exchange and the balance of payments are working in the same direction as the monetary expedients used primarily in the do-

[4] See pp. 103-4.

mestic sphere—open-market operations and government spending, primarily. Second, if the national money income is to be raised (for example) for the purpose of absorbing unemployed factors of production, it is necessary to consider at the time that such a change is planned what will be the end result so far as the balance of payments and the exchange rate are concerned. Otherwise it might be found that pressure from abroad makes necessary either an abandonment of inflationary plans, as appears to be the case in Japan today, or the establishment of a Four-Year Plan to render unnecessary dependence on cheap imported raw materials.

In a world without the business cycle it would be possible to discuss international trade in real terms and to indulge in pleasant academic debate over the merits of the sectional-price-level school and the shifts-in-demand school in relation to exports of long-term capital. When we live in a world in which the national income of a country can vary from $81,000,000,000 in one year to $38,000,000,000 four years later, and to $60,000,000,000 in another four years, it can be seen that the most important shifts in demand are those in the national money income. If in this world, too, monetary economists tacitly agree that a national money income which either remains stable or increases at a steady pace should be the objective of monetary policy, then it is necessary for the international trade economist to orient his thinking in terms of monetary, as well as real, factors.

APPENDIX

STATISTICS ON INTERNATIONAL SHORT-TERM CAPITAL MOVEMENTS

The present monograph has attempted to do no more than to outline some theoretical aspects of the role of short-term capital movements in the balance of payments, and to suggest a definition of foreign-exchange equilibrium which may afford a more comprehensive guide than gold movements to banking policy concerned with money in its international aspects. It has not dealt with the problem in statistical terms, however. The reasons for this are that, first, the original scope of the volume was sufficiently inclusive without a statistical exploration of the problems raised; and, secondly, the published data available to the student are still inadequate for a thoroughgoing statistical treatment of the subject.

The published data on the subject of short-term capital movements are of three kinds: (1) annual and (since 1934 in the United States) semi-annual balance-of-payments estimates; (2) banking statistics; and (3) capital movement statistics gathered by monetary and governmental authorities (largely since 1931) because of the inadequacy of the information afforded by categories 1 and 2.

Balance of Payments Statistics. Balance of payments estimates are inadequate as a guide to banking policy concerned with the preservation of foreign-exchange equilibrium because of their inaccuracy and their infrequency. The first charge is now losing force with respect to estimates of the capital items because of the fact that compilers of balance of payments figures in some countries are having an opportunity to rely on statistics gathered at more frequent intervals by monetary authorities, equipped with legal or other authority to require reports that were formerly on a voluntary and less regular basis.

It may be pointed out, however, that considerable inaccuracy remains in these data. This can be shown by reference to the residual items in the American balance of payments, which reflects errors and omissions which did not cancel out. Some part of this residual item may reflect movements of short-term capital;[1] but, on the other hand, part of it is undoubtedly due to other errors and omissions, particularly in estimates of long-term capital movements,[2] in merchandise imports improperly valued on consular invoices,[3] and in interest and dividend payments made to foreigners by Americans.[4] No justification exists for adding the residual item to the short-term capital item.[5]

It is perhaps necessary to emphasize the infrequency of balance of payments estimates. It is quite clear that movements within the year or half-year may take place in opposite directions, leaving no movement on balance and resulting in the fact that annual data have given an inadequate picture.[6] It may be worth while, however, to demonstrate this with a table of short-term capital movements for 1935 and for nine months of 1936.[7] It should be remembered that these data cover a period in which

[1] See the Department of Commerce, Bureau of Foreign and Domestic Commerce, *The Balance of International Payments of the United States in 1934*; "Trade Information Bulletin," No. 826, p. 14; and *Ibid.*, 1935, "Trade Information Bulletin," No. 833, pp. 3-4.

[2] *Ibid.;* and the 1934 study, p. 74.

[3] The 1935 study, p. 4.

[4] The 1934 study, p. 13.

[5] This is the procedure followed by Angell, "Equilibrium in International Payments: the United States, 1919-1935," *op. cit.*, p. 21, although he does not enter a strong defense for it (see note). Angell refers to the 1934 study on p. 74, where it is suggested that the 1927 and 1930 excessively large residuals may perhaps be accounted for by unreported American purchases of outstanding long-term issues in the international security market. If this was the case, then the residual item may have added to the net export of long-term capital and may not have offset the inflow of short-term capital.

[6] White emphasizes the point that monthly data are desirable (see *The French International Accounts*, p. 33 n.). It is a commentary on the accuracy of balance of payments data of several years ago that the figures used by White for the 1926-30 period were entirely revised in 1932 (see 1932 study, pp. 34-35).

[7] Derived from *Statistics of Capital movements between the United States and Foreign Countries* (hereinafter, *Statistics*), p. 12. A mere glance at the column of the weekly movements of short-term banking funds reveals the fluctuating character of short-term capital. The range is from a capital inflow of $91,586,000 in the week ended May 29, 1935 (at the height of the French crisis of that period) to an outflow of $49,535,000 in the week ended July 1, 1936. The latter figure, however, does not represent a true outflow of short-term funds but rather reflects a cash redemption of Canadian long-term securities (see opposite *Canada* for the week ended July 1, p. 60, "Purchases of Foreign Securities in the United States for Foreign Account").

the inflow of short-term capital into the United States by reason of the recurring crises in the gold bloc was extremely high.

IMPORT OF SHORT-TERM CAPITAL INTO THE UNITED STATES

1935	
Quarter ended March 27	$ 215,232,000
Quarter ended June 26	336,661,000
Quarter ended September 25	147,725,000
Quarter ended December 31	263,929,000
1933 (total)	$ 963,547,000[8]
1935 (quarterly average)	($240,887,000)
1936	
Quarter ended March 25	$ 19,203,000
Quarter ended June 24	293,761,000
Quarter ended September 30	76,561,000
1936 (total for nine months)	$ 389,525,000
1936 (nine-month quarterly average)	($129,842,000)
Total (twenty-one months)	$1,353,072,000
Twenty-one month quarterly average	($193,296,000)

Banking Statistics. Figures for net short-term capital movements are indicated by changes in banks' foreign assets and liabilities. Such figures are, however, not complete. In the United States, for example, foreign balances due to banks are the only items reported, and these for Federal Reserve Banks and Federal Reserve member banks combined make up only about 30 to 50 percent of the total foreign short-term liabilities as reported by the Department of Commerce on an annual basis.[9]

In the case of countries which habitually maintain an excess of foreign short-term assets over short-term liabilities to foreigners, however, it is likely that a greater portion of the weekly or monthly movement of short-term capital will be revealed by an examination of banking statistics. In Sweden, for example, the foreign exchange reserves of the Riksbank and the large joint-stock banks probably comprise the bulk of the foreign

[8] The discrepancy between this figure and that given by the Department of Commerce for the movement in net short-term banking funds, $970,000,000 (see 1935 study, p. 50) is due to the inclusion by the latter of the inflow of funds through brokerage balances (a reduction of debit balances owed by foreigners to American brokers) amounting to $6,039,000 for the year 1935 (see *Statistics*, summary Table B, p. 13).

[9] See Bank for International Settlements, *Sixth Annual Report*, 1936, p. 36.

short-term assets of the country, while their liabilities to foreigners presumably also make up the greater part of short-term foreign indebtedness. Thus, movements in the total "net short-term foreign assets of the Riksbank and joint-stock banks" may be taken as a rough approximation of the short-term capital for the country. Similarly, the net short-term foreign assets of the Issue and Banking Departments of the Commonwealth Bank of Australia and those of the so-called "trading banks" may be taken as a crude indication of the movement of short-term capital to and from Australia.

For the majority of countries, however, banking statistics are so incomplete as to be of little use in the problem of obtaining a continuous series at frequent intervals covering the movement of short-term capital. The difficulty is not with the frequency of such series, since the central banking statements are generally issued at weekly intervals and the commercial banks' statements usually appear on a monthly basis.

Under certain conditions and circumstances, however, the statement of a central bank may cast important light on the problem. Such was the case with respect to the Bank of France's holdings of foreign exchange from the stabilization crisis of August, 1926, until the eventual liquidation of the Bank's foreign exchange portfolio in 1931 and 1932. For the period between the Banking Law of August, 1926, and the Banking Law of June, 1928, it is necessary to make estimates of these foreign-exchange holdings, which are included under "Miscellaneous Assets."[10] But with the definitive stabilization of the franc in June, 1928, the gain in gold and net foreign short-term assets is clearly revealed merely by reference to the Bank of France statement.

Special Reports. Finally, there are statistics gathered by monetary authorities for the purpose of informing themselves—and, on all too few occasions, others—concerning the international movement of capital. The Macmillan report set the fashion in this regard, although it confined its attention entirely to bank-

[10] See J. H. Rogers, *The Process of Inflation in France,* p. 185.

ing foreign assets and liabilities.[11] Since the publication of the Macmillan report, especially since the setting up of the Exchange Equilization Account, the Bank of England and the Exchequer are believed to have instituted a continuous system of reporting for joint-stock banks, bankers, and discount houses. It is believed that international security transactions are not covered by the reporting system, although it is well known that the Bank of England, the Committee on Foreign Loans (set up by the Exchequer in April, 1935), and the Exchequer itself, examine all new foreign issues with a view to exercising a veto over them. The collected data are not made public.

Similarly, in Belgium a reporting system has been in effect since March, 1935, whereby member banks and bankers report transactions in foreign exchange to the National Bank of Belgium. It is not clear whether international security transactions are covered by these reports. In France, frequent reports of all foreign assets are required by a series of laws extending down to June, 1936. Although M. Auriol, French Minister of Finance in the Front Populaire government, reported in a speech before the Chamber of Deputies on June 19, 1936, that French holdings of gold abroad, foreign short-term assets, and foreign securities totaled 25,000,000,000 francs (presumably at that time); no further figures have been released to the public.

In Canada, where the international traffic in securities is of such peculiar importance to the economy because of the number of domestic loans denominated in sterling and/or American dollars, in addition to Canadian dollars,[12] the Dominion Bureau of Statistics has issued since the beginning of 1935 a monthly report entitled, "Sales and Purchases of Securities between Canada and Other Countries." Other data for long- and short-term capital movements, except for those that may be gleaned from statements of the Bank of Canada and the chartered banks, appear only in the annual balance of payments estimates.

In conclusion, we may devote some attention to the *Statistics*

[11] See Appendix, Table 9 (*op. cit.*, p. 299). For a discussion of the accuracy of these data, see above, p. 128 n.

[12] See Bank of Canada, *Annual Report* for 1935, *Federal Reserve Bulletin*, April, 1936, p. 258.

of Capital Movements issued by the United States Treasury Department[13] in November, 1936.

With respect to short-term capital movements the figures published in *Statistics* do not have as wide a coverage as those of the Department of Commerce, since they do include only data for banks, bankers, brokers, and dealers and do not include short-term capital movements which take place at the instance of corporations and individuals domiciled in the United States. Weekly reports from those corporations which transact a foreign business would impose an unnecessary hardship on them, and it may safely be assumed that the volatile portion of short-term capital movements is covered by the reports of banks, bankers, brokers, and dealers. The discrepancy between the Department of Commerce figure for total foreign short-term liabilities of the United States is on the order of $105,000,000.[14] Individuals in the United States with short-term foreign assets or debts, except known exporters or importers, are covered presumably by neither method of reporting.

In the separation of long-term from short-term capital movements, two important problems appear. The first has already been mentioned in this study,[15] viz., the problem of estimating what part of the international traffic in outstanding securities is speculative and hence essentially short-term in character. The second problem appears when the *Statistics* is studied in conjunction with redemption and refunding operations in international long-term loans (in the United States, foreign dollar bonds for the most part). It is a problem in timing the international movement of capital.

If a foreign government or corporation redeems bonds in New York, the operation involves an inflow of long-term capital to the United States in the amount of the issue redeemed from American holders. If the funds for the redemption are acquired

[13] The legal authorization for the Treasury's requirement of reports is to be found in sec. 5b of the Trading with the Enemy Act of October 6, 1917, as amended by sec. 2 of the Act of March 9, 1933, together with sec. 8 of the Executive Order of January 15, 1934, and the Treasury Regulations of November 12, 1934, issued under that order.

[14] See *Balance of Payments*, the 1935 study, p. 52.

[15] See above, p. 4 and pp. 223 ff.

in New York in the form of balances some time ahead of the actual redemption, however, the operation is reflected in weekly capital-movement data as (1) an inflow of short-term funds and later (2) an inflow of long-term capital balanced by an outflow of short-term funds. Evidently, the capital movement actually takes place when the dollar balances are acquired. For the purpose of obtaining a true picture of the international movement of capital the initial acquisition of dollars should be regarded as an inflow of long-term capital and no attention should be paid to the latter actual redemption.

Similar adjustments should be made in the case of refunding operations. In this case, if the refunded issue is all held by Americans and if the refunding issue be all bought by Americans, no international capital movement takes place. Yet if an interval elapse between the flotation of the refunding issue and the redemption of the refunded issue, during which interval the proceeds of the former are held as balances,[16] violent fluctuations in short-term capital movements and in long-term capital movements, each taken separately, will be recorded. If it be desired to study the short-term capital movement by itself, these fluctuations should be eliminated.

An illustration of the types of adjustment which should be made to eliminate the effects of (for example) refunding operations on statistics of short-term capital movements is afforded by the borrowing operations of the Dominion of Canada in January, 1936. On January 1, 1936, the Dominion of Canada floated an issue of $40,000,000 of 2 percent three-year notes to retire one month in advance of maturity $20,000,000 of five-month notes dated September 1, 1935, and $20,000,000 of two-month notes dated December 1, 1935. On January 15, 1936, the Dominion floated a $48,000,000 issue of twenty-five-year 3¼ percent bonds, of which the proceeds to it were $45,052,800. These funds were used, together with additional Treasury cash,

[16] This interval may be as long as six months. See, e.g., the prospectus of the $70,000,000 Argentine Republic 4 percent Sinking Fund Issue of February 15, 1937, p. 3, where it is stated that the proceeds of the issue are to be deposited on March 1, 1937 with the Fiscal Agents of the two issues to be retired, such issues to be called for redemption on September 1, 1937.

to retire (1) $40,000,000 of 4½ percent ten-year bonds of February 1, 1926; (2) $2,737,986.67 of 2 percent Treasury bills dated April 30, 1935, and maturing January 30, 1936; and (3) $5,418,000 of 2 percent Temporary Guaranteed Bonds of the Canadian National Railway Company, dated February 15, 1935, and maturing January 30, 1936.

The January 1, 1936, three-year notes involve no week-to-week adjustment in the figures, since the new notes were floated and the matured notes were redeemed all in the same week.[17] The summary table, without adjustment, records a net inflow of $45,051,000 among short-term banking fund transactions for the week ended January 8, 1936, and a net outflow of $8,234,000 among security transactions (including changes in brokerage balances).[18] But in this case no adjustment should be made between long- and short-term capital movements, since the redemption of the two-month and five-month notes by securities of longer than one-year maturity actually involves an inflow of short-term funds and an outflow of long-term capital.

When the $48,000,000 issue of 3¼ percent bonds was floated, however, an adjustment is required. The proceeds of the issue were placed on deposit with the fiscal agents of the securities to be redeemed, during the week of January 22.[19] The matured issues were actually retired during the week ended February 5.[20] The summary table reflects an inflow of short-term funds during the week ended January 22, an outflow of short-term funds during the week ended February 5, and a reverse movement in security transactions. The following table illustrates this.[21]

[17] See *Statistics*, p. 63, where foreign securities in the amount of $40,575,000 are recorded sold for Canadian account in the week of January 8, 1936; and p. 47, where short-term Canadian assets payable in U. S. dollars, belonging to banks and bankers in the United States, but other than "Loans to Foreign Banks" or "Acceptances Made for Foreign Account," fell by $35,549,000. Other transactions were involved in both cases.

[18] See *Statistics*, p. 12.

[19] See *Statistics*, p. 25, where Canadian deposits with banks and bankers in the United States rose by $44,138,000; and p. 63 where Canadian sales of foreign securities in the United States are reported as amounting to $46,998,000.

[20] See *Statistics*, p. 25, where Canadian deposits with banks and bankers in the United States fell by $44,503,000; and p. 60 where Canadian purchases of foreign securities in the United States are reported as amounting to $44,239,000.

[21] See *Statistics*, summary table A, p. 12.

NET CAPITAL MOVEMENT BETWEEN THE UNITED STATES AND ABROAD

Weekly totals in thousands of dollars; capital inflow or capital outflow (–)

1936	SHORT-TERM BANKING FUNDS	SECURITY TRANSACTIONS PLUS CHANGES IN BROKERS' BALANCES	TOTAL
January 22	41,997	–35,645	6,352
January 29	–15,414	2,302	–13,112
February 5	–42,587	53,969	11,382

If an adjustment of $45,052,000, the proceeds of the issue to Canada, is made in this table, being subtracted from short-term banking funds in the week ended January 22 and from security transactions in the week ended February 5 and added to the items under these headings in the opposite weeks, the resulting data present a truer picture of the capital movement.

NET CAPITAL MOVEMENT BETWEEN THE UNITED STATES AND ABROAD

Weekly totals in thousands of dollars; capital inflow or capital outflow (–)

1936	SHORT-TERM BANKING FUNDS	SECURITY TRANSACTIONS PLUS CHANGES IN BROKERAGE BALANCES	TOTAL
January 22	– 3,055	9,407	6,352
January 29	–15,414	2,302	–13,112
February 5	2,465	8,917	11,382

Finally, the question of adjustments necessary to give a true picture of the movement of short-term capital may be discussed with respect to gold-shipment financing. When an American bank buys foreign exchange and with the foreign currency proceeds to buy gold for importation, no movement of short-term funds takes place. When Europeans banks ship to New York gold which they themselves own and deposit the proceeds in New York banks, a short-term capital movement occurs and an offsetting gold movement accompanies it. If the European banks later pay the dollars so accumulated to

Americans, a short-term capital outflow from New York takes places to offset the original inflow and to leave simply the gold flow.

When, however, European gold shipments to the United States are financed by American banks, the problem becomes more complex. At the time of gold shipment from Europe, the American bank makes dollars available to the foreign bank and acquires an offsetting asset in the form of a short-term loan abroad payable in dollars. If the European dollar balances are not drawn down prior to the receipt of the gold, there is no net short-term capital movement until the receipt of the gold pays off the foreign loan. If the proceeds of the loan are drawn down prior to the receipt of the gold, however, the transaction appears as a short-term capital outflow, counterbalanced later by the repayment in gold of the American loan, which constitutes a short-term capital inflow.

In this circumstance, the effects of the loans on gold made by American banks to abroad need to be eliminated in order to give a realistic picture of the movement. The adjustment in this case affects the week-to-week total movement of capital as reported in *Statistics*, not the breakdown of capital movements between long- and short-term capital, as was the case with respect to refunding and redemption issues.

A case in point may be taken from *Statistics* covering the movement of short-term banking funds between France and the United States for the period of May and June, 1935. During the two months the net import of gold to the United States from France was $318,350,000 according to Department of Commerce figures.[22] Some of this gold was doubtless purchased directly by American banks, some was French-owned gold, but a large part of it was shipped by French banks (or the Paris branches of American-owned institutions) and financed by New York banks.

The movement of short-term capital as given by *Statistics* is as follows:

[22] See *Federal Reserve Bulletin*, August, 1935, p. 524.

MOVEMENT OF SHORT-TERM BANKING FUNDS

In millions of dollars; capital inflow and outflow (–)

1935 WEEK ENDED:	ALL COUNTRIES[23]	FRANCE[24]
May 8	17.2	– 2.8
May 15	24.4	–11.0
May 22	20.3	–22.9
May 29	91.6	57.5
June 5	23.2	–17.3
June 12	50.6	55.0
June 19	21.5	7.5
June 26	2.7	– 1.1

A glance at "Loans to Foreign Banks" among "Short-Term Foreign Assets—payable in dollars" (*Statistics,* p. 45) indicates that large fluctuations took place in this category, reflecting weekly changes in loans on gold in transit to the United States. To adjust the series, it is necessary to make an estimate for loans on gold to French banks. Approximately, it is sufficient to take the weekly change in total loans to French banks and add it algebraically to the weekly capital movement figure, thus eliminating the effect of those loans in the weekly capital movement.

The adjusted figures give a much better picture of the movement of short-term funds in the period considered. The spot rate on francs was at or near the lower gold point in New York throughout May and June. But the forward rate reached a discount of 36 percent per annum for three-months francs on May 31, and thereafter declined, although to still high levels. The return flow of funds to France after May 29th (in the adjusted series) reflects bear covering of short positions which were costly to maintain at the high discount on forward francs. The net movement of short-term funds from France, only $64,900,000, cannot be directly linked to the import of gold from that country, since the gold import reflected movement of

[23] See *Statistics,* p. 12.

[24] Computed by netting short-term liabilities and assets for France for similar weeks. *Statistics,* pp. 23, 39, and taking the algebraic weekly change.

ADJUSTED AND UNADJUSTED FIGURES TOGETHER WITH THE ADJUSTMENT FOR THE TWO-MONTH PERIOD

Movement of Short-Term Banking Funds Between United States and France In millions of dollars; capital inflow and outflow (−)				Discount on Three Months Forward Francs
1935 WEEK ENDED	UNADJUSTED	ADJUSTMENT FOR GOLD LOANS	ADJUSTED	WEEKLY AVERAGES IN PERCENT PER ANNUM OF SPOT QUOTATIONS
May 8	− 2.8	− 9 −	− 2.8	4.20
May 15	−11.0	+16.0	5.0	4.63
May 22	−22.9	+32.6	9.7	7.42
May 29	57.5	+62.5	120.0	16.06
June 5	−17.3	−34.8	− 52.1	20.28
June 12	55.0	−66.9	− 11.9	15.05
June 19	7.5	− 8.5	− 1.0	13.53
June 26	− 1.1	− 0.9[25]	− 2.0	12.70
Total	64.9	− 0 −	64.9	

funds from England in the short- and long-term categories as well.

[25] The actual change in "Loans to French Banks" this week (see *Statistics*, p. 45) was a $3,200,000 reduction. The present arbitrary figure, however, is necessary to balance the adjustment out over the period.

BIBLIOGRAPHY

Books

Aftalion, A., Monnaie, prix et change. Paris, 1924.

Angas, L. L. B., The Problems of the Foreign Exchanges. New York, 1935.

Angell, J. W., Theory of International Prices. Cambridge, Mass., 1926.

——— The Behavior of Money. New York, 1936.

Bagehot, W., Lombard Street. London, 1870.

Beach, W. E., British International Gold Movements and Banking Policy, 1881-1913. Cambridge, Mass., 1935.

Beckhart, B. H., Discount Policy of the Federal Reserve System. New York, 1924.

Bresciani-Turroni, C., Inductive Verification of the Theory of International Payments. Cairo, 1932.

Brown, W. A., England and the New Gold Standard. New York, 1929.

Cassel, G., Theory of Social Economy. 5th German ed. translated. New York, 1932.

Clark, J. M., Strategic Factors in Business Cycles. New York, 1934.

Copland, D. B., Australia and the World Crisis, 1929-33. New York, 1933.

Committee on Finance and Industry, Report. London, 1931.

Currie, L., The Supply and Control of Money in the United States. Cambridge, Mass., 1934.

Dulles, E. L., The French Franc, 1914-1928. New York, 1929.

Dunbar, C. F., The Theory and History of Banking. 5th ed., New York, 1929.

Durbin, E. F. M., The Problem of Credit Policy. New York, 1935.

Einzig, P., Exchange Control. New York, 1934.

Ellis, H. S., German Monetary Theory, 1905-1933. Cambridge, Mass., 1934.

Fanno, M., I Trasferimenti anormali di capitali e le crisi. Turin, 1935.

Furniss, E. S., Foreign Exchange. New York, 1922.

Gayer, A. D., Monetary Policy and Economic Stabilization. New York, 1935.

Gregory, T. E., The First Year of the Gold Standard. London, 1926.

Gregory, T. E., The Gold Standard and Its Future. New York, 1932.
Haberler, G., Der internationale Handel. Vienna, 1933.
——— Der Sinn der Indexzahlen. Vienna, 1931.
Hall, N. F., The Exchange Equalization Account. London, 1935.
Harrod, R. F., International Economics. New York, 1933.
Hawtrey, R. G., Currency and Credit. 3d ed., London, 1927.
——— The Art of Central Banking. London, 1932.
——— The Gold Standard in Theory and Practice. London, 1933.
Hayek, F. A., Prices and Production. London, 1931.
Heckscher, E. K., Sweden, Norway and Iceland in the World War. New Haven, 1930.
Hobson, C. K., The Export of Capital. London, 1914.
Iversen, C., Aspects of the Theory of International Capital Movements. London, 1935.
Jenks, L. H., The Migration of British Capital to 1875. New York, 1927.
Keynes, J. M., Tract on Monetary Reform. New York, 1924.
——— Treatise on Money. New York, 1930.
——— Essays in Persuasion. New York, 1932.
——— The General Theory of Employment, Interest and Money. New York, 1936.
Knight, F. H., Risk, Uncertainty and Profit. Boston, 1921.
Le Branchu, Y., Essai sur le Gold-Exchange Standard. Paris, 1932.
League of Nations, Gold Delegation, Report. Geneva, 1932.
Luthringer, G. F., The Gold Exchange Standard in the Philippines. Princeton, 1934.
Malpas, J., Les Mouvements internationaux des capitaux. Paris, 1934.
Mises, L. von, The Theory of Money and Credit. New York, 1935.
Mitchell, W. C., Business Cycles: the Problem and Its Setting. New York, 1927.
Moulton, H. G., The Formation of Capital. Washington, 1935.
Nielsen, A., Bankpolitik. Copenhagen, 1930.
Nogaro, B., La Monnaie. Paris, 1924.
Nurkse, R., Internationale Kapitalbewegungen. Vienna, 1935.
Ogilvie, F. W., The Tourist Movement; An Economic Study. London, 1933.
Ohlin, B., Interregional and International Trade. Cambridge, Mass., 1933.
Pigou, A. C., Industrial Fluctuations. London, 1927.
Rifaat, M. A., The Monetary System of Egypt. London, 1935.
Rist, C., La Deflation en pratique. Paris, 1924.

Robertson, D. H., Money. 2d ed., New York, 1929.
Rogers, J. H., The Process of Inflation in France. New York, 1929.
Shaw, W. A., and A. Wigglesworth, Principles of Currency, Credit and Exchange. London, 1934.
Spahr, W. A., The Clearing and Collection of Checks. New York, 1926.
Taussig, F. W., International Trade. New York, 1927.
Thomas, B., Monetary Policy and Crises; a Study of Swedish Experience. London, 1936.
Thomas, S. E., The Principles and Arithmetic of Foreign Exchanges. Rev. ed., London, 1934.
Viner, J., Canada's Balance of International Indebtedness, 1900-1913. Cambridge, Mass., 1924.
Whale, P. B., International Trade. London, 1932.
White, H. D., The French International Accounts, 1880-1913. Cambridge, Mass., 1931.
Wicksell, K., Lectures on Political Economy. Vol. II: Money, translated, New York, 1935.
Willis, H. P., The Federal Reserve System. New York, 1923.
——— and B. H. Beckhart, Foreign Banking Systems. New York, 1928.
Wilson, R., Capital Imports and the Terms of Trade. Melbourne, 1932.

ARTICLES

Adarkar, B. P., letter in *The Economist*, July 20, 1935, p. 127.
Angell, J. W., "Monetary Control and General Business Stabilization," in Economic Essays in Honour of Gustav Cassel, London, 1933, pp. 53-68.
——— "The 100 Per Cent Reserve Plan," Quarterly Journal of Economics, XLIX (1936), pp. 1 ff.
——— "Equilibrium in International Payments: the United States, 1919-1935," in Explorations in Economics, New York, 1936, pp. 13-25.
Bastable, C. F., "On Some Applications of the Theory of International Trade," *Quarterly Journal of Economics*, IV (1890), pp. 1 ff.
Bowen, H., "Gold Maldistribution," *American Economic Review*, XXVI (1936), pp. 660-66.
Brisman, S., "Some Reflections of the Theory of Foreign Exchange," in Economic Essays in Honour of Gustav Cassel, London, 1933, pp. 69-74.

Cassady, D., Jr., and A. R. Upgren, "International Trade and the Devaluations of the Dollar," *Quarterly Journal of Economics,* L (1936), pp. 415 ff.

Coe, V. F., "The Gains of Trade," *Canadian Journal of Economics and Political Science,* I (1935), pp. 568 ff.

Currie, L., "Domestic Stability and the Mechanism of Trade Adjustment to International Capital Movements," in Explorations in Economics, New York, 1936, pp. 46-51.

Einzig, P., "Some Theoretical Aspects of Forward Exchange," *Economic Journal,* XLVI (1936), pp. 462-70.

Gilbert, J. C., "Banking Policy and the Income Velocity of Circulation of Money," *Economica,* I (1934), pp. 242-45.

——— "The Present Position of the Theory of International Trade," *Review of Economic Studies,* III (1935), pp. 18-34.

Graham, F. D., "International Trade under Depreciated Paper. The United States, 1862-79, *Quarterly Journal of Economics,* XXXVI (1922), pp. 220 ff.

Hayek, F. A., "A Regulated Gold Standard," *The Economist,* CXX (1935), pp. 1077-78.

Henderson, H. S., "The Case against Returning to Gold," *Lloyds' Bank Monthly,* VI (1935), pp. 338-45.

Heuser, H. K., Review of M. Fanno's, I Trasferimenti anormali di capitali e le crisi, *Economica,* II (1935), pp. 491-93.

Hilgerdt, F., "Foreign Trade and the Short Business Cycle," in Economic Essays in Honour of Gustav Cassel, 1933, pp. 273-92.

Hohlfeld, H. H., "Die Struktur der zwischen-landischen Kapitalbewegungen," *Weltwirtschafliches Archiv,* XXXVII (1933), pp. 473 ff.

Huizinga, J. H., "Central Banks and Forward Exchange," *The Banker,* XXXVIII (1936), pp. 119-24.

Keynes, J. M., "The Arithmetic of the Sterling Exchange," *The Nation and Athenaeum,* June 13, 1925, p. 238.

——— "The British Balance of Trade, 1925-1927," *Economic Journal,* XXXVII (1927), pp. 551 ff.

——— "Reflections on Sterling Exchange," *Lloyds' Bank Monthly,* III (1932), pp. 143-60.

——— "The Future of the Foreign Exchanges," *Lloyds' Bank Monthly,* VI (1935), pp. 527-35.

Kindleberger, C. P., "Flexibility of Demand in International Trade," *Quarterly Journal of Economics,* LI (1937), pp. 351-61.

Machlup, F., "Theorie des Kapitalflucht," *Weltwirtschaftliches Archiv,* XXXVI (1932), pp. 512-29.

Machlup, F., "Why Bother with Methodology?" *Economica,* III (1936), pp. 39-45.

Noyes, C. R., "Stable Prices vs. Stable Exchanges," *Econometrica,* III (1935), pp. 129-46.

Paish, F. W., "The British Exchange Equalization Fund," *Economica,* II (1935), pp. 61-74; III (1936), pp. 78-83.

Paish, Sir G. A., "Commercial Policy and the Gold Standard," in Proceedings of the Academy of Political Science, XVI (1934), pp. 83-87.

Palyi, M., "Die Zahlungsungsbilanz der Vereinigten Staaten," *Schriften des Verein für Socialpolitik,* 1928.

——— "A Desirable Monetary Policy," in International Economic Relations, Minneapolis, 1934, pp. 236-45.

Robinson, J., "Banking Policy and the Foreign Exchanges," *Review of Economic Studies,* III (1936), pp. 226-29.

Shone, R. M., "Exchange Stabilization; an Industrial View," *Lloyds' Bank Monthly,* VI (1935), pp. 346-51.

Silverman, A. G., "Some International Trade Factors for Great Britain, 1880-1913," *Review of Economic Statistics,* XIII (1931), pp. 114-24.

Smith, L., "The Suspension of the Gold Standard in Raw Material Exporting Countries," *American Economic Review,* XXV (1934), pp. 430-49.

Syrett, W. W., "A Revision of the Theory of Forward Exchanges," *The Banker,* XXXVIII, 1936, pp. 202-6.

Vallance, A., "Foreign Trade and the Exchanges," in What Everyone Wants to Know about Money, New York, 1933, pp. 179-210.

Viner, J., "International Aspects of the Gold Standard," in Gold and Monetary Stabilization, Chicago, 1932, pp. 3-39.

Whale, P. B., Review of Ohlin's Interregional and International Trade, *Economica,* II (1935), pp. 114-16.

——— "The Theory of International Trade in the Absence of an International Standard," *Economica,* III (1936), pp. 24-38.

Whitaker, A. C., "The Ricardian Theory of Gold Movements and Professor Laughlin's Views of Money," *Quarterly Journal of Economics,* XVIII (1904), pp. 220 ff.

White, H. D., Review of Ohlin's Interregional and International Trade, and Haberler's Der internationale Handel, *Quarterly Journal of Economics,* XLVIII (1934), pp. 727 ff.

Williams, J. H., "The Theory of International Trade Reconsidered," *Economic Journal,* XXIX (1929), pp. 195 ff.

Williams, J. H., "The World's Monetary Dilemma; Internal Stability versus External Monetary Stability," in Proceedings of the Academy of Political Science, XVI (1934), pp. 62-68.

——— "The Adequacy of Existing Currency Mechanisms under Varying Circumstances," *American Economic Review*, XXVII, Supplement (1937), pp. 151-68.

INDEX

Bei Fragen zur Produktsicherheit wenden Sie sich bitte an:
If you have any questions regarding product safety,
please contact:

Walter de Gruyter GmbH
Genthiner Straße 13
10785 Berlin
productsafety@degruyterbrill.com